DORSET WOMEN

DORSET WOMEN

Interviews by JAMES CROWDEN

Transcribed by RUBY WRIGHT

Photographs by GEORGE WRIGHT

AGRE

First published in 2006
Agre Books
32 Highacres, Loders, Bridport, Dorset, DT6 3SE

Typeset by Andrew Crane
www.axisweb.org/artist/andrewcrane
Book production managed by Watershed PR
www.watershedpr.co.uk
Printed by Remous Limited, Milborne Port, Dorset DT9 5EP
www.remous.com

Text typeset in 11/14pt Octavian, headings 14/15pt Octavian
and Octavian italic. Cover font Baskerville Old Face

ISBN 0-9554327-0-7
ISBN 978-0-9554327-0-5

Cover photo :
Joy Michaud, Josephine Pearse and Ellen Simon with Celeste,
Fairyflax and dog Pedro. Tamarisk Farm, West Bexington

Abby Bunyard shoeing Chester

Sadie James with Fiona, Flower and Floss

CONTENTS

INTRODUCTION

Dorset Women is a complementary volume to *Dorset Man*. Both books document manual labour and rural life in twentieth century Dorset, highlighting the skills and determination needed to succeed in what is often poorly paid but interesting work. *Dorset Women* does not just look back at the past but has an eye to the future and includes many younger women who have chosen unusual careers. Dorset has a very rich rural history and is now at the cutting edge of a new food culture. Often it is the women who have had the courage and the foresight to diversify in the face of economic hardship. The rural tradition is adapting very fast and many of these stories document those changes. *Dorset Women* has a broad focus and looks at the way in which women have been able to follow their own paths in what was once assumed to be a man's world and have made very successful careers for themselves, often having to adapt and diversify for family and economic reasons. This research echoes previous work for a book called *Working Women of Somerset* and shows how rural women were often skilled in many different jobs.

Dorset Women is slightly different to its predecessor *Dorset Man*, which looked back to a pre-tractor age when horses ruled supreme on the farms. True, several of these women still work with horses, but the emphasis of these interviews is very much looking forward. In some cases I deliberately chose women who have made their own path in a man's world, whether it was in shepherding, scrap dealing, farriery, deer stalking, game-keeping, fishing, the church or undertaking.

The real inspiration for this book was an old shepherdess I met in Ashmore in 1980 called Ann Hodgson. She taught me about lambing and many of the basic shepherding skills. For a while, when I had sheep, we shared the grazing on Fontmell Down near Shaftesbury. Her next door neighbour in Ashmore, Mrs Morris, was then in her 90s, her father had been a shepherd, and he had died from pneumonia when droving sheep to Wilton. He often had to sleep out under the hedges and the weather took its inevitable toll. Her mother was evicted from her cottage and then had to make a living in Ludwell by taking in washing. A hard job if ever there was one.

Ann Hodgson has an interesting story to tell and luckily I managed to record her in 1985. Well into her 70s then she still ran her own flock of pedigree Dorset Horn sheep and did contract night lambing on large estates such as Crichel, Morrison's and Higher Bridmore. Her battered blue mini van was often to be seen out on the downs, when she was fencing or feeding sheep. She gave me one of her old shepherd's crooks and I have it to this day. She also introduced me to such interesting characters as Ruby James and Elsie Martin. I very quickly began to realise that there was an underground network of women's friendships that held the farming community together. Times were often hard financially but mutual help was an essential part of the fabric. Men did the work, women not only helped them but provided food, children and the stories to go with them. Raising a family on 53 acres was never easy. Sadly Ann died in 1998.

Not all of the women were born in Dorset, but many have interesting tales to tell about how they came to be living here. What impressed me most about the interviews has been the confidence and the guts of some of these Dorset Women. Imagine being the only woman on a farriery course with 45 men. To succeed they very often had to be better than the men. Dorset has also thrown up a home-grown rock musician of international status, Polly Harvey, but her roots are very firmly in Dorset, stone masonry and quarrying.

It is hoped that this book will inspire the next generation to adapt and invent jobs for themselves in a rural environment which is often richly rewarding in many different ways, and in so doing keep the old traditions alive by making new ones. It has been a fascinating journey and there have been many rich stories, most of which appear in this book…

James Crowden *November 2006*

ACKNOWLEDGEMENTS

First of all I would like to thank all the Dorset Women for their patience in being interviewed and photographed. Many have held their own in a man's world and escaped the pigeonholing of a suburban society. Many would have also made interesting central characters for Thomas Hardy's novels.

My main thanks also go to George Wright who once again has produced a fine library of photographs which will make an interesting and important archive in years to come. My thanks also to my cousin Jonathan Morgan who lives in Bournemouth who took the photographs of Ann Hodgson in 1994. She was a remarkable woman and without her this book would not have even started. My thanks to Ruby Wright who has intrepidly transcribed nearly all of the interviews and did three interviews herself. Thanks also to Carol Trewin who helped with transcription and proof reading, to Nell Barrington, my father Guy Crowden, and Rosemary Lewis who also spent long hours proof reading. My thanks to Sara Hudston of Agre Books for editing and publishing, Andrew Crane for book design and to Remous of Milborne Port for the printing. To Fergus Byrne of the Marshwood Vale Magazine for assistance with photography and lastly to Dorset Chalk and Cheese Leader+ in Sturminster Newton for the original *Dorset Man* funding which has been the inspiration for this second project. Chalk and Cheese supports sustainable development in Dorset's rural heartland.

1. Ann Hodgson – Shepherdess, Ashmore.
Born Concepcion, Chile 1915,
died Shaftesbury 1998.

*Then I thought 'I am going to do sheep if it is the last thing I do,' and sheep were very difficult to get into in those days, because it was a closed shop…
"May you live in interesting times."*

My mother, she came back from Chile with her husband. He had a tramper of his own, in sail too, used to go round the Horn. My brother had been round the Horn seven times before he went to England to his prep school. Her father went over from Portugal to the cod fisheries because he met my grandmother on the Grand Banks, Newfoundland, married a girl whose surname was Christiansen, so I suppose she was Norwegian, married the boss's daughter. Very sensible of him, my grandfather. Well I suppose he thought Chile was a good place to start. He took nitrates from Valpariso. Frightfully expensive the Straits of Magellan. "Pay us money or else." Pirates. And then he went up to New York and came back with wheat. Never asked him how long it took him but I know that she bore all of his children at sea. My mother was born at sea and so she had no birth certificate, simply had longitude and latitude in her passport. Same as my sister. But I was born in Chile, had a Chilean wet nurse.

Took a fairish time round the Horn. He carried nitrates. Lot of money in guano in those days, till they invented artificial fertiliser. He would carry anything even tea. Turn of the century. Father's father was a clergyman. And doctors! Never anything else. They despised anyone who had a title because they were all so thick, you couldn't do anything with them. They were what

you called the professional classes. Church, the services and doctors. Solicitors were thought rather little of.

I was brought up in a vicarage. Portishead, Bristol. Uncle George and Aunt Lillian. Here's a photograph. That's my uncle, George Hodgson. Look like that, one's relations do. Very respectable. Sweet clergyman's face. A sweet man till the day he died. Aunt Lily wasn't quite so sweet. One of her more standing jokes was that when someone appeared to be coming towards the house she once said "Oh dear here comes 'who ever it was'. Take the cake out."

I ran away from the vicarage exceedingly early. Ran away at 16. Went to London at 17. You were never expected not to run away mind. You wouldn't be expected to stay at home. I was so accustomed that you were only there as poor Alfred's child.

My sister was there for a bit but she went back to her mother. I went out to Spain only on visits. She trained at Barts and nursed and married from there. I went to the orthopaedic. You signed a form saying you couldn't come out till you had done two years. I was always getting people out. The food was ghastly and they took people far too young. It was a really Dickensian place. Funny thing was I was always getting other people packed up. Nobody ever has a trunk now. So they took the trunk away and left you with all your gear. You have legs, so they got paper bags and various things which people took to various spots in London. But I was the only one who ever got her trunk out. Determined to have my trunk and got it. 'Matron, I don't like the place and I don't think it is a good idea.' Wasn't much they could say. I learnt from a very early age if you really blow it they can't do very much, they can't put you in the cooler.

You see my mother had gone to Spain to run an estate. A citrus estate near Torremolinos. Just a bare beach then, sand and orange groves. All very beautiful then. Now it's like death. She

Ann Hodgson with crook, Ashmore

Photo: Jonathan Morgan

answered an advertisement in London, she was a very competent woman mind. She was bi-lingual and wrote Spanish far better than she wrote English and so she got the job. She controlled the whole kybosh. She came back at the beginning of the Spanish Civil War. Got out on a destroyer at Malaga. July '36 I should think.

Then I worked with the stallion man, that was all round the Cotswolds, Troytown the horse was. Never see a stallion man now on the road, all boxed up. Never dare risk it. He was fairly all right, a made up shoe, had a racing accident, stayed with them all winter. My friend, Rosalind, I used to keep a look out while she was behind the hedge enjoying his company. I was merely going on down the road… She got pregnant and in those days far more serious than now. She was determined to get rid of it, drank a bottle of gin, talk about being pissed to the eyeballs. She fled out of this place behind a pub, shot out to the back of a pub in a nightdress, bits of it and pursued by me. Her husband who was the stallion man. He was being pissed off in the pub so I fled after her. Oh dear, the trouble we had. Doesn't work.

They had pills too, but they didn't work either. In the end he married her which saved a lot of trouble. And it was about the worst thing she ever did. The stallion man. He was queer too, suddenly disappeared, went up into the hay barn and I found him, that was a bit awkward as well. Nearly nuts not quite. Got into a dangerous depression. It taught me not to think that drink was funny. She didn't wait up for him because she daren't and I had to, because there was no electricity in his place and so you had to wait up for him with a lantern to put the horse away. Couldn't leave the lantern out because it would set fire to something. That was in the winter when he got so drunk. This was in the Cotswolds, just before the war.

The day before war started I was staying with a curious woman called Martin Clay, must have been a roaring lesbian but I was far too green, brought up in the vicarage, to have realised that this was what the matter was with her. But I was quite safe. She wasn't attracted to me. She had a girlfriend staying with her. God they were funny too. She had horses there. Never entered my head, and dear old Uncle George and Aunt Lily who went there to interview her had no idea either. Two nice ladies they thought they were.

I remember the first thing of war and almost immediately I thought 'I am going to leave Martin Clay' and I did. Joined the air force and eventually got into the WRNS which was a feat in itself. I was on the plot at Chatham and at Liverpool. The only two plots at that time. One for the Channel and one for the Western Approaches. The Western Approaches were amazing to watch because as the Queens go across, quite by themselves they were so fast, quite safe to go and you saw these packs hunting about. They were all plotted, very seldom got out of a plot without people knowing. Convoys. Ghastly to watch. And of course the one down at Chatham. Got into trouble there, hit a petty officer in the showers, she was being a bit obstreperous and wouldn't let us wash after coming off duty. She slipped over and hit her head, silly woman. Got 28 days in jankers with the other wrens, they were a marvellous lot. All on the game of course, caught soliciting in Chatham. Nicer, more compassionate girls you wouldn't find anywhere. Completed my education all right. Hearts of gold, but they did find the uniform useful you see… Only did 14 days. One of the officers got me back on the plot because I was short and they could look over my head, made it easier for them.

Those plots are very interesting. Tin foil. We did not know what it was at the time, all we were asked to do was to watch on that wavelength, listening all the time and to see what you picked up, you did not pick anything up. Very successful. The Germans came in on a beam and they bent the beam, only trouble was they bent it towards Northern Ireland. The only time they bombed Northern Ireland. Northern Ireland very upset. Dropped it on Belfast.

Then boat's crew on trawlers. Couldn't use short wave radio. German and Irish spies in Eire listening out you see. You went out from Belfast to meet the convoys. We went around collecting all the captains of the convoy ships and taking them to the Commodore to open sealed orders to see which port they were going to go to. If Liverpool was badly bombed, then Milford Haven. Occasionally London. The trawlermen were really lovely people. They took all their fishing gear out. They weren't allowed to fish. And then we had to fish the Americans out of the drink that had fallen over the side drunk. No fun hauling them on board with a boat hook.

Then I had to drive an embalmer around. Very strange driving him round bombed out cities, taking him from airfield to airfield. Sometimes got held up for hours with air raids. I was once engaged to a bomber pilot. English mind. He felt very bad about bombing German cities and civilians, asked to be transferred to transports which was eventually granted, then on his last mission he was shot down by friendly fire, coming back in over Southampton water. So there… That was that.

After the war I went back into farming. Went to Exmoor. Suppose it was nearly '46 when I got up there just in time for the bad winter of '47. And I was up there for quite bit and then I came off and went to Castle Combe and then to the Duke of Beaufort's place. A few sheep there, mostly horses in the hunt stables. Once drove his lordship's Rolls Royce down the drive, the chauffeur let me have a go, his lordship was not at home at the time I might add. The chauffeur looked distinctly nervous but I only took it up and down the drive once or twice. Lordship was an awfully nice man, sorry they keep digging his grave up.

My great friend was in the laundry, never mind his underpants, the thing that was so interesting was the silk shirts. They've all got their names in and they just pass them on down to each other. The Duke of Clarence was one of his. And when they die they all re-distribute the silk shirts. "Old Beaufort can have these." His laundrywoman was a marvel. All the old stuff was there, rollers with stones in, enormous great rollers for rolling linen. Well pressed. All this damask rolled out on the vast table. He had these iron holders with the fire in the middle. She was using that when I was there, she couldn't stand electric irons. There were four faces with the irons just stuck against it. Three or four irons on a face and you just pick one up, use it and when it is losing its heat, you pick up another one and keep going. Just a kind of self-contained fire like you have under the table in Spain. Always thought that was a wonderful idea. Central heating is the death of half the children today. All you do is grab an iron spit on it, and iron away.

In the mornings everybody came in with their newspapers and we had a bookie in the village at Badminton and his runner was the maid. Everyone produced a paper and laid them out on these marvellous long tables then you all decided which horse you were going to back. Made a lot of money in those days, never lost much. And had cups of tea heated up on this iron, and gave Lucy her bets, and off she went on her bike.

Very curious place that, because you were there and they were all sorry for the fact that all the other servants had gone. You couldn't very well talk to a hoover. He had his own valet and his sister was her lady-in-waiting, and what else did he have? A cook, a chef and women up from the village, he lived up in a flat. Had all this property, can't sell it because it was all entailed and of course the hunt must have taken a bit.

When I left there I went into spraying just for the summer, the early days of spraying. A little Fergie. Little grey one, and set out from that lovely place in the Cotswolds, Turk Dean, stayed there, and went on up to Banbury, spraying bits here and bits there. Spraying for charlock, the next year they had their own equipment. The contractors had a bonanza.

Then I thought 'I am going to do sheep if it is the last thing I do,' and sheep were very difficult to get into in those days, because it was a closed shop. I went back up onto Exmoor as second shepherd. They have their allotment and the sheep stay more less where they are supposed to. They're brought into the 'in bye', Exmoor sheep are much more closely shepherded than Dartmoor sheep are. Did two stints on Exmoor one of three years and one of two I think. Had Cluns up there "Bloody great donkeys" the shepherd called them and Devon Closewools, very small Devon Closewools.

One time I was badly concussed. Champion method, sat on a tipping trailer, we had loaded it up with hay and I was sitting on top. Thing went right up and I went right down under God knows how many bales. Hit my head on the cobbles. I was a bit queer after that. Only for about a week. They took me down to the hospital. Never forget because the man held his watch to my head and said "can you hear that?" I said 'No.' He put it to my other ear and I said 'No I can't hear that either.' He put it to his own ear. And said "My God it's stopped." Could have got up and killed him…But he said "You've got the hardest skull of anyone I ever saw." Soon recovered. Only had two things in life, never work for anyone who hadn't got any money and never work anywhere which wasn't a beautiful place.

Then I came to Dorset. That was '56. Came straight off the moor. Went to Templecombe and Rolf Gardiner collected me.

Took me to Fontmell. Springhead. Started out with the cows, only for about a year then I went to work in the woods. I knew a New Zealand man and girl, he married her in the end, at Iwerene, Torrens was her name, they had some sheep, 'Would you train me?' I said. Went to them in the morning, and went to Rolf in the afternoon, half day. Didn't get anything for doing the sheep, life was like that in those days. They had me for lambing and all the summer after. I knew on the grapevine that Gardiner's shepherd was leaving.

Eventually I got the job. Then they built up to 600. Christopher took the farm on from his father. Very nice man, Christopher, John Eliot's brother. It was for him that I worked. Cluns crossed onto a Suffolk, talk about hat racks with cotty little waistcoats. We also had some Welsh mountain from Jack Houghton-Brown. Crossed them with a Border Leicester. Quite a new idea in those days. Welsh half-breds. Those Welsh sheep were quite something, fled in every direction. Knocked all the fences down and half of them were barren which was rather awkward. Never did take the ram and that was it.

Wages then: £8 a week went back to £6 when I stopped milking, had a free house and food was cheap, no different to now, if knocked down, no different today. About four times, four eights are £32. Easily go to Shaftesbury with a quid in your pocket. Can't even walk up the High St with a quid in your pocket now. Then they stopped free cottages, only me and the cowman. The others paid a little rent, but not much, no rates, no water, no maintenance. House fell down, round your ears mind, but they had maintenance staff originally, there were up to 40 people working there at Springhead one time. Photographs to prove it. It was a standing joke, they all crept out of the woodwork on pay day. They were doing things like brashing up, getting rid of honeysuckle, withy wind. Then there was chap who just spuddled about all day long, looked just about the same as it does now, but Christopher had a clear up when he came along.

There was one horse that we used in the woods, used for hoeing too. Frank Hellyer worked her. The mare looked like a Percheron. White. Ran away across that top road. Tossing out logs, full pole lengths on a chain. Just coupled them on in front horse so good and so quiet. Dashed off one of its funny days, the gate opposite was open that was the marvel of it. Heard the most terrible screaming of brakes, we hid. Lots of blasphemy. Didn't know what they were seeing. Went off with three poles and Norman Oddy chasing. Thought they had seen a ghost.

They had tractors, Fergusons but they still used horses on the steeper ground. Siegvart (Godseth) he always had a horse at Gore and in my day they always worked Gore with horses and for carting things about, they were much cheaper than a tractor. It is only the slowness and the amount of money you paid per hour that killed it. A slow transition. People died and retired, but every time there was a rise, someone went down the road, that was very noticeable. Nothing infuriated Rolf more than seeing men drive about in cars. "Their own cars, they've got better cars than mine," he used to say.

Combines came in during the Second War. But here they were much later. First combine came in at Gore Big Field, and we were stooking barley and we were going slower and slower and when it came everybody cheered like crazy, because stooking barley is about the most unpleasant job you can think of, because barley, the awns stand up on the inside of your arms. You can run with blood on the inside of your arms.

When my brother died he left me a thousand pounds. I then bought a flock of sheep. I was within five or six years of my retirement. I bought 30 horned Dorset Horn lambs, chilvers very well grown. £30 each. Dorchester July sales. Transport £6 from Dorchester. My wages never came to £40 a fortnight in my hand, and that was a man's wages. Ran them up to 50 nearly 100 at one time. If you don't own land you can get into dangerous trouble. Lambing moved earlier. Used to lamb in September when everybody else did. You were running into a very expensive season the whole time through. Your ewes have got to be caked right through the autumn and you have got lambs in bad weather just when you are fattening them. I came round to the idea that to lamb them earlier would be good. I found that the horns would be a drawback, the sheep are stronger than Poll Dorsets but they are always in trouble. Poll Dorsets are stodgy and difficult to lamb they aren't truly fertile in March, April and May. I had an Ile de France ram. They were very useful. Lot of very good tips from the shepherd John Randall. Actually an Ile de France is a better ram, fertile, active, a good carcase early. The first I bought was a very good ram indeed, and then Cadzow.

The price of having a flock shepherded is high and with a good shepherd worth every penny. Shepherd's wages have crept up because of their hours. But not as high as a dairyman, but then their hours are different. I mean a shepherd can have time a bit spare at certain times of the year where a dairyman never can. At other times he works all the hours God gives. Lambing bonuses. Always been part of the system same as a shepherd always had a free house. I never paid rent also you have a dog allowance and the other perk in those days was free firing. Two loads of wood a year. Everybody is now on electricity.

Dogs, I had out of the nest. Bought one and lost one. I like to see how they run, determined to have a wide runner. And I got this beautiful wide runner from Wales right out over the down and never comes back…used to drive round. He had got the message and got up onto the main road and was hit. Slung up into the hedge. Two days before I found him. So a dog that you have from a pup will know what you are and vice versa. I train them to stay with me, Kyi is so good with traffic. Turk needs to sit in the car. Heartbreaking thing to lose a trained dog, lost two on that top road. The first one I was bringing lambs along the hedge by the road, two lambs shot out with them and a lorry was on him. Both sheep and the dog. I never did sheep after ten o'clock in the morning. I could ask for a sheep day. When I want my dogs, Turk and Kyi I simply yell 'Turk-kyi'.

The crystal ball long term… Organic farming has a lot going for it if it is not done in too crazy a manner. I think to ease up on the use of artificials on grass and less animals. Sheep are very organic in many ways, but then again I wouldn't like to manage a large flock of sheep without good strong drugs behind me. You are not going to find a real organic sheep that won't get worms. And no organic business for worms is anything like as good as a good wormer. I use very few drugs indeed on mine. No covexin. Closed flock, foot vac and then I have cleared it.

Meditation. Excellent when you are on your own a lot. Leaning over a gate…First started reading about it on the trawlers during the war. Christmas Humphreys, all there was at the time. Buddhism made a lot of sense, but no one to talk to about it apart from the fish. The mind is like a hunting dog, you have to give it room to come back to heel. I now understand why I lived my life the way that I did. As the Chinese say "May you live in interesting times."

2. Josephine Pearse – Organic farmer, Tamarisk Farm, West Bexington. Born 1931.

In some ways we feel that we have been farming with a mission, as stewards of the land, and as an example of how one should live.

I was born in Brackenborough, Lincolnshire, 1931. My father was a farmer and a timber merchant, a Methodist family in Lincolnshire. Liberal. He was importing timber from Latvia, Estonia and Sweden. It came into Grimsby. It was a family firm which began with the rise of Methodism. It was ethically a good thing to do, I'm sure. My father took me round the docks once. You kept your big trunks in the seawater, in the harbour for seasoning for two or three years. The timber trade was relatively flourishing which then got turned into farming. Land was fairly cheap and people bought it up. He used to spend all his spare time farming.

Earliest memories? We lived on our 500-acre mixed farm which was 100 feet high on the last hill towards the sea, ten miles of flat marshland to the sea. And going for walks with my father, listening to birds and looking at flowers. Yes. We grew corn. We had some very heavy clay fields, some lighter. We had a little medieval village which I noticed, nobody noticed before me. We had parkland and a good rotation. Yes sheep, and Lincoln Red cattle. A fairly traditional mixed farm. Louth, there were lots of little markets, special lamb markets, Parkney, and Lincoln, we always had three of our best bull calves to go to the Lincoln Red Bull Fair, very traditional.

My mother came from Bristol. Her father was the youngest son of 13, farming at Huish, on Exmoor. And being the youngest he couldn't do farming so he went to Bristol to seek his fortune and married his corn merchant boss's daughter and did very well in the corn industry. His name was Hosegood. There are Hosegoods about here, and Stoates. Cann mill is Stoate, they're distant cousins of mine.

I went to the grammar school in Louth for a while and then kicking against it very strongly, I went to a Methodist boarding school which I hated. During the war we were evacuated to Chatsworth House, and that was quite fun. We used to lie looking at the painted ceilings, looking at the cherubs. It was extraordinary. Methodism was quite strict. So we had the opulence of Chatsworth but the regime of a Methodist boarding school. We weren't allowed out at weekends. The Duke and Duchess of Devonshire went away. I'm sure they came back and kept a small portion, but we didn't see them at all. I was only 14 at the end of the war and I can remember our headmistress saying what a tragedy that we'd dropped that atomic bomb. She thought it was immoral but we felt great exhilaration.

Both sides of our family were steeped in Methodist ethics, which meant a lot of welfare to our farm labourer families. My mother took them into Louth to shop once a week. We had 12 families living on the farm. Each man had his own job: shepherd, cattleman, carter, we had 14 carthorses and as a little girl I would go down to the field when they were finishing ploughing and ride back.

At school food was really fairly tight. I can remember feeling hungry at the end of the war when for tea we had just a bit of bread and a teeny spot of marge. Earlier in the war my father used to shoot rabbits, and everyone had one pig a year, every household used to help at pig killings when we feasted on fresh meat and the sausages we made, lightly salted down the small joints but heavily salted the hams and hung them up on the kitchen ceiling. My nephew still farms there with just two men.

Joy Michaud, Josephine Pearse and Ellen Simon with Celeste, Fairyflax and dog Pedro. Tamarisk Farm, West Bexington

After the war I went to Somerville, Oxford. Both Arthur and I studied geography. Absolutely ideal. I think having farming in my background was an immense advantage because it gave me an understanding of regional geography. Things were very tight in England after the war. My mother was ill and I nursed her for a year. Arthur stayed at Oxford studying anthropology. My father said that Arthur should have a job before we got married, and so instead of doing anthropology in the field, which he was all set to do, Arthur took up a teaching job in a grammar school, on the edge of Harlow. We lived there for three years and two children were born there.

After that we went to Nigeria for another three years and we lived in the north. We walked a great deal and took a lot of photographs. In 1961 Arthur's mother died, she was much loved. It was a very hard time to come back and we were very nostalgic for Nigeria. Arthur wanted to garden on a large scale rather than farm, that was his first interest. Very fortunately we had bought this house in 1958 and let it when we were away. We came to Bexington because Arthur's parents lived in Litton Cheney, and Arthur had loved coming to Bexington, he always cycled here to bathe, it was his favourite place. But the house had no land attached. It was labourers' cottages, four labourers' cottages and the hotel was the farmhouse. It was always just called West Bexington farm.

We were incredibly lucky. Arthur taught for a while in Lyme Regis which he hated, and then we met the person who owned 60 acres to the west of the barn. We asked if we could buy a strip for Arthur to do some market gardening, about six acres, and he said no, he wouldn't split it but we could buy the lot! A sudden vision came to me of wonderful space, 60 acres of wide open slope to the sea, wind, sun, Chesil beach, freedom for our children just to be…We bought the barn separately, that was Arthur's foresight.

So we got into farming by a series of steps. After this first windfall of 60 acres we never had any more capital to buy anything, we always did things bit by bit. We never got into debt because we always had Arthur's salary coming in before he stopped teaching. We did a lot of research into the time that Bexington Farm was a 999-acre farm, which a property developer bought up in the early 1930s and sold off in acre plots. We tried to find the owners, advertising in papers in the south east, particularly. Ten houses had been built before the war, but then came planning and nobody could build. In fact to begin with we rented from about 30 plot owners! They didn't allow infilling along the road until the water and electricity had come, about 1960 and never any building on the agricultural land.

Gradually we got these extra acres and our farm began to take shape. At first we had goats, we used to get stuff from the roadsides for them and to make hay. Then we had one cow, I liked to have fresh milk for our six children, then Arthur gave me two sheep, everything grew very organically! If you have one cow, her milk dries off before the next calf is born, so you need another cow and another! I can remember our first steer calf which lived in luxury all winter and got 'Best' at Yeovil spring market! So now we had a beef suckler herd, Hereford x Friesian, then Charolais, and I'd wean the calves and sell them off the cow at about eight months old in October, and then buy in calves at Sturminster Newton and rear another 20 or so calves on the cows. A major difficulty was that we had no fences at all, so we had to put money into fencing. We used to do what they called set grazing, as opposed to paddock grazing. It worked very well.

I never noticed that I was a woman in a man's world, except at Sturminster Newton calf market, because there they had a cartel, a mafia, and they didn't like me coming in to buy calves. I was much aware of that. They would let me bid but only just.

There were no other women there except farmers' wives of course. This would have been in the early '60s. Now Sturminster is no longer. It was a wonderful big, big market. I used to go to other farmers asking for advice quite a bit, there was somebody at the top of Little Bredy who was so helpful, he used to come and look at my calves and say what he thought they'd be worth. That's highly valuable information. John Cooper helped me too and Nigel Werritt. He used to be a big vegetable grower in Chideock.

The horticulture grew in different directions at the same sort time. I did the farming and Arthur did the horticulture. We've always tried to grow as many varieties, as many crops as we could and always sold on a very wide front. We've never done any monoculture. Fifty, sixty things we'd find we were growing when we tried to write them down. Soft fruit to potatoes. Any number of different types of lettuces. Well we first had a glut of tomatoes, I think, and said 'What on earth shall we do with these?' When you've got a big family, you want to feed them well, and we did. Then we had too much produce, so we put a little stall on the roadside, and that went exceedingly well for about 25 years. It was almost like a wayside shrine. That was very successful. We had an honesty box. You used to hear fishermen putting money in, in the middle of the night sometimes. But then it got rather less honest. We'd put honey out sometimes when we were doing bees and that would go. Different people seemed to be coming by car from further away, so we stopped about 12 years ago and did the organic box system for nine years. We are rather proud about our box scheme, because we never bought anything in except for carrots from the Chapmans, north of Dorchester. We managed to produce 12 or so different vegetables every week for 51 weeks in the year for nine years. Most people find they have to buy in, and in effect become greengrocers but

we weren't going to. We were very small, only up to 35 deliveries. We had a £5 box at first, and then an £8. Ten mile radius. It was fun, I liked doing that very much. That's been extremely popular and very successful till a couple of years ago.

We used to grow 15 or so varieties of cauliflowers each winter. It was great fun because you'd have Australian ones and French ones and Arthur was absolutely brilliant at it. We have had fun messing around with different varieties. Then we felt perhaps we'd try and do a little less, start a little shop near the house twice a week, Tuesday afternoons and Friday mornings when Ellen and Adam have their meat and flour farm shop open too. What's left over goes wholesale to Fruits of the Earth in Bridport and Washingpool farm shop in Salwayash and residential homes like Harbour House in West Bay. We once sold two tonnes of leeks to one of the supermarkets. They had to be one uniform size so half were wasted, we had to take them to Bristol and then they went to Spalding. It was absolutely hopeless for us, and definitely not in the spirit of being organic!

Oh yes, you have to register as organic, very much so. A very tedious registration, there's a lot of work involved. We registered very early on. The first people who inspected us were Peter Joyce, an Archdeacon and Ralph Coward. We are P07W, about 1963, and that was only for vegetables. We did use nitrogen for hay for many years and I liked to be able to worm my sheep too, and not have to get permission, which we have to now.

Of the 60 acres Arthur used about seven. That's a lot for one person. But we fallowed and did half the bottom field regularly. The soils - heavy Fuller's earth clay. Arthur had an idea that it would be nice to grow down towards the sea, but it was a total failure, not because of the salt, but because gales blew the little plants, leeks and some brassicas, right out of the soil!

So we've been organic for 40 years. The soil's improved

enormously since we have been here. On the top market garden it's beautiful, absolutely lovely. We couldn't grow carrots at first because the soil was too heavy, but now we grow beautiful bunched carrots, not the main crop, we haven't got the area for main crop. The top land is very intensive. Arthur describes himself as an organic market gardener.

Very early on we started with cloches because that's what there was then, but very soon it turned to tunnels. Little story about our cloches, you'll like this; I started keeping shire horses with one mare from which we bred registered shires. Every year I bred a foal and kept the fillies, and I tried to train them. It was pretty heavy work for me and Arthur had no interest in horses. One year a Ministry of Agriculture, as it was then, man, came to check on how I'd got on with a shire horse course with Charlie Pinney. Victoria, my first mare bought from Charlie went a little too fast and I went straight through a row of cloches with her, and he was absolutely appalled and got out of the way. Shires have a habit of going very fast when they're pulling, and that's what she did. We started with one polytunnel in the '60s, now we have 12, we use them rotationally, tomatoes, cucumbers, lots of different salad crops, oriental leaves and herbs…we make a very popular leaf and herb salad bag nowadays.

In the '60s our vet lent us a beautiful big hunter and we bought a little pony so we always had horses for the children to enjoy and for me to ride round the stock every day. But we bred a lot, after shires we bred Thoroughbred x shires which were most successful, and shires x Arab, which are equally successful. We also had a little tractor, a little Fordson Major, excellent. Then a David Brown and now a Massey Ferguson.

Sheep. We had Dorset Horns first. There was a good Dorset Horn flock in Burton Bradstock. Bunny Lenthall, he went to Australia just as we were starting. He was a loss because he was a big man here. I bought in some mules once, and they were very easy for lambing. I realised how much I'd been struggling with the Dorset Horns which have big lambs and the males have big horn buds at birth too. I put Texels on everything. I got more Texel blood as time went on, just to get a nice backside and I got very good grades. I used to hire really good rams from North Devon Meat. The lambs I sold them to North Devon Meat. That was an extremely good arrangement. Collected. There was no in-between, it was all direct. I had a quota of 129 ewes and kept round that figure. Ellen and Adam have increased numbers a little. One hundred and twenty-nine is quite a nice little number. It's enough to get out for and not too much to overwhelm you when you're dagging them.

Lime Kiln Hill has always been National Trust, 16 acres. That has a history of its own, and quite useful that we did rent that. Through the first agent, Mr Gaze, we covenanted our land to the National Trust west of here and down to the sea because of the possible nuclear power station a mole in the CEGB had warned us about. The National Trust would have helped us to fight it. Our relationship with them has always been very constructive. We went into Cogden in 1991 as a partnership, Adam, Ellen, Arthur and I, and we stayed in it for about six years, so the first business arrangement with the National Trust was with them. And that was a sort of idealist thing because it was conservation. And at that time the National Trust was still thinking they should take a lot of rent, and they charged us the heavy rent of £20 an acre for very poor land, but within a year they'd halved it voluntarily because they realised that what we were doing was wardening. And I think we've influenced them, they've become quite different in their attitude now. Later Ellen and Adam rented 'Labour in Vain' as well.

Children in farming. Well, only Ellen and Joy, my daughters, but Mark gardens in Brussels and he and his wife got the compost award for Brussels one year, although they've only got a pocket handkerchief-sized garden, just next door to the art museum. Christopher has a lovely garden near Aberdeen. Henry is a GP in Devon where he's got 20-odd sheep, a pony or two, and lots of good garden, and a keen interest in breeding small poultry and ducks. Andrew teaches paragliding in Dorset, a dab hand at building a stone wall, gardens when he can.

Woofers? Well a Woofer used to be called Willing Workers on Organic Farms, at that time, about 25 years ago, we'd get people who wanted to have a holiday for a weekend in the country. And they'd come and get their fingertips dirty. But now it's called Worldwide on Organic Farms, the word 'Worker' has been left out because East Europeans couldn't come over, they were sent back at the port if they said they were working. We once had two Polish students who came over and were sent back, it was very distressing. So now it's Worldwide. We have all sorts of people coming through our door, from all over Europe, Oh yes, and Korean and Japanese, lovely people. We get many more people who come for long term, such as the young man who is here now on his two month practical before he goes to Cirencester Agricultural College. He is from the former East Germany.

In between the weekenders and these more serious students we had a lot of unemployed people because they wanted to be doing something and they couldn't get a job, but could always have taken a job from here at any time, so we had a number of long-term very nice people who came, so the social side of my father's farm comes through. Yes, actually, I've never made the comparison, but that is so. The early Woofers would often have emotional difficulties and we would be there to help them along.

Arthur is astoundingly patient, but it does hit back at him sometimes because he can't necessarily get the work done which needs to be done. He really is wonderful. When people who have been here come back they say how amazingly good and patient he was in teaching them. We have with us now a girl who was at Tinker's Bubble, and is used to community living. She's writing on the challenges of being an organic farmer and maintaining your mental and spiritual life. You always think you're going to have lots of time for it and you have no time at all and if you do have time you don't have the energy.

The sea is important for our climate. Absolutely. Oh yes we have had frosts. When the times were a little colder the children used to skate every winter on the very shallow fleet just behind Chesil, here in West Bexington, '62-'63. Oh that was a wonderful winter. Arthur was teaching full time in Weymouth and he couldn't get in at all. We had skiing as well. Cross-country skiing. It was a wonderful time for children. And toboggans with ponies. That was much, much loved. Ponies would take you up hill nice and fast. Fertiliser bags? Well we've used those too. They are so useful for stone picking in the fields, the frost pushes them up every winter, or potato picking as well as tobogganing! You have to go to your neighbours and ask for them, but of course when the Soil Association inspectors come you have to say how you got them or why you got them. About 30 years ago Arthur and I bought about 10,000 turkey pellet bags, paper, and we're still using them. They are invaluable, still. We've had to explain them each year as well!

Storms? Well when we tried to grow leeks and brassicas down to the sea they were blown out. The only thing that really suffers on the market garden is runner beans. They will catch a storm in September and stop producing. They don't like salt. Arable crops are ok, we don't get any trouble at all, though you might get a bit of browning off with grass. We've put in thousands and thousands of trees as windbreaks. On the market garden we have put in every tree there except the elms which suffered with Dutch Elm Disease but are now growing high saplings.

Seine net fishing was just about stopping when we came. Arthur, as a young man, had helped seine netting quite a lot, I only remember seeing it once or twice. That was the Puncknowle gang, yes. Arthur would know the names. If a shoal of mackerel came the farm workers would dash to the sea. We have always had two little chalets, which have never made very much, but they were very useful, yes. For many years our four enterprises: cattle, sheep, market garden and chalets all made about £4,000 gross each. Then we built our first cottage in '89, that was built with a small builder's firm, followed by Arthur and Adam building the next one in 1990. We build with our own stones picked up from the fields, Forest Marble limestone, it used to be quarried from the bluff above the farm. Increasingly we get people now who are interested in organic things or people come because it looks over the sea…In 1999 we started building a cottage for the disabled, and that has been more success than anything else. A lot of disabled people come and I find it extremely interesting and rewarding.

The future? That's difficult, isn't it? Dorset has always been its own beautiful self…I can't see that dissipating entirely, I think it's too precious. I think the big farms in other parts of England will have immense difficulty, but I think Dorset will keep its good little farms. I think basically it's the immense variety of geology, the vales and downs and hills and streams.

In some ways I feel that we have been farming with a mission, as stewards of the land, and as an example of how one should live. You can't always be protesting against the wrongs of this world, but you can try to live well.

3. Ellen Simon – Organic farmer, Tamarisk Farm, West Bexington. Born 1956.

We had tomatoes and fantastic peaches… for years we had peaches and apricots. They were just so luscious, it spoils you for eating other ones.

I was born in Harlow and came here permanently when I was four. I remember Mr Mayall coming with his cows from Puncknowle walking down the old road. It was great, you had so much space. We were in and out of the scrub on the back of the hill, just ordinary pleasures, damming the stream and catching damsel flies and newts and things like that. And the beach. We had plenty of space. Everybody in the village went out and did that sort of thing. I now recognise that it may not be so common, but I still think it's right and perfectly normal.

I should think I was about eight, when we had horses, whereas my children were riding from about four days old. The sheep didn't come in again until I was about eight, it was arable before then. O & J House, big contractors in those days, I remember we had to take out the gateposts to let the first combine through, but we had mostly arable then.

The market garden was organic, and that was really why we slowed down the arable. My memory as a child is that I remember them discussing that they were now being instructed to use fertiliser and growth restricting hormones to get short straw and it seemed a bit mad and contradictory throwing chemicals on to counteract the effects of other chemicals and they decided that they weren't going to do that any more. Then we started fencing everything, because everything was open, bear in mind that the farm didn't have any existence before my parents brought it in together, so we started enclosing and from

my point of view that was very annoying because when you go riding you have to keep opening gates, whereas before you could go at any speed you fancied. So I suppose that happened when I was about ten or twelve. So that's when the animals came in more and that's when it went organic, remember there was no certification then. The market garden was always organic, that was from the start, about 1960.

That was really my father's pride and joy. My mother put a lot of time into it as well, though she managed the arable. I remember brilliant fruit, anywhere, any time you'd find something to eat, so you'd pull carrots and wipe the earth off them and eat them, sneak out and eat baby cucumbers, when they're six inches long. The intensity of flavour is fantastic, and you know you shouldn't really, and peas…I should think we were like locusts at times.

They experimented with different crops. We've still got Russian comfrey as a problem weed, the idea was to do good compost with it, but it is very prolific. Experiments with things you wouldn't expect.

Companion planting? Yes. I think over time it became less, because you were experimenting with different things it became 'Let's leave that there and see what it does,' So you go from relatively ordered to less ordered over years and years and years, because you accept what's come and try to find what's good out of it the whole time.

We sold into Bridport. I remember taking trays and trays of strawberries and tomatoes into shops in Bridport, but that's a long time ago, and then we started selling from the wall here. That developed more and more, and really even from quite early on people were coming from long distances. Some had allergy problems, I remember one person wanted our potatoes because they hadn't been watered with mains water, so therefore they wouldn't have inappropriate things in, so he'd be able to eat them. And I remember people coming from Bristol and Bournemouth because of cancer, we had quite a lot of goats at one stage, we had pigs before that, but the goats, we sold quite a lot of goat's milk. Hand milking? Oh yeah. We milked when we felt like it. When I look at it now I realise there was remarkably little pressure. You joined in when you wanted to because it was fun. I now hand milk pretty routinely, so it didn't put me off.

My sister's here, my brother lives nearby, and the others, we see a lot of them but they live at other ends of the country. Two of them aren't in farming at all at present, one of them has a small area of land in North Devon, and has also planted some vines here recently, he's keen to experiment, it's a nice idea and they're coming on well.

If you harvest late, you do often get a serious blow at the end of August, beginning of September, that blows down the runner beans and signals the beginning of autumn. We had Dutch lights before polytunnels. It's a standard-sized frame, they seemed big to me, maybe five foot by two foot six, you could walk in, they were glasshouses, relatively unsophisticated, we had tomatoes and fantastic peaches growing in there, don't get peaches at the moment, but for years we had peaches and apricots. They were just so luscious, it spoils you for eating other ones.

Then raspberries, loganberries, strawberries, gooseberries, blackcurrants, redcurrants, whitecurrants, we had cultivated blackberries as well as wild blackberries. The loganberries were very good indeed, they were better than the raspberries, but people didn't realise, they used to pick them too early. Loganberries have to be left until they're pretty black and then they're good. Other vegetables? Loads. Kohlrabi was relatively ordinary, salsify, things like that, Japanese leaves, a continuous good range of vegetables.

After Colfox, I went to university in Exeter. I did biology and psychology, but the course I really wanted to do was what the Open University did which was the biological basis of behaviour, and I thought biology and psychology would do that but of course it didn't mesh the two together. At Exeter one had to specialise in zoology and psychology. I ended up having to do botany instead in the end and I found it very interesting. It worked out really well. I did come back from time to time, do some fencing and fighting with the scrub and I'd go back lacerated and aching because I'd been riding and pulling blackthorn to bits, covered in sores on my hands which had got soft in the time I was there.

One summer I went to Northern India for three months, I stayed in Dharamsala and studied Tibetan Buddhism. That was '74 or '75. it was very influential, I stayed very near the library. You had to think about the world very differently. It has now sunk in and I am enjoying immensely, what it then worried me to label as Samsara. You have to be aware of what you're doing the whole time, the immense pleasure in the immediate life that surrounds you.

When I went back to university it was very difficult. I had a hard time being settled. Here on the farm there was the rich and beautiful and vibrant and lovely life, and at university things were a bit on the grey side for some time. People were not doing the intense worthwhile understanding of themselves or the understanding of the world.

I finished off the degree, and that's when I stopped the zoology. When you're a Buddhist it's rather difficult to wantonly pull things to bits, as I saw it. After university I just remember May and June this unbelievable freedom of not having exams, it was a great pleasure.

I then came back here, worked on the farm, and then got

what turned out to be a fantastic job, working with the Dorset Wildlife Trust and the County Council who were doing a botanical survey of West Dorset. And it involved travelling around in Dorset, walking around every field you could find and seeing what was growing there. Mapping every bit of it and it was just fantastic. That was for about a year. I remember finding Herb Paris in a woodland near Loders and being so impressed with the Marshwood Vale. Where there was corn you still found daffodils in it. I remember finding barley with daffodils. And around Lambert's Castle, around Fishponds Bottom, some of those little, to my mind, completely out of place bits, because they're acid and I'm used to everything being largely alkaline, you've got these little areas of acid bog, nothing terribly rare but marvellous, and ponds which were fairly isolated, we've got some of them on the farm now we've got 'Labour in Vain' as well. You've got different flora on different ponds, but then they're only two fields apart. The geology differs so you get different water. Lovely.

We did a report, we mapped it in colour, coloured it in bit at a time and had a card for every field of any interest. We were told to use footpaths as much as possible and do things from a distance but of course you can't do that, so we had to go and find the farms. You didn't know where the farms were, and of course you knock on the door and ask if you can look round, and then of course you realised you weren't necessarily on their ground. I have memories of getting on top of hedges and things and thinking 'How do I get over there?' and going to places where I definitely shouldn't have gone. Some of them were fantastic, I remember one dose of cider in the Marshwood Vale that left me sitting under the hedge for a bit. We're talking about '78, '79, I think I sneaked in rather a lot of the Marshwood Vale, rather than letting anybody else do it because I liked it. I loved other

areas as well, up on the chalk you'd find lovely edges and things like that, it was great. You'd talk to the parents, rather than the people that were farming now, and they said that everything started disappearing as soon as you started putting nitrogen on. They hated it. They had taken such pleasure in the range of plants that were ordinary and they weren't there any more and it was sad.

I then worked in the Dorset Environmental Records Centre for a bit, in Dorchester, at the top of the museum, it was lovely. You were right up there in one of the attic rooms, and it was a great place to work and I really enjoyed it. The previous place had been great because we were supposed to be working in County Hall, but there wasn't much space in the planning department so we were moved out into Woollaston House, which is now the NFU building right in the middle of town. It was a great big town house in complete disrepair, and County had put us and the Heritage Coast and a few other bits and pieces in there. It was really quite a bizarre place to work and on top of that they were excavating outside and finding Roman pavement. A bit of which I took to Litton School. I brought home bundles of Roman pavement because nobody wanted it, they were just chucking it.

Also during university holidays I had worked at Herrison Hospital, that was another influential thing. I'd worked on their therapeutic farm which was a market garden run by a couple of employed people for the inmates, those places were desperately unpleasant, as I conceived it, the tea came out of the urns with milk and sugar already in it, nobody had any control of their lives at all, as I saw it, it was a desperate place. The farm was good, very good, it actually had a combination of the long term people, and people who were coming in and out of Forston Clinic, and in the people who were coming out of Forston you could see the immediate good of it. Forston is a short-term place, acute problems. I worked there during various holidays, it all tied together, voluntary work when I couldn't get a job after the survey had finished. I also had part-time work at the Record Centre.

I then went and got a teaching qualification in London. I went up and knocked on the door of the Institute of Education because they had what looked like quite a nice course, and they said "Could you start tomorrow?" so I did that year in London. Being in London is great in some ways, but you get to the point, you know what you think when you see ragwort growing here? When you see it growing round the lamp posts in London, you feel very differently about it. I looked at it with great admiration, it was marvellous! Look what it could do! If it could survive, I could survive.

From there I got a job in Somerset, it was a joke really. I was qualified to teach science or maths, but I actually got a job teaching rural studies in a comprehensive in Langport, Huish Episcopi. It was a great place, I loved being on the moor, it was totally different to being here, but great. Flooding? Oh yes! Flooding. Camping nights on the ice and geese and swans coming in. So different to here. I only stayed there a couple of years because in the middle of that time Adam and I got married and then we moved up to the Lake District. I really enjoyed being in the mountain environment, finding enormous expanses of the plants that I mentioned growing in little pockets of acid soil, but growing in great expanses there. I had a baby which was great because I could shove a baby on my back and traipse all over the mountains. Adam was working quite a bit so I did it by myself or with friends. We lived in a great big rambling house which we'd persuaded somebody to let to us, right by a river. Adam was teaching outdoor activities. A lot of it was about giving people a

sense of success, which relates to what we do here on the farm, giving them something which you hope they can take back into their ordinary lives, feeling they've achieved something. It was a good thing.

After that we came down here with two children and Adam working, furniture making. The process of becoming part of the farm has been incredibly gradual. We had one of the first nature reserves in the county so now the conservation covers a large area with the National Trust bits either side. I almost feel like I'm recreating the past, I can lie with my face down in the grass and get the smell of wild grass, which you couldn't easily around here when we first came back.

At the time the farm here was consolidated it was about 180 acres and quite a lot of scrub. That's down to the sea, fairly narrow down to the sea, then broader on that slope behind us. We don't go over the main road, we stop just this side of it. If you start at Swyre and turn right it's two miles out towards Abbotsbury. We now have the National Trust land as well. First we got the National Trust land at Cogden which is separate, it's not connected to the farm, then 'Labour in Vain' came up as well and so we're now running 600-odd acres. We still think of ourselves as small farmers, but to my ears 600 acres is not a small farm any more, but because it is rough and wild and the productivity is very low, we're only running 150 ewes and 30 cattle and followers.

Sheep? Dorset Downs. My mother did some very good work with Texels when they first came in, and we used to have Dorset Horns before that, but we found the Dorset Downs will fatten on not very much. It's really a traditional sheep for folding on the downs, so we're really not using it for what it was bred for, but it seems to work. They're hardy animals and we're lambing outdoors now. These Dorset Downs lambs are nice solid little beasts and they don't die in the cold. The cattle are North Devons and they are just so lovely, we've got so much blackthorn which goes red in the autumn and you've got these dark red cattle and purpley red blackthorn. We do have problems with sheep in the brambles. Silly little things sit there, they think they've been struggling, you get there with yourself and a dog and they're away, they didn't need to be there. But they will still die if you don't help them.

The arable is all organic as well. The flour, we mill it here, and we sell it either from the farm or through three farm shops, Modbury, one in Abbotsbury, and Washingpool in Bridport, but we sell wheat to both the Town Mill in Lyme Regis and Otterton Mill. First of all when Upwey mill was working, we took loads over there, it was great using the mill, humping the sacks in, and taking them up on the hoist. Then unfortunately he had to close, so we bought a little electrically-driven stone mill. It works well and makes good flour but it is not as satisfying as the water mill.

Town Mill do a good job with our wheat and the work is beautiful to watch. The bread is good.

Sheep gathering on horseback. Yes. Quick and effective. It makes all the sense in the world to gather your sheep on horseback, if you think in practical terms, you can't take the Landrover out half the time because it's too wet, and every time you go through a gate you have to get out, open the gate, get out, close the gate. And that's always a waste of time. Horses are very good at slopes, they're also good at wet ground. You can go out on a horse at any time and do minimal harm. One dog and a horse. The horses learn to do things, you sit on the horse and she does the work. We had one that was magically good at it a while back. She's died, but now there's two or three others that are leaning down and nipping the sheep and telling them where to go for me.

So we're surviving. Yes, definitely.

4. Joy Michaud 'Peppers by Post'
    'Sea Spring Photos'
    West Bexington, born 1958.

Our Dorset Naga, the hot chilli. That's got serious legs to it, I mean there's potential there. It's our variety, it's our chilli.

I was born in Nigeria. That's where my father were teaching then. They came back in 1960. So I spent my first two years living there. I went back to Nigeria when I was 21 and the smells were so familiar, everything smelt so normal, and so familiar, it was very strange. I remember going on a little motorbike along the road and suddenly I could smell a fruit. We stopped and there it was, and I'd never smelt it since and it was right there and I identified it immediately.

That was some imprint. That was interesting. I came to Bexington when I was two and for my whole childhood I lived in Bexington. Went to school locally, primary school at Litton Cheney, Colfox in Bridport, and then university, Aberystwyth in Wales. I studied agriculture. My first degree was in agriculture. I enjoyed it immensely. I felt I learned a lot. It was conventional agriculture, and mostly big scale, so very different to everything I knew.

Machynlleth was there, and we also had the Welsh Plant Breeding station, and fairly early on I realised my interest was in grassland and plants, so having the plant breeding station right next door was good. We did a lot of field trips and I really enjoyed it.

My parents' farm wasn't fully organic when we were children but the market garden was. Being organic was such a natural thing to be doing that it wasn't an issue and it was long

before it was anything special. It was just a different farm system and I didn't have any trouble learning conventional at all, it was just part of the industry. I didn't take a gap year, and when I finished my degree I then took a bit of a gap year. Afterwards I went back and did a PhD.

That's when I went to northern Nigeria. I liked the Third World, I liked working in a cross-culture situation. I immensely enjoyed experiencing different cultures. I wouldn't say it inspired me but there was no question that was the direction that I could see my life going in. So I came back and did my PhD on grasses.

When you do a PhD you end up knowing an enormous amount about a tiny subject. And basically mine was on grass growth, so mostly rye grass but some other types. I was just measuring these tillers and how fast they grow. I'd manage them in different ways. I'd measure the width and I'd measure length, numbers, growth rate. I did a lot of other things and in the labs I'd measure photosynthesis rates.

Well, I'm very much a plodder sort of person and to do that type of research you've got to be a plodder. You've got to accept that you just go out and you spend 12 hours in the field measuring. It was quite a big field divided up into 36 plots, and each plot was cut in different ways or fertilised in different ways. That was my main experiment, I had lots of other small experiments. Agricultural research is like bucket chemistry anyway. So it was just seeing how grass responded to the different managements.

When I finished my PhD, I applied for a job with ODA (Overseas Development Agency) and I was actually offered a job in Bolivia. But about that same time I met Michael and it was one or the other. Bolivia versus Michael. Michael didn't stay in America, and we ended up in the Caribbean.

In the end I did a post-doctorate at Texas on digestibility of grasses which was quite interesting. I enjoyed that. And then Michael got a job in the Virgin Islands and we went down there. When I was down there I got a job at the University of the Virgin Islands. So he was the programme leader in the Agronomy Department, and I was the natural resource specialist, which was a wonderful job though it did take me away from agriculture a bit. Natural resources in American terminology means the wildlife, the plant life, what's growing, short-term natural history, which meant a lot of learning about plants, wildlife, trips out to the coral reefs. It was a fantastic job. We stayed there about four and a half years.

Then we came back to Dorset. We did this very foolish thing but we were immensely lucky. There was a farmer in the village. He was just retiring and we bought 15 acres off him with no easy access to the land, no water or anything. Our house had access to the land, and one small field which was completely surrounded by the land we'd bought. So we mentioned to the man who was living here that if he ever sold up we'd be very interested. Two years later when he died, his nieces offered the house to us. We were incredibly lucky, you just cannot imagine. We bought the land in '86, the house in '88 and we moved here in '89.

Although I'd done an agricultural degree I'd never really intended to work on the land. It's very hard work. It's wonderful but it can also be soul destroying as well. Having done my PhD I did see myself going into research side of agriculture, but it was always Michael's dream to have a smallholding and grow vegetables, not mine at all. So that's why we did it. He wasn't attached to the States and all the consumerism at all, and so it seemed like the right way to go.

So growing vegetables was a dream that Michael wanted to get out of his system. I don't think he ever intended to stick with it. Michael grew up in a very small town, very isolated town in

Maine, northern states, and nearly everybody there worked in the paper mill. Normally people left school, went straight into work, and would be grandparents by the time they are 50. They have a lot of money, they might buy a second house, a snowmobile, three cars, and never achieve their dreams. That was what Michael didn't want. So we came here and we grew vegetables.

We put up a few tunnels, we didn't really know which direction we were going in. We went to markets, we sold and grew vegetables, so it was ok. We also had two young children by that time. You have to be incredibly good to make a living out of growing on a small piece of land. If you're growing vegetables and you're growing a million lettuces you can have a profit of 1p a lettuce and you're ok. But if you're only growing a hundred it doesn't work. So we quickly realised this.

Originally we went to Weymouth and Dorchester markets, farmers' markets didn't exist then. Michael was the seller then and he enjoyed it. He quickly got regular customers. But markets are actually soul destroying. You grow all week. Twice a week we picked everything for that market, but if it it rains that day you come back with everything. And then what do you do? You haven't got another market for several days and by that time the vegetables are old. It's a very hard life. And the profit is always so low.

By the mid '90s we gave up markets and started doing wholesale, which was much more satisfactory. We always sold to the end-user. Shops, restaurants, that sort of thing. We would find somebody we liked to work with like Washingpool. I'd phone them up, they'd give me my order and then I'd pick to that order. Suits them, suits me. And we were much happier with that, it worked really well.

For a long time we had a big van and that was good, I

enjoyed that. But it's still very hard to make money out of growing vegetables. I take my hat off to anybody who genuinely makes a living off it, and has a mortgage and has a family. If you haven't got a mortgage, haven't got children it's a completely different kettle of fish. You can afford to work long hours.

To live off the land, directly, is in a sense a little bit self-indulgent. If you've got children you've got to be able to give them what they want and deserve. For a long time we actually rented our house out in the summer and we lived in the caravan. When Ben was about seven, he pointed out that when we lived in the caravan he never invited his friends home. And that was it, we stopped doing it at that point, we realised it was impinging on the children.

Also in the early '90s, Michael got a part-time job as a Soil Association inspector. Without that we wouldn't financially have succeeded. In the early days it was Michael's inspecting, renting the house out and selling vegetables. He also did international work so he went anywhere in the world.

So when somebody wanted to become organic, Michael would go and sit there and ask them a lot of questions. It was a very powerful position but in actual fact Michael enjoyed it a great deal because he made a lot of friends, but after a while it got a lot more serious. When the EU came in, the EU regulations, there's a lot more legal side... What happens is you've got the EU regulations, and every EU country has to conform to that minimum level. And then above that other governments, and other private certification bodies like the Soil Association can add their own standards. But it can only go up, standards cannot go down. So anything sold as organic in Britain conforms, it is organic, there's no ifs or buts about it. He was right in the centre of the Soil Association for a while.

Supermarkets were coming into it. They have their own set of standards as well. And if you're organic and sell to a supermarket, you've got to be registered organic and then the supermarket will have their own system. There are so many other systems which aren't organic. There's one called EurepGap which has a very organised system of paperwork, so there's a paper trail so you know exactly where it comes from. And a lot of supermarkets insist on that as well. It's not easy selling to supermarkets and being organic. So Michael was doing that a lot, but eventually he got tired of it because it got a lot more serious, a lot more political, a lot more legality came into it and he started being a policeman rather than a friend. Before he used to go in, inspect and advise, and help and chat. And then after the inspection was done they'd all have a bottle of wine and spend the night there. Well fairly soon he couldn't accept meals, and he couldn't drink with them and he couldn't stay with them, you couldn't be friendly and be an inspector... And so he had to stop being friends. And then all the ones he'd made friends with he'd tell the Soil Association he couldn't inspect. I guess he did it for about ten years.

The peppers started in '96. I think we realised, right from the beginning that if you're doing a market stall, you have to have your potatoes and cabbages but there's no profit in any of that. The profit is on high value crops, and not only that, you also want to have high value crops which require as little labour as possible. And so we were always searching for crops that fitted that criteria. We grew flowers a lot for that reason. Peppers are a high value crop, the actual labour involved is relatively small compared to a lot of other crops. We also found that tunnel culture suits us better than field culture. You are much more in control of the system.

Our land has a good outlook, we get plenty of light, plenty of warmth, and light reflected off the sea as well as good, clear skies: so in every way it is suited to polythene tunnel growing. You often find that growers are either field crop growers or they're tunnel growers. You rarely get someone who likes both the field crops and the tunnels. Completely different environments. Tunnels clearly suited us a lot better than the fields.

Our tunnels are all on a slope. We get good air movement and on some days we'll often open the backs and not the front because the hot air accumulates at the top. And so we open the backs just to let them cool off, even if the sun's not shining we'll often do that. We get tremendous gales, so we bury the plastic on the sides very thoroughly for obvious reasons. But the doors, we have the door frames very large to get optimum aeration. We have trickle irrigation. Conforming to our system we use black plastic, drip irrigation underneath, black plastic reduces weeding to almost a minimum. Drip irrigation means we just plug the hosepipe into one end at the bottom tunnel in one place and it drips, it waters the whole tunnel.

When we started as far as we know, nobody else was growing chillies in England commercially. But several others have since started – there's a very big grower in Bedford who started at about the same time as us. Nice fellow, we communicate quite a lot with him. He sells to supermarkets, whereas we went completely the other way, we had to. It is a matter of scale. He has very large areas of greenhouses.

We're always trying out different chillies, our catalogue never stays the same. Before a chilli goes into our catalogue we've grown it in pots, we've grown it in the soil, we've looked at the yield, we've cooked with it, we've done two or three years of testing at least before we feel confident that we can put it in the catalogue.

We also learned that if you want to grow, say a jalapeno chilli, there are hundreds of different varieties and we work to find which we think is the best one. We learned after a while not to tell too many people what that variety is, because if you've spent three years work finding that variety, your knowledge is valuable.

People benefited from our early research. So I must say we now code all our seeds, and we never actually mention the variety names. You learn, you do learn. We'll be as helpful as we can but that's just part of it. We've got a lot better than we were. Every year's a different situation, so every year you learn. Certainly we're better pepper growers than we were. This year we're actually doing courses on how to grow chilli peppers, because we feel confident that we've now got something to tell people, enough information.

Now if you're selling chillies, only a small proportion of the British population is going to buy them. So we couldn't expect to grow a lot of chillies and sell them all in West Dorset. You can either do it wholesale, but we were worried that we would lose control and have to sell to a middle man, which is completely against how we wanted to do it. Then somehow or other we came up with the mail order idea.

This is long before we'd heard of the internet. We sell our chillies entirely fresh. We pick them and they go out the day I pick them. And they always go out by first class post – labelled bags in cardboard boxes. So hopefully they'll get to the buyer the day after it was picked. So really they get there fresher than our customers could ever hope to buy them in a shop. Most chillies are relatively light and the system seemed to work. It took off straight away.

To start with we had just individual buyers. We've got a friend who has a business called the Cool Chilli Co. which sells dried chillies by mail order. Dodie, she knew that we were growing a lot of chillies so we did up a brochure and she included them all in her mail out. She was buying in dried chillies from the States, and selling them by mail order. She felt that us selling fresh chillies might take some sales but it would complement her business and just generally raise awareness of chillies. She was our mentor and she helped us through those early years.

So now we're completely separate. We have a website, but we don't yet let people order off the internet. Partly because we're as big as we want to get and we're getting more orders in than I can cope with at the moment. We don't want to get any bigger.

Up until last year the balance was perfect. We'd been doing it for ten years. By this time the wholesale side had taken off and we were probably doing about two thirds wholesale, one third retail. Then suddenly it turned out that we had a very hot chilli. The Dorset Naga. It hit the international news. This has completely skewed the whole thing and we were getting orders in April, four months before we had any chillies to sell.

Yes, it's certainly too hot to handle. For a while orders were coming in thick and fast. To be honest I was very happy with the way it was working before. By the end of the year we always sold out. We were comfortable with it all.

The plastic on the tunnels will last about five or six years, sometimes less, sometimes more. If you look at the actual land we grow from, it's highly intensive but we get a lot from it. Every year we have a big problem with aphids. It varies from year to year but it is an issue every year, we have to think about how to handle it. In our catalogue this year we've got nine varieties, but we actually grow 50 other types, just trying them out.

I do have other jobs. Photography. I sell pictures of vegetables and I also do editing work. My bread and butter editing work is a monthly magazine on organic standards. The publisher is Swedish and my co-worker lives in Malaysia and then we have correspondents all over the world. So it's completely internet-based. I do the editing of the articles, mostly written by people who don't speak English as a first language. So I've developed that skill of how to interpret what they mean rather than what they said. I also do the layouts, then I send the magazine off as a pdf file to Sweden, where it's sent out to subscribers.

It's only small, it's one of those magazines that is highly specialised for the business, with an expensive subscription, about £300 I think. A lot go to libraries. People who are in an organisation pay a group fee so it may go further afield. So we don't know how many actually read it. I'm reading very specialist articles all the time, I'm pretty much embedded in it.

I photograph mostly vegetables, because that's just what I'm best at, but also a lot of farming pictures, and it's a library so I take the pictures on spec. I do sell, give some pictures to other libraries but I never seem to have enough time to send pictures to other libraries.

So if a magazine wants a specific photograph of a certain vegetable they contact me. They say "have you got a picture of e.g. primo carrots?," and I say 'Yes I have,' and I'll send it off and they'll put it in the magazine. Waitrose might say for their magazine: "We need a picture of somebody washing carrots." Well I've either got it or I haven't, and if I have, I send it to them. And then they may not like it, it may not suit their requirements. Again, my photo business is one of those things which probably could blossom into a full-time business, but it plods on. It certainly contributes to the family income, quite significantly. And without it we'd be the poorer for it.

There are other directions. We're selling chillies in pots, that's a diversification…as edible houseplants, and that's been working very well. It's labour intensive but it's less physically demanding and is a different approach. We're trying to figure out what we want to do with our Dorset Naga, the hot chilli. That's got serious legs to it, I mean there's potential there. It's our variety, it's our chilli.

We made selections from a very variable population to produce a clean line that is uniform and separate, and generally looks rather different to this wild population that we started with. So needed to define it, so called it Dorset Naga. We were looking for something very specific and it just happened to have a very high heat measurement. We are being asked by chilli fanatics all over the world if they can have this chilli. There's one Bangladeshi family we sell to, and they do a lot of sauces. But most of the other sauce makers are British and they've just come up with their own recipe. We are forever being given people's sauces and asked to see what we think of it.

We have an open day and every year it's got bigger and bigger. I'm absolutely dreading this one. I just can't imagine how many people are going to come. They come from all over the country. It's extraordinary. 'Peppers by Post' is a lot bigger than the business is itself. And, it surprises us immensely because we're just tiny, an absolutely tiny business. Within the chilli world though it shouts a lot louder than it feels. But as far as I'm concerned, my editing work is my main work. I sit at my computer and I work hard there. Michael also writes articles, he's doing a lot with the RHS (Royal Horticultural Society) right now. He's worked with the Eden Project, gives talks. His big thing is working with immigrants, ethnic food and how to produce it in Britain. Any one of these could be a full-time job and we're loathe to give anything up. So we keep at them all and struggle to keep up. We're always looking for something new.

5. Elsie Martin – Farmer's wife & jam and pie maker, Drone's Farm, Twyford and Motcombe. Born 1939.

We often had to pull a calf out. And the first calf that we had to pull out, Ted had hobnail boots on and I had slippers…
Now I just make a few cakes and pies. Country Markets. It's a great institution. It's like a family, and we have a terrific following… It's the first time in my life I've ever had a jammy job! My speciality is Bakewell Tart and Dorset Apple cake.

Actually my name is Elspeth, everybody calls me Elsie, but my name is Elspeth McDonald Martin. I was born in Perth in Scotland in 1939. My mother and my father were both Scots. Dad was in the Black Watch, I didn't know him because I was a very young child when he was killed. He was in the Palestine Police. It must have been about 1941. I didn't know him at all.

I was eight years old when I came down to Swindon where my stepfather's mother lived. I remember my mother not having a husband to provide for her, I remember taking my brother through the snow when he was about two, two and a half, I used to push him down to the nursery and then I used to get to school late, and I had the strap for that and it was very sore too. I used to try and pull my hand away but they made sure you kept it out, and it depended how many bands was on the strap, how much it hurt, which looking back was quite cruel to have the strap at such a young age. We were quite poor. I remember also going up with my gran and picking strawberries she used to pick for jam in the school holidays.

My stepfather used to be in a foundry up in Scotland. He was a foreman of the foundry. He got a very bad chest which he died of in the end. He had to get an outside job, he worked as a milkman. We used to move around a lot because he kept changing his job. We moved to Holt then, near Trowbridge. I used to go with my stepdad on the milk round and then he'd drop me off at the bus stop to go to school, because he had quite a big round. It was just something we did. And then after I stopped the milk round I got a paper round instead. I bought the papers and then I'd take them round and deliver them and I'd keep the profits.

Then we ended up in Salisbury and when I had to leave school, the headmaster called my mother in and said "I don't think she ought to leave school because she's got more to her," and Mum said "Well she's got to because we can't afford to let her stay on." That was just coming up 15. So I got a job in Percy Churchfields in the office when I went in there and I saw this big book which the milkmen would come in and give you their books and I thought 'I don't think I'll ever manage this book' and I didn't realise that you had to have three! And I used to keep the poor manageress in the office until about half past six, most people went home at five and I was still struggling through and I thought 'I hate this job.'

Then one day Mr Thompson who was the owner came in, he was a fiery Scotsman and he said "That lad that goes with Mr Smithy" he said, "hasn't turned up again. I don't know what I'm going to do. He's got the biggest round." I said 'I'll go' and he said "Will you lassy?" And I said 'Oh yes please.' I thought 'anything to get out of that office.' And he said "Yeah, but you start at four in the morning." I said 'I don't care!' and he said "Do you think you'll get up for four?" I said 'I'll get up' and he said "You'll finish at two." And I thought 'That's alright' and that's what I did. I did that for about four months because I was

Elsie Martin in Shaftesbury Town Hall – a jammy Lady

still officially an office girl but I was standing in because the boy didn't turn up and he sacked him when he did turn up, which they could do in those days.

The round was Alvediston and Broadchalke, I loved it. Yes, loads of watercress beds, a lot of wildlife. I rather enjoyed it. It was only for four months. That was about '55, '56, and then after that I thought 'I'm not sticking this job, I can't bear it,' you know in this boring office and that and I thought 'what shall I do?' But then I got TB. I was quite ill, because I'd always had bad asthma. And I had to go to the sanatorium in Salisbury, at Harnwood, and I was there for five months, and they said "You've got to have an outside job," and I thought 'What can I do?' I didn't want to go back in the office, so somebody said "I know somebody wants a girl outside, on petrol pumps up on London Road." So I said I'd go and see, and I thought 'I think I'm going to like this,' because I was going to be on my own. I got to know so many people and I loved it, and then I got TB again. So I had to go back into the sanatorium and then I went to the Royal Pay Office, I went for a job there as a telephonist, and I had a room on my own, out of bounds to all, but everyone used to come in, and that was good fun. I made a lot of friends there and had a happy time.

A couple of years later I came to Dorset where I met Ted, my husband. We married three years later. He was managing a farm for Young up at Kilmington. We used to have the manor house which was rather nice, an old-fashioned place, but awfully hard work, I didn't know how to cook, this was 1959, coming up to 1960, because we moved down to Twyford in 1960. His dad was a small farmer, he bought a smallholding, he used to work for a general as a driver and chauffeur, and his mother used to milk cows by hand. Ted told me lots of stories when he was young, how he used to have to walk back with a piece of bacon on his back from the bacon factory in Gillingham with his sister and when he got home he used to have to get churns of water from the river because they had no running water in those days, no electric and it was a very hard life.

Waterloo Mill. That's where they had the cider press. They made quite a lot of cider there. That's how they used to pay the men who helped with the haymaking, they used to come and do the haymaking and then go down and sit and drink the cider. It was made through straw wasn't it? Actually Ted's sister was killed on that press, she'd ran into where they had it in an out shed, and where the handle spins round, it caught her dress and smacked her round and killed her outright, it was terrible really. She was about four. I don't think Mrs Martin ever really got over that, she would often talk about her to me, even years and years later.

Ted was born in 1926 and he died when he was 74, six years ago, so he would have been 80 today if he'd been alive. We lived at Drone's Lane. It was a county council farm, 1960. I remember when we went down you had to be interviewed, and we were sat on the gate waiting for our turn because there was quite a few people in those days that were after those farms. We were pretty keen to have it as Ted always had the ambition in his life, he used to save so that he could maybe one day have a little farm.

He was 33. It was very good time to take on a farm, but we went in there with £1,500, paid the ingoing and we only had six cows and we didn't have a tractor. So for the first six months we used to take the dung out on a wheelbarrow, and spread it around the ground, which now seems ridiculous.

It was wonderful and we thought we were so lucky to have that place. The house was small and we had four children, four girls, and it was quite a hard working farm, it was only small, it was 53 acres and we used to have to go miles for ground, we used to rent fields from different people, and one or two gave us some, there was a nice man at Fontmell who gave us about eight or nine acres, but a lot of the time we were driving around to rented land.

Six cows and a wheelbarrow, and Ted said, as we were living down this long lane, "Well at least we won't have anybody looking over the field in a year's time saying 'They've still only got six cows'." But we saved up, he wouldn't borrow money, the council offered us £1,000 to start…They knew we had enough to start that small farm. Just!

He bought a second-hand tractor from his father for £350 and he bought an old bailer at a sale for about £100, and he went bailing for other people, so I'd do the milking and he'd go off and do the baling and there was three or four cows that I couldn't milk because they'd kick, and I was too nervous, so he'd have to come back, maybe at ten o'clock at night and milk those cows. He really worked terribly hard. We had churns and we were the first pick up. They came at just the back of seven to pick up the milk, we had to be up very early to do the milking though. The lorry driver used to be very irritable if we weren't ready, and one day I just lost it. He came down a bit earlier than usual, he'd been away for two weeks, we had one more cow to milk, he was banging the strainer like he was trying to get the milk through quicker, and I said 'Did you enjoy your holiday Tom?' he said "Yeah, I did actually." I said 'Well we bloody haven't had one,' I couldn't help it, and he never did it again.

Our holiday was three hours in Weymouth! I felt sorry for the kids because I used to see people there lying out on the beach but we'd be straight down, let them have a kick in the sand, fish and chips and back home. Later on of course, as things got better, we had a week in a caravan, which we loved.

We never got into debt. We were very careful. Actually I suppose we could have been big farmers if Ted had been the sort to take up money but he was brought up by his father not to. We were happy. We didn't want too much out of life, we enjoyed the life we were having. At one time we had about 90 head of cows with young ones coming on.

Haymaking, of course we did all our own and Ted did other people's as well, and he was an excellent hedger. He loved the land, he loved everything about it, he was a real Dorset man. If he had a cow that was going to calve, or a pig, he would be up with that pig all night. He would go to market and someone would say "Bit of bad luck, I lost a cow or calf last night." And he'd say to me "That wasn't bad luck, that was neglect." He didn't believe there was such a thing as bad luck. I used to lie in bed at night, and the wind and rain blowing and that, and I'd go down to help Ted pull the calf out with my nightie on and come back with some afterbirth on the bottom of the nightie! When I think of the friends I've made now, I tell them things like that just to see the shock on their faces. And I used to lie in bed and think 'Please let him be alright' so I don't have to go up there in the wind and rain.

We often had to pull a calf out. And the first calf that we had to pull out, Ted had hobnail boots on and I had slippers, 'cause he'd said to me "Quick, there's a cow and she's got a hell of a calf in her," 'cause he could tell. And I went up to help, I put my foot in front and he was behind me, and he didn't realise until after, but I had the imprint of his boot on my foot. He didn't know, and I was just thinking 'She's having contractions,' but I didn't feel it, when you've had children yourself, you know what she's going through. We were there until 1989, we were there 29 years, then we moved up to West Melbury.

I started cooking for the WI, when I was down at Drones, because somebody came down and said "Ooh, look at all those damsons you've got." I said 'Help yourself, there's so many here,' they were hanging like grapes, but nobody would, they couldn't be bothered to pick them, then a friend of mine said "Why don't you pick them?" She said "I belong to the WI up in Shaftesbury market, I'll take them up there and sell them for you." So I let her have them and she said "What about your honey?" Because we had three beehives. I used to take the honey up and I thought 'Well I can't expect something for nothing,' so I offered my services to sell coffee. They were glad of an extra hand.

That was about 1984, just before we finished at the farm, and then I used to look at the cooking at the market and I thought 'I think I could do that,' so I made some pies and took them up, and then they promoted me to the jam counter. It's the first time in my life I've ever had a jammy job! So I'm the jam lady. Now I just make a few cakes and pies. Shaftesbury Country Markets. It's a great institution. It's wonderful. It's like a family, it really is superb and we have a terrific following. We open at 10 and shut at 12. The customers come in, everything is gone in a flash!

We had a market at the town hall once with the Farmers' Market and they complained because our prices weren't as much as theirs. We were charging what we usually do. My speciality is Bakewell Tart and Dorset apple cake. I make anything really, sponges, apricot and pineapple flans, biscuits. I make steak pies and chicken pies. I don't usually have anything left.

It was quite a feat to raise a family on a small acreage, especially girls. The oldest one is Mary who's now 50 and lives in Australia, also Chris, Jane and Tracy. Three of them worked in banks and one was a civil servant, so they all did quite well. The girls all helped. Because we had daughters, especially Chris, she used to come up and do the milking a lot, she used to help a heck of a lot, but they all had boyfriends. And we were very lucky

because we didn't just have the girls' help, but we had their boyfriends too. Once they befriended our daughters they used to always be made welcome in our home. They didn't get used to milk, but they used to do an awful lot of haymaking and my son-in-laws were wonderful, and still are.

We had all Friesians but we used to have an Ayrshire now and again and a Guernsey just to keep the milk solids up. The milk used to go to Wincanton. It's all changed so much, it is 17 years ago since I was down Drones. We used to have a lot of primroses. Terrific amount. There were lots of different vetches which you don't see now.

The old chap that used to have the place came home from the war, Mr Stone, he used to have a bike and a wireless, no car. The first year Ted ploughed up one of the grounds, and I was walking down from milking one day and I looked up and I thought 'It can't be snow in September,' but it was a mass of white, and we had thousands of mushrooms where they had been disturbed. People came from all over the place to pick them. Ted'd disturbed them after years of being dormant.

We kept everything, my brother-in-law, Peter Martin, who lives over at Silton, used to be friendly with the relief milk driver. He was talking to him one day and said "Do you know Peter," he said "There's only one place I'd call a real old-fashioned farm." He said "Where's that?" "Drone's Lane, down Twyford," he said "They've even got two or three pet rabbits eating on the side of the road." We had a donkey at that time, sheep, about 65 bantams, ducks, geese, it was all there, just like it should be.

You go into a farm now and it's so clinical, not a way of life just a business. We didn't get rich, we weren't there to get rich. We enjoyed the life. I remember when we bought the first cow, it was 100 guineas and I said 'My God, how many are we going to be able to afford' because I thought we'd get about five for that and Ted said "It's a really good cow" and it was the worst cow we ever had for milk, it was the most beautiful looking beast, we got it from Sturminster, it was called Titch. I'll never forget, it was our first cow and I thought 'My God, we'll never be able to make money on these prices. We'll never be able to have a family or anything,' but we did.

Ted always used to go to Sturminster every Monday and I used to go with him. I used to love the sales. It was a bustle, it was lovely. We used to go into the pig part and it was all dust in the air and just that feeling of excitement and people used to jump up on the side with the auctioneer, as he walked along they used to walk behind him and he was so fast I had a job to pick out what he was saying. That pub was great on a Monday. Oh yes, that was always a bustle, wasn't it? And then Johnny Burden started up having his sales outside the pub. I went to the first sale he had there, and I bought some knives and forks that I thought were solid silver, but I should have known because they were two shillings at the time, but they looked like solid silver. He sold everything; cabbage plants all mixed up with eggs and rabbits. We used to go to all the markets. It depends on where we found the best place was to take the calves. Ted bought a trailer and we used to take our own cattle most of the time. We used to like Shaftesbury Market.

We always kept Poll Dorset sheep, wonderful sheep. Ann Hodgson the shepherdess from Ashmore used to bring me down her orphan lambs because she said she knew I would, as she said, do them well. That was worthy praise from Ann. She was a wonderful woman with sheep. Sometimes I had ten on the bottle when her ewes had too many lambs to suckle. It was a wonderful experience to meet and find out about her life. At shearing time Ann always managed to drop in just as were sitting down to lunch and of course joined us.

Many years ago they had a seminar at Springhead about small farms and some clever clogs got up and said "Oh the small farms are wonderful because you see them on the skyline, they will always be there." And I put my hand up and said 'They won't exist in time because they're not viable,' I was tutted down, but I knew what was coming. There won't be any at all in time. They've sold two or three off this last few months. The small farmer can't afford to take on the ground now because he's not getting the money for the milk. I read all about the small farmers even now. I've got a terrific feeling for small farms, being one ourselves, it's hard work and people say it's cheap food in this country, it never was cheap food because you only have to go to market and see the men walking around on sticks. It was dear to the farmer.

Damson wine? Oh yes, I used to do all sorts of wines in those days, I used to pick all the heads from the dandelions and parsnips, carrot wine, potato, really anything can be made into wine. One day Ted was working in a field by the road when he saw an old chap going by on his bike with milk cartons of soft fruits which he sold locally each year. Suddenly there was a screech of brakes and a bang. Ted jumped over the gate. The poor old boy was lying in the road, fruit everywhere, luckily just winded. Ted saw the young man in the car was slumped over the steering wheel, so he opened the door and said "Are you alright mate?" The man said "I'm ok, but I can't bear to come out of the car, I know I've killed him." "Why do you think that?" said Ted. "Because I can see all his blood over the windscreen" came the reply. "That ain't blood" said Ted "that's raspberries." We had quite a laugh about it afterwards.

I could tell you a story about rabbit. In those days before freezers my brother rang up from Salisbury, he said "I tell you what, is it alright if we come down, Maureen and myself and the children?" He said "I've got a lovely rabbit, I bought it when I was working down at some place near Salisbury and I bought it in a butchers shop. I'll bring it with me." We only had a joint for Sunday, that's all we ever had and I said 'That's fine, you bring it on and we'll share it all out between us.' So Ted said to me "I haven't had rabbit for years." I said 'Well I'll make sure you have a good bit of it.' So Roy came and they went off down to the local pub and took the children with them. And Maureen, my sister-in-law and I, we put the rabbit on, and put vegetables with it and cooked it, and I kept pricking the rabbit and it was so tough, and I thought it must have been really old, and it didn't go a nice white colour, it was sort of red. And round about that time there had been a spate of cats being napped, and we were all sat round the table, there was eight children and us four adults, we were all sat along my long table, and I'd given Ted quite a fair bit of this rabbit, and we were all sat there eating and I said 'I'm sorry about the rabbit,' but it just wasn't very, you know, it had been on for about two hours, it should have been really tender, and Ted stuck his fork in and he picked it up on the end of his fork and he said "This is no bloody rabbit, this is a CAT." I said 'Oh God, you don't really think so do you?' and he said to my brother "Was there a head on it when you bought it?" He said "No, it was jointed." And after my brother went home Ted said to me "What did you give him all my beef for?" I was in the doghouse for that.

Ted's dad made cider. He used to get the apples from different people, he did have a few apple trees with the old apples on there, but it was lovely cider, but it knocked your head off. Damsons? We had loads of them. Ted used to put the kids in the bucket and swing the bucket up and they used to pick them off the tractor and that, and I'd take them to market and sell them.

We had our own vegetables, and we had a stream going through the whole farm where the cows used to drink off from. We had our own meat and vegetables and eggs, there wasn't very much that we didn't have really.

There were nights when I would get indoors and sit by the Rayburn, honestly, I'd have a job to walk up the stairs. We had an old-fashioned house with a door on the bottom, and I thought 'Oh God, I've got to walk up those stairs,' and also the mess that a house like that brings, wellies and straw, you take your boots off and there's straw everywhere, you try to keep it basically clean and it was very hard work. You always had piles of ironing coming on because there were more important things to do. The animals come before us. Equipment had to come before us. I remember an old aunt gave me some white, old flour bags, she sewed round them because I didn't have any tea cloths, and I was really thrilled at those. Can you imagine today somebody being thrilled if somebody gave you a few tea cloths made out of white bags?

One Christmas Eve Ted went up to the local borstal for a drink, 'cause he was an outside member, and I went to feed these little lambs that were behind the barn, I took my big torch up and the bottles up with me, and I was sat there and it was so quiet, and I looked up and the sky was really dark, the stars seemed like they were right in my face. I thought 'There couldn't be a better feeling in the world to what I've got right now.' I sat there behind that barn and all these little lambs tugging away, I had about six of them on the bottle, and had to keep the other four off, and I thought 'This is what life really is about,' I miss it terribly.

6. Phyllis Tuxhill – Wartime memories Weymouth. Born 1925.

We heard the whine of the plane diving, then the whine of the bomb, and by that time most of us knew how many bombs the planes carried and that there would be a rack of four or five or whatever, so we learnt to wait and count them off for each explosion…we heard the whistle…it was very close.

I was born in Weymouth District Hospital. My father was then an engineer in Whitehead Torpedo Works, my mother trained as a tailoress. My grandparents both lived in Weymouth but my father was born in London within the sound of Bow Bells, of which he was very proud! My mother's father was a dour Scotsman.

My father was working in the gyroscope department which is quite a critical part of the torpedo. It's what keeps the torpedoes running straight. He was on the manufacturing side. He didn't talk much about it. The torpedoes were tested across Weymouth Bay, and occasionally one would turn round and come back again, but they never had warheads on them when they were being tested. It was quite sensitive work. They used to get a lot of visitors from overseas. I remember at the time when the Japanese-Chinese War broke out they had a visiting Chinese delegation there and my father came home and told us this, "I said to them you must be worried with the Japanese invading and people being killed? And got the reply 'We are overpopulated, it doesn't matter'."

Well I was born in 1925, so when the war started in September '39, I was just 14. I was at Weymouth Grammar School. On the Sunday that war broke out on September 3rd, I and various friends had been to a church service at Holy Trinity Church, which is down by the harbour in Weymouth, and from there we went down to sit on the rocks down by Newton's Cove where we always went swimming.

You wore Sunday best in those days with hats and all the rest of the palaver, so we sat on the rocks, a whole group of us and one of the boys said "What would you do if a German submarine came out of the water now?" And I think we all said we'd run like mad, but at the same time we heard the church clock chiming and somebody said "We're at war" and there was a silence and we all sat there and then we somewhat sheepishly went home for lunch. It was a beautiful, gorgeous summer day, really lovely.

Then the next day the evacuees started arriving from London. It was a grammar school from Plaistow, and family evacuees, mothers with young children who had come from Stepney. They were very poor. I hadn't ever seen people with as few possessions. We had to collect clothes to kit some of the children out who really were not dressed suitably. Some of their shoes were almost non-existent. They all had their labels.

At the reception centre the WRVS were organising who would go to each billet and whether families could be kept together. My parents took a mother with a baby of eight months and a toddler. Looking back I'm not sure where we put them all because we didn't have a very big house. I was helping up there; it was an eye-opener. They were just so poor and they had so little. We weren't wealthy but I felt as though I had so much compared with those youngsters. I remember that they were all given a tin of corned beef, two pounds of sugar and a large block of Cadbury's chocolate which some of the kids fell on - I guess they hadn't had anything to eat.

We shared our grammar school with Plaistow; we went in the mornings, they went in the afternoons. Their teachers came but they were completely separate. The whole school came and we

Phyllis Tuxhill with Chesil Beach

used halls in the town in the afternoon and they used them in the mornings, which didn't make life very simple for people who were doing examinations, or for the staff trying to teach them.

First of all it was the phoney war, and then in the spring the raids started. They had built air raid shelters in the sports field behind the school by digging trenches and piling the earth on corrugated iron over the top and sand-bagging the entrances and there were benches to sit on. And whilst we were doing our exams every time the siren went we had to go down to the trenches and we were supposed not to talk to anybody and certainly not to talk about our exams, and the poor teachers had to walk up and down trying to make sure that we weren't discussing the exam papers or the answers to anything.

I remember one morning when I was going to do my art exam the siren went just as I was going to go out the front door and a Plaistow boy was running down the road to go to school and my mother said "Come in, there's going to be an air raid" and he said "I can't, I've got an exam" and I said 'Well so have I and I'm not going until the air raid's over.' So he came in and waited with us. It wasn't frightening, I don't remember being frightened, it was exciting.

The phoney war went on for almost a year, then at the end of May, early June the raids began, 1940. But they were the daylight raids, and because there were a lot of airfields near us there were a lot of aerial combats. I usually made sure I had a roof over my head while I watched it, but the boys stood out properly and were passing comments on who was winning and who wasn't, because we were near the sea, most of them went over the sea, people baled out. That was the year that it built up with more and more raids and then the bombing raids.

Portland. Well quite apart from the fact that it was a naval base, it sticks out into the Channel, it's a landmark and it was a submarine base and it was also the base for teaching people the Davis Escape apparatus used for submarines, there was a school there. It was a prison too, of course. There was a railway line between Portland and Weymouth in those days.

The raids built up, gradually they got more intensive and more fighting took place overhead, and then the daylight bombers, they were heavy, you knew the different sounds and you knew whether it was a German bomber or whether it was English planes overhead because their engines weren't synchronised in the same sort of way. I'm sorry to say people got hurt, I had an elderly great-aunt who was bombed out three times, just moved to the next street along, living in the same area, by the harbour in Weymouth, refusing to move anywhere else. You went on with your life.

Dive bombing was a bit different. That was a bit later. I should mention the day, I've forgotten the date, it was in September, when so many planes got shot down and the whole of the South of England was covered with dog fights right through the day and I think it was about 130-odd that got destroyed. Well it happened to coincide with Whitehead's sports day, the annual sports day which was on the field immediately behind the factory at Littlesea, between Weymouth and Portland, and my father was one of the stewards and they had all the prizes on a table. We had gone along just to watch and the raids started. The fighting started overhead and we all had to go to the shelters. I remember my father and a couple of men with him decided that they ought to move the prizes to safety because there were silver cups. They put them under the trestle table that they were standing on and it wasn't until later that evening that my father suddenly burst out laughing and said "Wasn't much use putting them under a trestle table was it!"

The dog fights. Oh yes there were a lot over the bay. We

didn't actually get any bombers coming, it was mainly Stukas and Spitfires from the airfield near by and a lot of dog fights and breaking off coming back, with gaps inbetween when you went and sort of tried to run the sports. That was quite a day.

Then after that date there was a sort of gap and then they started night bombing. Because of Portland being such a landmark into the sea which you could pick up in virtually any weather, they used Portland as a landmark. They bombed it because of the dockyard and there were warships in, they were refuelling and things like that. They bombed Weymouth harbour as well. They also used Portland as a landmark to go inland to Bristol, Birmingham and up country. We usually knew where they had been by the length of time it had taken and then on the way back if they hadn't found their targets or the anti-aircraft guns had been too strong and they hadn't been able to drop their bombs, they dropped them on our area as they came back. I think it was the fact that there was Chesil Beach and the sea on one side and Weymouth Bay and the sea on the other made a tremendous difference. I once saw a map where the sea was littered with marks where the bombs had dropped but although a lot landed on the land, the sea saved us.

Well then soon after that my father got sent up to Street because part of the Whitehead's factory was sent to Street and he was in digs in Glastonbury. We stayed at home and his oldest sister came and joined us as well. We went on with life as usual, we had a Morrison shelter, if the raids were bad at night we went to the Morrison shelter and it was '42 I think and there was a lot of night bombing, it was particularly bad. I'd had a particularly bad attack of flu that year, and for the first and only time, I had chilblains because we couldn't get enough coal. We got a ration but it didn't go round properly and there was no central heating.

Food was boring at times but adequate. Mum was a good cook and stretched it somehow or other. There wasn't supposed to be any fishing but men did go out and neighbours would come and say "I've got some mackerel for you." Somebody else might come back and say "I've managed a few extra eggs this week, would you like these?" It wasn't luxurious, it was dull. There was always enough. The evacuees from Plaistow went back and they went back into the first London bombs. They were much worse off than we were, definitely. But somehow the children flourished and life went on.

In Weymouth I was a messenger in the ARP service, and it just so happened that the ARP post was right next door to where we lived so I never had very far to go. My father was a warden and he saw more than I did. Apart from my aunt when I saw her in hospital, I didn't see any bodies at all, I was told about them and that they had got so and so out and my father relates a tale when one Sunday lunchtime we had a short daylight raid, they nipped in and out like this, they'd dropped some bombs on the school at the top of our short road and some houses had been demolished. He with some other wardens had gone up to see and they'd rescued a lady who'd been cooking the Sunday lunch. There weren't many people at home, fortunately, in the homes that were damaged, and the kitchen table had blown over on top of her and had protected her and when they got her out and Father and another man were helping her onto a stretcher to go to hospital to be checked and Dad said "How are you feeling?" she said "I'm fine, I was as safe as houses." But she didn't have a house left.

So you know, it was an odd period when you look back. People made jokes out of everything, and people listened to Haw Haw and they treated it as if it was an entertainment show, I don't think people believed anything! In the morning you'd hear people saying "Did you hear old Lord Haw Haw last night? He got that wrong didn't he?" You know "We know very well they didn't go there!"

Then it was a particular night raid, it was the Thursday before Good Friday, this was '42 and the raids started at about nine o'clock at night, there were lots of planes going over and ack ack fire and searchlight and all the usual things and then we started having dive bombers. We had all four of us, my aunt, my mother, my aunt was a large lady I may add, a young boyfriend of mine who had come to supper and myself all crowded into our Morrison shelter. Father had put a mattress at the bottom so there was something soft under us, and it was in the small dining room in the house, in fact it became the dining room table because there wasn't room for the table as well as the shelter and it was nasty, I must admit. We heard the whine of the plane diving, then the whine of the bomb, and by that time most of us knew how many bombs most of the planes carried and that there would be a rack of four or five or whatever, so we learnt to wait and count them off for each explosion. The boyfriend I had was in the air cadets and he used to produce all this information, he did join the Air Force and became a navigator, actually, so we lay there counting and we knew that there was one more to come and when we heard the whistle it was very close. We had a small garden at the back of the house, very small and behind it was the town cemetery and the bomb pitched over the wall but it didn't explode, it was unexploded and they had to get it out next day. But it was enough, even without exploding, to take the tiles off the roof, to bring down ceilings throughout the house, to break the glass which we had already stuck tape over as we were advised to do behind the blackout curtains. My mother had just made four cups of cocoa before this had happened and they were still on the top of the Morrison shelter next morning, each with a thick edging of plaster cream on top of them! Silly the things one remembers, isn't it?

We left my aunt in charge of the clearing up and left to catch the train, you changed at Wytham Friary to get on to the Somerset and Dorset line to come into Wells where Father was meeting us and we came up for the weekend. My mother's nerve had gone and she just wouldn't go back. My father's works had moved to the Clark's factory, to what they called the big room. So there they were working on gyroscopes for torpedoes in a shoe factory. In a Quaker shoe factory! Of course, I think they were told they had to have something, and by having the gyroscopes I imagine that salved the conscience. It was a very large room, ideally set up for small machinery. They kept making shoes. They made flying boots and were the first people to make desert boots.

Yes, it was trying, life wasn't easy, but I don't remember at any time thinking that we weren't going to win, no matter how dark the news got. VE Day. Well I remember a whole crowd of us we had a bonfire on top of Wearyall Hill in Glastonbury where the Holy thorn was planted and there were masses of people and people were dancing around the Cross, in the town but at midnight, they'd lit the bonfire and a whole crowd of us went up and danced round the bonfire on top. I think there were about six of us, three girls and three young chaps. It was bright, it was lively and next day you went to work.

Until of course the atom bombs in Japan and that I found horrifying. We knew about the Japanese prisoners of war... But the holocaust, we didn't really know about the holocaust before the end of the war. You didn't get the pictures that quickly. There was the Picture Post. Yes, but a lot of the national papers had black and white pictures anyway. And of course they were restricted by the amount of paper they could use. It did make a difference, you couldn't always buy a newspaper, there were limited numbers that came out. And if you hadn't got one ordered you couldn't get one quite often. Then they were finding the people who'd been in the Japanese camps.

The atom bomb. The Hiroshima one was on my birthday. So I'm never going to forget it. It came over on the radio. They used the word 'atom bomb,' but they didn't use the word 'nuclear,' or any mention of nuclear war. They said that a very large bomb, the equivalent of however many tons of TNT it was, had been exploded in Hiroshima and that it was a special type of bomb that sent up a mushroom cloud and that there was an enormous fallout of radioactive dust. At that stage, nobody realised the damage or the effect that it was having on people. I'm amazed, looking back, that they didn't give in after the first one. I think that's what they expected, quite frankly. But the second one was very close, I think, about a week. And then of course the more we knew and the more we learnt about the Holocaust and the Jews and the people, not just Jews but people who had been put in prison for absolutely no reason and killed or worked until they dropped and then the people coming back from Japan, and I think it was then that the horrors began to come.

You were told about bombs, you were told about Bath and Coventry and the Baedeker raids and the damage that was done and you saw newsreel pictures of it, I mean you didn't have television, you didn't have it inside your home, it was only the odd black and white picture in a newspaper or a magazine or a newsreel at the cinema, which was very limited and very edited, looking back. But you did realise how bad they were. I had an aunt and uncle living in Bristol, the area that was bombed, Wine Street, Castle Street, which before the war was THE shopping area in Bristol with the big department stores, just went. There was nothing. I remember going back before they'd started clearing everything, walking around and not being able to work

out which street was which any more and then thinking 'Oh yes, well I know that church, don't I?'

Soon after the war had started they stopped you going down on the beaches in Weymouth, but they didn't put the barbed wire up overnight, it came up over a period and I have swum during the war off the beach in Weymouth, having gone through gaps in the barbed wire to get there.

The beaches weren't mined, just barbed wire, because they were using them, when the Americans came and they were practising the landings and that type of thing. They were using the beaches all along the south coast. Whether they were steep and shelving or whether they were shallow and went out for miles, but I wasn't living in Weymouth then, although I used to go and visit and stay for weekends with a friend. The Americans of course were in Glastonbury, they were billeted at Millfield school. It was just Millfield House then, with huts all over the grounds which eventually became the buildings for Millfield school, there were two big camps near Street and Glastonbury

Cider, they couldn't really handle it. Some of them learnt quite quickly, but whenever a rookie came who hadn't been in the area before, he was plied with the rough scrumpy without realising, thinking it was apple juice I think and not realising that the effect it would have as soon as he hit the cold air outside. But my parents had people home for meals, they were young lads of 20 and 21, I think they just tried to provide a bit of home life. They were appreciative, they were very pleasant. I never fell for any of them, the dances were lively, we used to have weekly dances at Crispin Hall in Street. The friend I usually went with, her mother came to do the refreshments so we were always walked home afterwards…

7. Ruby James, Scrap dealer & Spitfire Girl, Cann Common, near Shaftesbury. Born 1924.

I used to help my father do the scrap metal. I used to go with him on the pony and milk float to pick up the iron…Then I went to Westlands in Yeovil…We were making Spitfires. So I am really a Spitfire girl. I was working on the rear fuselage, rivetting. After Spitfires we did the carpets.

I am Ruby James, born at Wincanton in 1924, 82 in April. I have been in Cann Common 50 years and before I came here, I worked on a bread round in Shaftesbury, Nicholas and Harris in Salisbury Street. My mother had married from Wincanton and came to Shaftesbury to live, because my father was a Shaftesbury man. Of course I was only three weeks old when I came to Shaftesbury and I've been here ever since. Father was a scrap metal merchant. It was a very good occupation then, very good. He collected anything and everything. Farm sales, you know, he did all that, he bought machinery, second-hand machinery and sold it on. You know in those days it was just the one-horse plough, you know, that sort of thing.

So what he was dealing in then, in the 20s and 30s, would now be museum pieces. Governess carts. Lovely. We used to drive one, my mother and father couldn't drive a car and so we used to go out in a Governess cart. Almost everything was horse-drawn then. But I was one of the first lady drivers in our road. Taught myself! My brother said "You'll never be able to drive, you know." But I proved him wrong. First I went from Shaftesbury to Fontmell Magna. I went up Cann Hill and I don't know how I got up there! I didn't know which gear I was in or anything. Oh dear!

Grandfather was a confectioner. My father and three brothers were in the First World War and they all came back, the four brothers. My father was a mounted policeman on horseback like, going back to horseback days. Father talked about it, yes, he told us some lovely stories about orange groves and things like that. He was in India. He had this one brother that was in the Army, an older brother and he was a bit of a one for the cider and that you see, and he was on the quay in Bombay, but they call it a different name now, don't they? Mumbai, and he said to his mate "Well that couldn't be anything," he said "But our Reg!" And the brothers they met on the harbour or whatever it was the quay in Bombay 'cause he was drunk! And my father recognised him, his brother! And later both of them finished up in Salisbury Infirmary in the same ward. No they weren't injured. But one had a ricochet bullet in his neck or something but they all came back quite well really. They were very, very lucky.

My first memories? I didn't go to school until I was six. That's about the first memory, I should think. I liked school, there was no problem, we had a long way to walk. We lived on the Salisbury road, the A30, Five Square, you know, and you used to have to walk to what was the little Cann School it was then, and then we had to go right up by the hospital. It's flats now, like. And there were no problems. We left at 14 and then I took a job, my mother had to give £2 for a second-hand bicycle for me and I had to cycle in to Ludwell to clean up two houses made into one, like, you know. And this one particular morning she came out to the gate to see me off on this bike and it was snowing heavens hard, and I went there a month on trial, and she said to me : "Phew, some weather. If you're worth that," she said. "Seven and sixpence a week for that woman" she said. "You're worth that to me to stay home" she said "Give your notice in today!" And I did, I came home, I didn't do anything

Ruby James with her Rayburn   *'Rumour has it…I have even got a crystal ball…'*

then, other than be at home, until I was 17 and I went to Westlands in Yeovil then, you know.

We were making spitfires. So I am really a Spitfire girl! And Seafires. It was a branch factory at Bradford Abbas. They had two, one in Sherborne and one in Bradford Abbas. We used to make all the bits and pieces of the planes and then they took them down to Yeovil. I was working on the rear fuselage, rivetting. You'd have different colours and different sized rivets and four of us girls were put up like, on the men's department of the big RAF hanger and then we'd work with them. We got better wages then. A lorry used to come up and pick up the bits and pieces that we'd done and take 'em back to Yeovil and they were assembled there.

I did that for nearly four years. There were a lot of women there. You had to get your overalls and oh it was cold. I used to leave home at six and get home at seven at night. I came home every night. A coach used to pick me up, and you picked up all the way along. It was a long day, but at 17 you don't think about it. It wasn't too badly paid. Oh no. It was 34 shillings a week when I went there and after a year I supposed I went up onto this rear fuselage and then you got about £4.50 which was quite good then. I don't recall any overtime, no 'cause it was set, you got there at seven and left at six.

So when the war stopped, well I was the first to leave! It was all right up to a point but of course I'd never been shut in before, had I? You didn't like that regimentation sort of business. It was very cold in winter and very hot in summer. Well that's how it was. They had some sort of heaters which were right up in the roof if you know what I mean. Nice people.

Before that I used to help my father do the scrap metal. I used to go with him on the pony and milk float to pick up the iron and course while I was at Westlands he had nobody to do that so he cleared out the yard and everything and then he took this job, well it was from nine o'clock until four, that sort of thing, to help a farmer. The scrap metal went to a firm…Wilton, they used to come and pick it up. They had lorries and men to sort it. You used to get a heap of iron. I went with him in our cart, it was a milk float, he'd get this heap of iron, quite a good heap, and he'd sell it twice a year. Then after that was all finished he went to work on this farm you see. He didn't often weigh it, he was a pretty good judge. He lumped it as they call it, you know. But if people came in with scrap…Oh yes they weighed it then, yes, 'cause we had some of those sort of scales, you know, my mother had bought them second-hand, and course the Customs and Excise come and condemned them and I remember having to drive to Salisbury to get a new pair! Oh yes we had the higher value metals, we had all that and we used to have to keep a book and the CID used to come in and see that book, what you'd bought in, you'd put that in one book and when you sold it you'd put that in another book and they used to come and see your books, like. As it was just over the border in Wiltshire, they used to come from Trowbridge, the CID officers or whatever it was at that time used to come and see that your books were straight and that. It might have been that because you used to buy batteries and that sort of thing, you know, and often the police would pull up outside and say "Can I have a look round?" and we'd say 'Certainly you have a look round' but we'd never get anything, you know. The batteries? Well you moved them very quickly like, you'd get perhaps 30 and they'd go and you wouldn't have a problem, but I think you have to have a drainage thing or something, you know, that sort of thing.

Recycling metal was good business, must have been quite good business, 'cause you had like copper and you knew that if you got more of that that was a better price than anything else.

Aluminium hadn't really come in then, and of course you needed so much aluminium for big hundredweights, you know.

We were getting old cooking pots. Half of them would be antiques these days. We could have kept some but we didn't. Everything went in the bag in those days, you know. Thinking back, you went to a sale and there'd be six or seven brass lamps, you took 'em back and you threw all the tinny bits away and you put 'em in the bag. People would pay an arm and a leg for them now. Good gracious. Never kept a thing, never kept a thing.

It's rather funny because I can remember going with my mother to a farm sale in Handley, and she gave a pound for this pony plough, you know, and my father said when we got back "What the hell did you get that for? How're we going to get that home?" You know, she said "I'll get it home somehow." Well a friend of ours came from Frome and he had a little lorry and she said "Jack will you take me to Handley?" And he said "Yes, course I will." And she went with him and got this plough from this farm sale it was. And all of a sudden the next door neighbour, he used to grow swedes and all that and he said "I don't suppose you've got such a thing as a pony plough?" It was funny, the farmer just down the road. And "Yes I have, Mr Hall" she said. And that was the end of the pony plough.

After Spitfires…we did the carpets. It was interesting. They were beautiful really. It's a lovely pattern, that Turkey pattern, isn't it? Did you see that man Cruickshank with the carpets? Well we used to sell them too. Never kept one of those for ourselves. If you sold a new one you see, you took the old one back. And the old one was worth more than the new one!

Well I got married in 1953, and came to Melbury and been here ever since. It's technically Cann Common but Melbury Abbas. It's Cann Common right to those fields there and Melbury starts up the top…And Matthew's Vice Chairman of the parish council. That covers Melbury and Cann and that goes as far as Guy's Marsh. He has to go down to meet the Governor down there sometimes to say what's happening and that. It's actually high security now. We get them from Portland. Some of them are very bad boys I believe, really quite high security. I did work there for a short while when it was a military hospital, an English military hospital, then the Americans came, I'd left before the Americans came and, not for very long, for about a year, I suppose. The sisters' mess.

When they had the young offenders first of all they used to take them for a walk from there all up over those hills and then they come back up this way and walk back. And one chap, he was about 15 or 20, when they escaped they always came this way 'cause they knew it you see. While we were down at the bungalow, the neighbour over the road she said, what did she say, oh she said : "Did you hear the Landrover and the police," she said, "that were out last night" she said. "Oh," she said, "they went all round your bungalow, with a torch," she said. "There were some borstal boys out!" We never heard a thing! So ignorance is bliss you see.

I knew Lucian Freud in his younger days. He lived in the same village as me when he was married to Lady Caroline Blackwood. She was Irish, from the Guinness family and she couldn't drive a car because she only had an Irish driving licence and she used to come in and talk to me and my mother on the Salisbury road. And he used to drive up and down 'cause we knew him like, we saw him walking about. Coombe, a little village over there, and he used to drive that car like mad. This was in the 50s or 60s the Priory, that's where they lived in Coombe, but somebody's painted over it, there's a whole wall that he did in one of the rooms there that he did of fuschias or was it irises? But somebody's stupidly painted over it. Whether it would be still there or not I don't know. Garbo stayed there as well, didn't she, Greta Garbo? It was a shame really about it because he was only renting it, Ashcombe. Bitterly upset about it, Cecil Beaton was only renting it and he asked "Could he decorate it?" and the owner said "Yes he could do it." And then he pulled the rug out of under his feet and wouldn't give him another lease and now we've heard that Madonna won't come there to live until the building's finished. She's caused some controversy, put up some gates without permission and then had to get it retrospectively…Then there was a thing about some footpaths, wasn't there? I don't think she knew that when she bought it, 'cause she did get some moved.

No, Lucian Freud, he lived here with Lady Caroline. She had two sisters besides and a brother. She used to ride a bicycle up and come and talk to my mother and I. Then we had Sandeman, the port man who lived there, and they divorced. But I must tell you a tale about my brother. He used to walk down through Coombe like, he's always been a walker and that, and he used to talk to this Mr Sandeman and his wife and they had a little girl like, and they were all together there talking, and they had a flat somewhere in London where they lived, I think it was near Trafalgar Square. And my late husband was in hospital at Salisbury and I had a cousin that was standing with a stall in Salisbury market every Tuesday and Saturday that was living in Maldon in Essex you see. So my brother had some business to do, metal business at Battersea. So he said "Would you take me" he said "to Salisbury" he said, "catch a lift with Peter" he said "back to London?" 'Course I will' I said. Well, we were going to see my husband, dropped him in Salisbury, picked up with Peter, he went to London. Well he knew that we had a cousin staying at Croydon at that particular time, so he went and saw his business, what he had to do at Battersea, how he got there I don't

know. He knew he could stay with these cousins at Croydon overnight like, and he, well, he caught the train or something back to Croydon, and he got there at ten o'clock at night and shouted her up you see and she thought it was the milkman. Well anyway, 'cause of course she let him in and he'd worn out his socks with walking, he was a terrific walker and that and she had to find him a pair of socks to go on, he didn't have the sense to go and buy any, so course he stayed there that night and the next day he had to get back into London to get home you see. So he got back into London and he thought to himself, "Well this Mr Sandeman had told him that he had a flat and he lived by the Marble Arch," well he went and found him out. Doorman there, rang the bell, whichever number it was, so Mrs Sandeman came to the door, he said to her "Is Mr Sandeman going back to Coombe today?" "Wait a minute," she said "I'll just go and ask him." So he came to the door so he said "Are you going back?" So he said "Yes I am." He said "In about an hour's time. Would you like," he said "to go and get yourself a drink," he said "and something to eat?" he said. "You can go back with me." And he came all the way back from Marble Arch in a Mercedes car, a new one, with this Mr Sandeman and the two dogs, and he dropped him outside of our house and he went into Shaftesbury and got some dog meat, and he never had to spend a penny, well he had to get from London to Croydon, you know but…He's a very good person for knowing his way, you know, he never really gets lost.

No. We have sold everything here at one time or another: stone bird baths, stone pineapples, great big ones, urns, stone troughs, staddle stones even gnomes, refined ones of course, furniture, antiques, house clearances you know. Our house is made from Purbeck stone, came from a small quarry over there, we built it ourselves, went over there in a lorry and collected it bit by bit. One day Matthew will finish it off, yes we sell peat, logs, compost, all word of mouth, never advertised, all recommendation. We had Andrew Lloyd Webber in here one day and that lady from Cadbury's. She turned up one day, lived in Bournemouth, we have had cider presses, fish kettles, old post office vans, red ones, green ones, a couple of lions…

Rumour has it…I have even got a crystal ball…

8. Rose Whitcomb – Kennel man.
Toller Porcorum. Born 1932.

Oh yes. I just liked hounds. I've only ever liked the bloody hounds! Plain and simple. You don't need money to go hunting. All you need's a bicycle.

The puppies have been chewing the furniture. The sofa. They've been chewing the carpet as well. That's why I have a new carpet every other year. I have actually got one in the bedroom. I took this sofa out, well the one that was here, then I couldn't get it through the bloody door, that was square you see, finished up with a spade underneath it, had to take the door off, couldn't get the bloody door back on! Well yes. When you live on your own you either do it yourself or it don't get done.

Me proper name is Margaret Rosalind, but I've always been called Rose. I was called Rosalind at school, well Rossa by the kids and Rosalind by the teachers, born in 1932 in Walton-on-Thames. Mother was born in Newcastle-upon-Tyne, her mother come from Alnwick which is a bit further up and her father was a border shepherd who married a gypsy. They lived in a little place above Newcastle-upon-Tyne called Alnwick and the father and the two brothers was killed in the Tweed, when the bore come down the Tweed, getting the sheep out the Tweed, you know the water bore, same as the Severn. You never hear about the Tweed Bore, but you hear about the Severn Bore, I think because the Severn Bore is more spectacular. They were drowned. Which year? No. Couldn't tell you. It'd be before 1900 because she was born before 1900 and she was getting on a bit when she had us. I'm a twin.

Dad was Petworth, Sussex, which is his ancestral home. Him and his brother, they joined up in the First World War, 'cause everybody did, but they sent his brother home because he couldn't get away with being older than what he said. They were both big chaps. Dad was an aeromechanic in the First World War. I'm very proud of me father being in the Flying Corps before it was in the Air Force.

Mother actually was one of the first kennel maids that there ever were. Below London in Bellmead Kennels. Looking after dogs for boarding. After she got married she used to take puppies to house train. Yes. There was always dogs. Cinder. She was us kids' dog, a little cross bred thing. We was 16 when she died. When I say 'we' it's always me and my sister. My sister's Juliet. Mother was all into Shakespeare you know! She was actually a well educated woman, was mother. We lived by the main Southampton to London mainline. You see, when Dad come home on leave we were in the shelter they would be shouting "Your husband's just got off the train Molly!" Mother would shout back "He know where to find us." And our neighbours always used to stand outside the shelter where they'd got us bunged in it, we slept in the shelters for however long, the Battle of Britain was and all that, Fire of London and it wasn't till Dad came out the pub. As I say we lived on the main Southampton to London line and the railway was on a viaduct, and he come under the bridge from the pub was the other side and there was two bombs dropped in the road. He had got our side of the bridge and he thought it was time to shift the Mrs and the kids. That was when we moved to Derbyshire.

It must have been '41-'42 The only time I can remember being frightened was when there was a lull one afternoon and the parents had all rushed down to the school to get the kids and I lost my mother. That's frightening when you're a kid.

Me twin sister. No. We don't really look alike. Some of them called us 'Twinnie Whitcombs'. Me with me gammy leg limping

Rose Whitcomb with Poppet, Toller Porcorum

about all over the place, and she's taller than me anyway. She was normal. Well she was into more young female things, whereas I wasn't. I was always a bit of a tomboy. Oh arr. Yeah. I could always climb trees better than the other kids. I've never called meself crippled. I had polio when I was a baby and me mother was determined that I would bloody walk. I did have a calliper. The doctors in the hospital said "Oh she'll never walk" so mother said "Sod that for a game of soldiers, I'm not pushing her about in a wheelchair all her life." She was determined and I were determined. Oh yes. I don't know whether the bloody mindedness is there to start with or whether you get bloody minded but you remain bloody minded all your life. Teased at school? Not likely, I used to hit 'em! I couldn't see why anybody else couldn't get over it! Polio I'd had it in '32 you see, I was only six months old when I had it, they never actually got the vaccine until the 60s you know.

Me grandparents on me father's side was farmers and builders, down Petworth, and oddly enough, me great grandfather was the one with get up and go 'cause he built Leconfield Kennels at Petworth. More hounds. Dad had hunted as a child. He'd hunted with the Leconfield. Now it's Chiddingfold, Leconfield and Cowdray. Chiddingleck they call it nowadays. Fox hunting. Oh yes. Oh we didn't know nowt about beagling until I was in me 20s actually. 'Cause there was no beagles about much.

Where am I? Dad went, he was in the RAF stationed in Derbyshire. He wasn't a flyer, he was a motor mechanic by trade. He drove his car on Mother's hairpins! "Mother! Lend us a hairpin while I mend the car!" when it broke down. He went to North Africa and Italy and before he went he bought a hound pup, a white bitch called Parachute. I thought she was the best thing since sliced bread, and have never changed my mind.

Derbyshire'll be '42 about, so nine or ten. Very rural. When I left school, 1946, you had two choices where we lived, you either went into service, or you went into Nestles. There was about five of us from Sudbury, the village where we lived, went to Nestles. They did tinned milk, they done army composite packs, and in the spring when there was a flush of milk they was condensing. But what you used to get was every fortnight, and this was still rationing you see, you used to get a bit of chocolate, tins of Nescafe. You had them cheap, you know, half price or something.

Yes, it was a production line. I was filling things up. Very, very… boring. Oh Ha ha! Your mind goes off, you know. Radio? Oh arr yeah, you had Worker's Playtime! It was ever so modern in them days! You didn't have much of a social life because we lived too far out. On your bike in the summer and on the bus in the winter, and you carried the hurricane lamp to see your way down in the fields 'cause we lived up, what was it? Two lanes and three fields when we caught the bus, used to leave the hurricane lamp in the bus shelter which was the drunk hole! We had a drunk hole in our village! It was half as big as this with a bloody great door, anybody that was drunk they used to push them in it years back! The village used it as a bus shelter, about the first one I should think. The factory was about five miles from home and when you heard the ten minute bell go you had to go! Clock in, clock out.

Mother had her own dogs, the Scotties and Cinder, the little cross bred dandy, and she was us kids' dog 'cause she'd always come to bed with me. I went into Uttoxeter the day before I went on holiday, I was going on holiday with Dad down to Petworth and I was 17 and I come back on the bus with Mrs Stone who was the housekeeper to the master of the foxhounds. And she said Johnny was having to go, that was her son, Johnny was having to go to do his national service and that they hadn't got anyone as the second kennel man at the kennels, so I said 'I'll go.' The kennels was at Sudbury, the same village that we lived in. The Meynel Hunt. I said 'I'll do that.' Second kennel man. I was offered the job, the Mrs went round to see Mother. Unusual for a woman to do that job? Oh yes, but I just liked hounds. I've only ever liked the bloody hounds! Plain and simple.

I was four years there. You was tidying up, washing down, scrubbing down, making grub. They used to eat anything. You had your knacker meat, you know, your dead stuff, and you'd skin that, That was horse, cows, sheep and that was all cooked, you boiled it. Just smelt like meat cooking, didn't it? It's not a bad smell, you cooked it on the bone and boned it when it was cooked. In cauldrons. They come out of Bass' brewery and you had a big steam engine and the steam went round the copper and that boiled the grub in the copper. That was every day. It was always fresh.

We probably had 50, 60 hounds. You was restricted on how many because of how much grub you got. Used to have a basis, you see, to put the meat on. We'd cook stock feed potatoes. You didn't get a lot of meal, it was barley meal, and brewer's grains. You'd put the meat and gravy on it. Fox hunting through the winter basically. Then in the summer exercising. There was four of us that worked in the kennels, three men and myself. I was the one that walked behind, they call it whipping in, you know 'Go on, don't sit there all day, hurry up and finish and get on.' You have to leave them to empty, like, but not let them stay there sniffing about. You've got to keep them up together.

I've never liked walking dogs on leads. They were walked twice a day. Morning and afternoon. The kennels is the whole of it, the lodge is where you keep your hounds. They lay up on the beds with straw, always straw. Ah, you'd feed them when they come back from hunting. You don't feed them before the hunt.

The hunt went out three days a week. The kennel huntsman and George, they hunted, they'd be on horses. One man, the kennel man and I did the work at home. The master hunted the hounds, he was the master huntsman. Charismatic my eye, you ain't got the faintest idea what charismatic means 'til you come across him, matey. He never had any money but he was ever such a clever feller with the hounds.

The master, the kennel huntsman and the whip. They was the three from the kennels that went out. Mostly they was farmers, they was servicemen on leave. Oh people get this idea that it's only people with a lot of money that go hunting. You don't need money to go hunting. All you need's a bicycle.

Foxhounds hunt foxes, otter hounds them days used to hunt otter and beagles hunt the hare, and staggies, stag hounds, which is a bigger hound than a foxhound, they used to hunt the stags and you got the deer hounds. It's horses for courses. You don't hunt what somebody else hunts, and if you do it's riot. You get your arse slapped.

I went to Cirencester when I was 21, yeah. That was foxhounds. Cirencester Park. There was two VWH's – VWH is Vale of the White Horse. The country had been divided then between Cricklade and Bathurst and they'd made two separate kennels. They're all back in one country now.

I went on interview to see Lady Apsley, and she said to me, she'd broke her back hunting, been in a wheelchair for donkey's years, and she said to me "Of course, Rose" she said, "living so near the town, we don't want any talk!" And I said 'Oh no, M'Lady, I don't think you'll have any trouble like that with me!' I thought 'Too bloody right you won't! I'll keep my nose clean, Mrs!'

I was there six years. Then we had a new huntsman come in and I got instantly dismissed. There'd been a barney because I'd objected strongly to leaving puppies without any bloody dinner. Old Alf was keeping his head down. I was feeding the puppies and I was feeding them nine o'clock in the morning. Tom came in, and he didn't feed 'em until 12 o'clock, after they'd been on two hours exercise on horses with the hounds. I said it wasn't good enough. They, the puppies, couldn't wait 'til 12 o'clock for their morning meal. But it was me that got the sack. They had me on the carpet, Lordy and Tilbrook did, and he says "Tom's father was a huntsman and his father before him", which is a load of old cobblers, i'n't it? And I said 'Yes' I said, folding me arms, 'my father flew aeroplanes but it didn't make me Amy Johnson!' And Lordy said "Well that doesn't really matter, you know, Rose." And I thought 'Well, sauce for the gander, sauce for the goose.' So I got dismissed, I'd have shot the bugger. I'd have shot bloody Tilbrook.

I then went to the Isle of Wight next. We had the beagles and foxhounds there as well. That didn't suit me at all so I went to the through the winter and then this Chilmark beagles next. The job was advertised. I went one day into Salisbury and I saw one of the grooms that was at Cirencester and she was working for the sister of a chap called Commander Oram, and he was amateur whip at Cirencester, I'd known Dorothy, 'cause she was his groom and they only lived just down below the kennels, and I saw Dorothy and I said 'Where are you then?' and she was working with Mrs. Oram's sister. Anyway, it turned out Mrs Oram's sister Miss Abbey who lives here at Chetnole and is moving to Yetminster, and she was talking over dinner and the Commander said he was looking for another kennel man and he wished he knew where I was, 'cause I'd known him at Cirencester and she said "Oh I know where she is" so I got the job at North Hereford. I was there nine years. That was foxhounds of course.

Then Jack Stevens, the huntsman, was retiring, a more honest chap you couldn't find anywhere, he went into Securicor. I went to the Grove and Rufford in Nottingham. Mother and me, we'd been there about a fortnight and John was there as the whip and Fred the huntsman went on holiday. John got married and did a moonlight flit a month later! And I helped him flit, it was that sort of a job! We was both taken in and I couldn't flit 'cause me father had died by then and me mother was living with me, and she was getting a bit gaga and I had to stick it out 'til the end of the season. I'd said at Christmas time that I'd be leaving, and I picked the phone up and come to Cattistock, and that was the only job I had offered.

Cattistock the kennels. You always got accommodation when you was working in the kennels 'cause it was seven days a week. I came in as second kennel man! David who was kennel huntsman, he'd say to me to walk the rest hounds, he'd feed one lot and I'd take the other lot out to walk and dodge him coming in, like.

Otter hounds? Well, after two years, I was coming up 40-odd, and I thought to meself 'It's time I bloody got out.' And I liked it down here. 'Would I go up to Badminton to fetch this bitch back?' He didn't want to go there 'cause he'd come from there, would I go back there, so I went and got her and I come back along the top road, you know, the Yeovil-Dorchester road, bloody lovely. And I come down in the kennels and I said to David's wife, I said 'Do you know what? It's bloody lovely down here, i'n't it?' She says "It's not bad!" I said 'Do you know what? I'm not going to go back there, I'll go along there a bit but I'm certainly not going back there!'

So I came to Toller. I bought the thatched house down there, it was derelict then. There was two old folks living in the bottom side. My sister paid for it to be done up. Was it £500 I paid for it? It was quite a lot for the one house, but I wanted all the garden and I had to get the other house and that was more derelict than the one I was in. That was '72 . Just down the road. I built the boarding kennels that was down there. My sister done the stone on the porch. She come down here on holiday for a bit and she carved the stone out. She's quite handy with the paddies.

I was up with the otter hounds, they're bloody great hairy things. I was offered the otter hounds by Mrs Van der Kirst, she was in with the Courtney Tracey otter hounds since the year dot, about 40 bloody years she was mixed up with the otter hounds, and I met her when I was at Chilmark, 'cause that was Courtney Tracy country round there. But when I'd tried to go out with the otter hounds I'd never seen anything, all I did was walk along the river as far as I could see. They was genuine Courtney Tracey otter hounds.

The last ten years they had a 'no kill' policy on otters because they reckoned they was getting shorter. From a conservation point of view the otter hunters themselves put a ban on killing otters long before any law was made. Oh they just had a bit of a hunt round. Sport? Oh yeah, no determination to catch them. Towards the end of it they was finding mink. After putting the 'no kill' ban on the catching of otters, they turned them into mink hounds. And Mrs Van der Kirst came to me and she said would I take the otter hounds. So I had the otter hounds. We had four couple of dogs and four couple of bitches from the kennels at Wilton.

You encouraged them to catch mink. They do kill everything, and stuff a lot bigger than themselves too. I've always maintained that a mink will kill a baby otter but a full grown otter will kill a mink. You see they talk so much bloody rubbish about otters, you know Trigon, below Wareham, all wild as everything, because the Frome runs through there, there must

have been otters there all along. There's places where it's so wild like that, down in the West Country, where there were never not otters. On the Somerset Levels, I was talking to a chap the other day whose family were otter hunters up north, and he's always been, his whole family, his grandmother was master of otter hounds, and he was saying, I said 'We aren't finding any mink this year' he said "No" he said "on the Somerset Levels," he said "there's a fluke in the fish and the mink are catching the fish and getting the fluke and so are the otters." They have found some otters, not as many as they have the mink.

I've only ever seen an otter one once in the wild and that was this dead young 'un that had been killed by a dog, but it had been killed about a fortnight beforehand. The ban did nothing. You know we're not hunting mink now, we're only hunting rats… and only when they jump out at us…

About 16, 17 years I had them, 'til I had a very bad road accident, which was the Antis, 'cause they'd done this silly trick, and 'cause it was Christmas Eve and I wasn't thinking of Antis, what I'd got to do was go to South Dorset to get some meat for me dogs, 'cause I used to walk hounds for South Dorset, and Cattistock weren't knackering, so I couldn't go there, and I was going along and a car came out from Stratton and it crossed the road in front of me and I slapped me brakes on. Old car it was, old Marina, went down the road in front of me 'You silly bugger, pull your choke out, you'll get on then!' and it slowed and I hurriedly stopped and we got going again and he did it again, and I was going far too fast and I went off the bloody road so as not to go up his arse and hit a tree and a branch come down across the cab. It would have come down across on me, but I dislike seatbelts. I reckon I threw meself sideways, 'cause I have got quick reactions. I broke all sorts of bloody things as well as having concussion and double vision.

Hunting. I wouldn't like to see the end of it. It has got a lot of following. You can go out, you know, who wants to go hunting when it's pouring down with rain or it's freezing bloody cold or pouring down with rain, but when you get older you say 'sod it' don't you? But I hunt all the year round really. I used to go out with the beagles in the winter, I go out with the foxhounds, I go out with the Cattistock foxhounds, I go out with the Blackmore Vale, I go out with the South Dorset. Legally you can catch rats and rabbits.

Hounds too old to hunt? You never shoot one hound in front of another. Well, I wouldn't, the majority of people I know wouldn't. It's the hardest part of your job. Oh yeah. Your own, other peoples, you do get asked and I've never refused to do it but I do think it's an imposition, somebody will bring their dearly beloved pet because they don't want to take it to the vet, and "Would you put it down?" And 'No, I don't want to put it down. Take it to the bloody vet's' and I think to meself take it to the vet's and sit there, I suppose it's kinder, it just gets out the car 'cause they know when they're sitting in the vet's, but no, I don't like it, I object strongly to people bringing their pets. When I was at Cirencester I put a couple of his dogs down that had been the kennel man there, and he said would I do it for him and I said yes, but that was in the trade.

Any other women done what I've done? No. They've got more bloody sense. They get married and let their husbands do it!

A happy career? Oh yes. The first woman kennel man. I don't think I've ever contemplated anything different. In fact I am quite sure I haven't. I was the first female kennel man you know.

9. Peggy Darvill – Pig breeder & pork butcher. Toller Whelme. Born 1947.

I was a Rocker, not a Mod. I used to have a 350cc…A 3TA Triumph motorcycle…It went fast enough for me. My mother totally disapproved.

I was born in Suffolk. My father went there when he was married and he farmed it for many, many years as a manager. We did soft fruit, pigs, then a bit of cereal. Blackcurrants, raspberries, apples, pears. And then the owner turned up one year, in about July time and announced he was selling the farm in Michaelmas. In those days there was no protection and my mother and I were heading for the so-called workhouse. My father'd just got to lodge where he could. I would have been, about ten I suppose. That was Lower Summersham, which is about six miles from Ipswich. One brother was in the Navy and the other brother was in the Army, so that didn't really affect them as much as my mother and I. But another farmer, who my father had done some part-time work in the harvest, offered us a cottage and that's where we went.

Just a very basic farm. Mother used to have two pigs at the end of the garden which she used to kill for bacon and pork for us. Then my father used to sell the pigs in the open market. Right from when I can remember there was always pigs, always pigs, yes. They were just a white pig that was probably Landrace. There weren't sort of hybrids like they are today.

Did you cure bacon? Only my mother used to do it for our own use, that's all. We didn't do it in any commercial sense at all. Yes it was quite a shock to be moved off the farm. I expect it was about 100 acres. But in those days you did as you were told and went didn't you? My father, although he'd farmed it, I don't think

he was paid huge amounts of money. He changed his life completely and worked at the British Steel Pylons at Claydon. Totally different, his health improved and I think secretly he liked it better, because there wasn't so much responsibility there for him. The pay was regular. We moved to a little village called Nettlestead, into a council house, where I lived with my mother, until I moved away from home myself.

When I left school I went into a departmental store in Ipswich, which I believe Debenhams own now. I was just a normal counter hand really. There was a food department but I was on hosiery department, just a little minion. And then I got fed up with that, and our family all had motorbikes, my brothers had motorbikes, and then I went as a store person in a motorbike shop, which I thoroughly enjoyed and got a lot more money for. Just the spare parts and accessories. Those days were the heydays of motorcycling. Oh very much so. The Mods and Rockers were around in them days. Mostly English bikes, Hondas had hardly started to dribble in then. And they were pretty basic in those days but obviously they went on in leaps and bounds and overtook us in no time at all really. I was a Rocker, not a Mod. I used to have a 350cc… A 3TA Triumph motorcycle…It went fast enough for me. My mother totally disapproved. Reckless biking days. Yes and then became sensible, got four wheels.

Then I moved to Wendover in Buckinghamshire, met Steve. We ran a construction business in High Wycombe, which we worked very hard at…street lighting and telecommunication cabling on the motorways. We did that for several years and then I think we both got to the end of our tether when all the legislation and all the rules kept getting tighter and tighter and tighter, and we moved down here in '87. So we've been down here nearly 20 years. We did eventually sell the business. Stephen

Peggy Darvill with Gloucester Old Spot and Saddleback, Toller Whelme

came from a farming family as well. We couldn't afford any property in Buckinghamshire, so we bought Lake Farm. The owner had beef cattle but it was originally a dairy farm. There was an original proper Dorset house on this site. We bought the 60 acres and the farmhouse and buildings.

We had an outdoor pig unit. Yes, with arks. We did that, and we sold weaners to start with. They were called Peninsula and then we went on to Cotswold, which are a hybrid sort of multi-breed really. And we did that for a time and finished the pigs for pork weight, which we sold locally through Normans. They were very good. And then, I think Steve got a little bit fed up with the mundane work of that, although he enjoyed the space and the farm, he started going and working for someone else, temporarily. He liked variety. So he was working on farms. And then we got some beef cattle, which we used to finish. We used to buy them in as calves. And I said well if I can't have pigs outside I want some rare breeds. So that was when I started having the traditional breed pigs. I had one of each to see which ones I liked.

We had a Middle White, a Large Black, a Tamworth, we had a Gloucester Old Spot and Saddleback. We didn't have a Lop, think that was it. And I finished up with the Gloucester Old Spots and Saddlebacks. Well it's market forces isn't it? You know, the Gloucester Old Spot and the Saddleback, as long as you rear it correctly, so it don't lay huge amount of fat down, they are nice pigs for pork. The Gloucester Old Spot in particular makes nice bacon. And you have to sell these animals, you have to get a business, you have to get an outlet. If you send them to the normal abattoir you get very little for them because they don't like inverted coloured pigs. But if you get some of the traditional butchers or butchers who want something other than what the supermarkets produce or sell, as long as you keep a sensible fat level on them, and produce a nice pig, I've been very lucky, I've

been with one butcher for at least ten years, and he has pigs off me every week, and two local butchers in Beaminster both have them. Then we do a few for the freezer here, and we only breed the quantity that we can sell.

There's no point breeding any more because you don't get any money, you know you're wasting your time really. But there's a huge market out there I think for them. People have become aware that if they eat this traditional meat from a traditional pork pig, it tastes totally different but they have to accept there is a level of fat which makes the cooking easier. Yes and that's where the flavour comes from isn't it, as well, you know. The Tamworth can lay a lot of fat down, but actually they make beautiful sausages, to be fair. Some people put the whole pig into sausages, that's not sort of financially viable really.

Pigs inside? They are some of the time. The adult pigs can go in and out as they wish, but we've found the weather, with our land and the rainfall we get here, normally, it's not sensible to keep them outside, they need to be indoors, to finish them how they need to be finished.

Feeds? We buy in from Bridgwater, from it's like a family mill. Bowerings, because you can still get hold of the owner. It has no GM products in it. I just think it's a nice, straightforward feed that these pigs seem to do well on. It's just barley and wheat and things like that. You get soya and things like that. But they don't put any by-products in it like biscuit and things like that. It's all straight.What you see is what you get. That's right.

We have usually two boars of each breed because obviously we have to keep at least two to be able to keep the lines going. We don't closely breed our pigs. I don't like putting father on daughter, although it is acceptable I think. We like to keep a variety and I do change my boars quite frequently for that purpose as well. They're not hugely expensive, not like the commercial boars. But there's obviously a cost to it. And we tend to try and breed some pigs that we could sell to people. But basically we do breeding stock, but the majority of the boars especially go on the hook, because you know you can only sell so many boars.

Well we have about 12 sows, so you're looking at about over 100 pigs most of the time. I'm very fussy and Steve has become very fussy. We do a lot of cleaning. We clean them out every day, they're fed twice a day and they do get quite a lot of attention I suppose really. That shows in the growth rate? Well yes, and the temperament of the pig, you know. I don't like pigs when you go in the pen that they crawl up the wall. I like to be able to handle them. We wean the pigs from the mums, at six weeks old, because they're normally pretty fed up with them by that time. And then, if the pig is in good condition, if she is not milked off her back, but if she's had a big litter and she's milked off her back, I'll let her miss a cycle, but normally they come off the piglets and within about five days they'll come on to heat and we'll serve them again. Only two litters a year. We let them rest by themselves until we know they're in pig and then they go out in the pig hotel with all the others. VIP conditions here.

The British Saddleback, all I know, is in about 1963 there used to be an Essex and a Wessex, they were differently marked. They all had a saddle, but one had a thin saddle which goes over her back and down her front legs and all the back end would be black, everything black. And then the other one had got a wider saddle, and it would have white-tipped feet and tail. Well they were amalgamated because the breeds were obviously getting less and less, in about '63. So now we get a mix and match of that. I've got some old sale books for Gloucester Old Spots upstairs and they were making megabucks in the 1920s.

I got my Gloucester Old Spots from Mr Stiles, George Stiles.

And me Saddlebacks, I actually bought from locally, over at Burton Bradstock. The Gloucester Old Spots I paid a lot of money for, but the Saddlebacks were just big weaners. And actually the Saddles did me better initially than the Gloucesters.

On the rest of the farm we've got a small suckler herd of Aberdeen Angus cattle, which we breed stock from and kill for beef. And we've also got some pure Suffolk sheep to remind me of home. That's right. I get tormented up hill and down dale by the commercial shepherds, "what on earth do I want those things for?" I think they're lovely, we put a Charollais ram on them and they produce some beautiful little carcases…I think the Suffolk rams still are the 'in thing,' they like to cross them on the mules don't they?…They're lovely aren't they?

We do process our own meat here. Not all the time, but it's usually just for freezer meat, it's never fresh. We do a bit of bacon here sometimes but not very often. There's a great demand for good bacon, I must say. If I had enough pigs to be able to take some on to bacon weight I would probably do that, because there is an awful gap out there. There is.

Hams and gammons? No, the only time we'd do it probably if we'd got a big animal is at Christmas… But in the normal event I don't do it, but you know it is a good thing if you've got a heavy pig that's a gilt, I wouldn't do it with a boar. We do make sausages. I've got some trade that I do in the wintertime for shoots. Just a basic pork sausage.

We always hang the meat for about five or six days, yeah. It needs to dry out you see, it's a very wet process, pig killing. They deliver it here as a whole carcase. I do all the cutting here. I must have started about '98 I should think, when we just had a block, you know, to do the odd pig on. We started with an old chiller body, off the back of a lorry, but they don't work really, because unless you've got three-phase electricity as they link into three-phase when they're stationary.

In the cutting room you're sawing up? Yeah. If I'm working in there, Steve then does all the farm work. Butchering's quite hard work. I try to keep it to a minimum but customers don't always let you do that. People are much more fussy these days and I think quite a lot of people just don't want a bone on their plate. They want a chop whether it be pork or lamb and they just want to eat it without having to do battle with a bone… Picking the bone up and chewing it and throwing over your shoulder, I think them sort of days are starting to go a bit.

Yes, we do whole animals for pig roasts. Yes that we do. It's a real good way of feeding a lot of people, you know. We do them for weddings and birthdays, and it is a very economical way of feeding about 150, 200 people. Usually we just supply the pig and the tray with people, and they go to Halstock bakery and have them cooked.

Hugh (Fearnley-Whittingstall) got his original pigs from me, but he is organic now and we're not organic. So he has another organic source that he sources pigs from. We did the basics with him. Yes he is a quick learner. He listens to what you say, that's something. Lot of people don't, they think they can have a pig and just put it out on the grass and forget about it. People do ring me up and ask me a lot because I'm on the website with the Saddles and the Gloucesters through the BPA (British Pig Association), and so you do get people ringing up. And people do need to be educated a bit really.

Pedigree sales. Because I show them I sell them from the shows. Yes it is quite good really, we have been very lucky… We've won the breed champions, with the Saddles, we've won the Royal (Show) twice…and have won the Bath & West outright for the breed and we got reserve breed champion at the Bath & West again this year, for the Saddles. But I sort of dropped the Saddles, I'm still showing them but I'm promoting the Gloucester Old Spots a bit at the moment…Well I just think that I've neglected them.

For grooming we use our pressure washer which we turn right down to a nice, power wash shower…they love it. So they get a nice warm shower and shampoo the night before, and then they're all bedded down nicely on straw…and then the next morning they're loaded on the lorry and they're gone. They do get too high and mighty sometimes, "I'm a show pig, I don't have to do that."

We've just now got to select our stock, July stock, this year for next year. And then in January we have to select our pigs for January, for the January class, and then the sow. And usually the sow will come from the gilt you've shown the previous year, and it rolls on really.

Showing is an integral part of our life. Yes, very much so. We do a lot of shows. I select my pigs and then isolate them for the show season. The sow that won at Bath and West was pregnant. She's now had her piglets so she's pulled out of the system, so you have to mix and match a bit. Competition is very stiff, but Saddlebacks seem to have taken on this year. There was 57 Saddles at Bath and West this year… I walked in and I thought 'Oh my word.'

Yes, we show the pigs down Melplash. Thursday yes. I'm always late, local show… I think showing starts about 9.30, I think it's 9.30, ten o'clock time, we usually get down there about half past eight. Because everything should be clean, and we just feed them and then we get in the ring.

Yeah we get rosettes and you get cards at some shows, and obviously when you hit the big time you get the silverware with it, but you have to give it all back. The big shows actually I find are a bit mean, because you'll win the breed championship you'll get nothing for it, only a cup, you don't get any money, and yet you go to a small show, you win the breed champion at a small show and you get money. So somebody's got to learn something here.

I have had a couple or three Saddles that have won the gilt class one year and then gone on and won the sow class the next year. I have been fortunate that I have had some Saddlebacks which have done that. I had two Saddlebacks about three years ago, sisters, and they just won, I put them in the ring together as a class and they'd normally get first and second, and I used to do the pairs and they used to win the pairs, and which is quite satisfying really. And that year we won the interbreed at Dorchester show, with them. We had a very good year with those two girls.

I go to a small show at Sherborne, which starts on May Bank Holiday, and then we go to Bath and West. I haven't been to the Royal this year because I find it very expensive, so we went to the Royal Cornwall Show, which is absolutely wonderful show. And then I went to the Three Counties which I hadn't been to before and the Mid Devon at Tiverton in July. A couple of weeks ago we went to Okehampton, we're going to Melplash this week, we go to Dorchester the following week, and then in about the second week in September we go to Newbury and that's the last one.

We have had one or two chefs coming here wanting our meat. As I say, some of them don't mind paying the money as long as they get what they want. That's why I say there's just a huge outlet out there. Here I cut up maybe a couple of pigs a month, sometimes more, it all depends really. I never have the heads back if I have a pig back, don't want its eyes looking at me.

10. Annette Lee – Cheese maker. Woolsery Cheese, Up Sydling. Born 1948.

Radio's got a lot to answer for…Goats' milk is so fragile. It's very delicate…it's lovely to work with.

I was born in Birmingham. My father was in the Central Electricity Generating Board and died very young actually, early '50s. I worked in the utilities in the Midlands and then in London before having a complete career change. We set up three new companies. There was Nuclear Electric, National Power and Powergen. I was involved in the nuclear one. They wanted new, sparkling people for these new companies, and to do away with a lot of existing people, so I saw that as an opportunity of getting out of the rat race.

It was quite daring when I look back, quite a big step to take. I had friends in farming and I'd always thought it would be lovely to escape from London. One set of grandparents are Spanish and they had vineyards in Spain. So I think farming comes from that side. My grandmother was from Santander and my grandfather was from a village near Madrid. Small scale really. But they left Spain and decided to come over here because of the Civil War. There was a Spanish community in Wales. There are still remnants of the family in the Rhondda valley. I used to love going to Wales as a child. It was beautiful.

Friends in Somerset had a farm. I used to spend quite a bit of time there and I loved the animals. They had a dairy herd. This was in Wiveliscombe and I thought to myself what can I do? I was determined not to go back into office work. Well, I hadn't thought of goats till I heard a radio programme which said that there was a shortage of goats' milk. Radio's got a lot to answer for. It has really. Because this idea just came into my head and I

thought 'goats,' right I need to do research. So I joined goat clubs, got in touch with the Goat Society and found out that there was a shortage, and perhaps it would be a good idea. I went to South Molton where a lady was milking a commercial herd. She makes yoghurt. I thought 'Well, if she can do it then I can.' I read loads of books, got involved with goats and thought they were great creatures. They're very different to sheep. So I did a business case and decided that it would work.

I was still working but my friends in Somerset said that I could rear some kids there as it would take a couple of years before they were ready to milk. I bought 50 kids from the lady in South Molton and they were my foundation goats. British Saanen. They were on the farm in Wivi and while I finished off work. I had two years to find a place, which was in Devon. Woolfardisworthy near Crediton and Black Dog. It was great. That's why the cheese is Woolsery. A smallholding of about 16 acres. I then decided that I needed more than 50 goats. I found an outlet for the milk. Goat Farmers UK and the lady at South Molton needed milk, so I'd got two possible outlets. So I became a goat farmer. I went out and bought more dairy goats. I went all over the place and that was really exciting and interesting.

They were fed hay and silage. They'll do anything for food. They were in huge open barns and I had three groups of goats kidding at three different times of the year, so that there was a continuity for the milk. To begin with it was a nightmare. I was hand milking about 30 goats twice a day and they started to kid before we were really ready. You actually get quite a lot of milk out of a goat especially when they first kid. So we got the parlour sorted out and got the goats trained, which was quite amusing. I used to play them music. If I wanted to milk quickly I'd put on some very fast music and that seemed to work. No they were great fun the goats, and I did enjoy having them. I also used to

Annette Lee with goats' cheese, Up Sydling

deliver milk, and supply Vulscombe, who's still making cheese. But there was a point when I'd been going about three years I suppose, '95 when my customers had as much as they needed and I had to throw milk away. Not a pleasant experience. That's your income down the drain, and when you think of all the hard work, and the goats' work. I tried to find outlets or people who could make a cheese for me. Nobody was really interested. That was only ten years ago.

I needed to be self-sufficient and in control, so I contacted Rita Ash. Rita came out to the farm and brought this miniature equipment and she showed me how to make cheese. Came out of retirement, which was great really. What I said to her was that I want to make a cheese that will keep well, and that is nice and savoury, because I wanted to enjoy eating it myself. And so she showed me how to make a hard cheese. I hadn't a clue about cheese before Rita. She left me her equipment and said "What we'll do, you have a go at making the cheeses, if you get stuck give me a ring." But she said "It's better if you experiment and try yourself and you'll get to know how to handle the milk."

She said that if I experimented with different temperatures and different ways of handling it would actually make a different cheese. So I made several cheeses and she came back after six weeks to have a tasting session. I'd got all these cheeses lined up. We tasted them and she said "This is great, I like them. I like them even better than my own. I think you've got it." And I said 'Right, ok, then I need to get going. I need equipment.' So Rita helped me to find my first cheese vat, curd knives, curd mill, moulds. They don't come cheap being stainless. I had to set up a room as a cheese dairy, and that had to go through planning. I said 'Look this is a dairy farm do I need permission?' "Oh yes you need full planning permission." We got that, but building regulations got involved and said "Right it's got to be to factory standard," and this was for a room 20ft x 10ft. And it was set up to factory standard. Anyway, we got through all of that, at great cost. End of '95 because I started selling in '96.

I had about 300 goats then. They were different ages because you've got the young stock included in that, so I was probably milking about 150. I was doing the milking and the cheese making. Some milk was still going to Vulscombe, some went over to South Molton and the rest I made into cheese. I only had a small 40-gallon vat.

So I started making cheeses and they started piling up. I'd never gone out to sell anything like cheese, or any product to anybody before. It was totally new to me. So I got the first cheese that I made, cut it up, wrapped portions in cling film, typed a label and stuck on it, very amateurish, went down to Crediton Deli, Treloars was the first shop I went into and I shall never forget it, because I stood outside for about ten minutes, working myself up to going in. Anyway I did go in and Guy was actually serving, so I waited until he was free and I said that I was a new cheese maker, this was my cheese and could I leave these samples for him to try? To my amazement he said, "Hang on I'm going to try them straight away." So he tasted it in front of me and I thought 'Oh my God!' He said "Fantastic, it reminds me of France. I'll have two truckles please." And that was the start.

So that was my first sale, and from then on I wasn't bothered about going into a shop. I went round all the local delis and went to wholesalers and that's how it started. Then Farmers' Markets started. Cullompton was the first Farmers' Market in Devon. I went along and I was amazed at the interest. It also became very good promotion for the cheese.

Yes it's very important being seen, because then people who had got shops themselves, wholesalers saw it and thought "oh yeah, cheese." Then people started contacting me. Other

Farmers' Markets sprang up like Crediton, Taunton, Bridport. They have been an absolute godsend for farmers, including myself.

I do deal with Waitrose and Sainsbury in a small way. I think it's best to have a finger in a number of pies. But as the cheese became more successful my friends in Somerset, who were having difficulty in the cow industry, offered to take the goats and just provide the milk back, which is what we did. We had a little tanker and trailer going backwards and forwards.

I could then concentrate on cheese and found my vat wasn't big enough, so I said to Rita, 'Look I need a bigger vat. Can you find me one?' And I said 'Also I'm running out of space here in Devon, because it was all really set up for the animals, not for making cheese.' There was no way I could expand where I was, because it was right on the side of a road and there were problems with electricity supply. So I thought 'Well, it might be better if I were to find a place to rent and then move across once the other one's ready.' And that's what I did. So I moved to Up Sydling to much bigger premises, with room for expansion.

Rita found it for me, because she knew the landlord. So she did all the talking, and he said ok because what he wanted was to have a farm shop, which is on the front of the dairy and have the cheese as an attraction. So that was what happened, and I came here in December 1998.

Unfortunately the goats at Wiveliscombe were lost to foot and mouth but the farm here had started with goats, because they saw it as the thing to go into, with Goat Farmers UK being the co-operative collecting milk. Foot and mouth, that was really tragic because that came right at the end. It was traumatic. It was something that you don't really get over, because I had been getting the bloodlines so that we had really good milkers and the herd was becoming really fine-tuned over there. And it was such

a shame to have lost all that work.

It was awful. They can't have had foot and mouth because they weren't out in the open. It happened at the end of May 2001. The Ministry went in and said "Right, these goats are going to be put down." I think that was on the Tuesday and on the Friday they all went out in skips.

Very quick, and very shocking. The assessment? They were going to go out as cull goats, which had a value of £5. So that had to be fought. So Tony on the goat farm, sorted it out. But the farm here, it was just so fortunate that they had goats here. Because they then came and said I was welcome to help myself to their milk. So that's what happened.

The Ministry also decreed that four weeks worth of cheese had to be destroyed. FMD in the cheese? No. They couldn't prove it. And it's not going to harm people anyway, it's all pasteurised. So it's absolutely ridiculous. The vet said "I'm sorry about this but these are the instructions we've got. We've got to destroy the cheese back to that date." And I said 'Well there's nothing wrong with it.' And he said "I know but we've just got to get rid of it." And he said "We'll come over and we'll deal with it." And all they did was they came and dipped the cheese in disinfectant, put it in black bags and it went to the tip.

Ridiculous, isn't it? Because those black bags could have been opened by crows and eaten anyway. They did compensate me for it. The thing is that you've got a gap in your supply, to the customer. But we managed to get over that, fortunately, and I was able to catch up by taking extra milk.

The people in Wiveliscombe? Well, they've gone out of farming. It's too tragic, too raw for them. You never want to go through it again. What they made them do with the buildings is incredible. They had to dig up concrete and re-lay it all.

When my landlord sold the farm the new landlord didn't

want to keep the goats. So a local farmer, down in Holywell, took them on and he is my supplier. It's just up the road, literally. The A37. So he brings the milk along. Once a day normally. There's about four or five hundred goats and I use all of the milk.

The cheese? A lot of it goes to London, and to the wholesalers. For Farmers' Markets, I decided that it would be nice to give people a choice and not just to have hard goat cheese. So that's when I experimented with a soft cheese, and found people liked that. Farmers' Markets are great for trying things out on people. You know you get feedback, whether they like a thing or don't like a thing. And then somebody said to me "Could you make a feta cheese, because we keep being asked for an English feta cheese?" So I spoke to Rita again and she came up with feta, so that went on to my list of cheeses. It was called feta until last year. We're no longer able to call it feta, although I do on the market, put a label on because otherwise people don't know what type it is. It's like Cheddar, if you call a cheese Cheddar people know what it is. I called it Fiesta… Well it's quite close, if you miss out the I and the E you've got feta. So I thought well, we'll call it that. Having lost the goats to foot and mouth, I needed to have an alternative in case anything happened to the goats again. So that was when I started making cows' milk cheese. Because you can get cows' milk quite easily, whereas goats' milk might be more difficult. I did have organic standard but the cost to do it was greater than I could justify at that time. Because with making so much goats' milk cheese I can't fit in many batches of cows' milk cheese.

The cows' milk cheese is a young Cheddar. I haven't got storage to mature it. You need lots of space. The longer you keep it the more tasty it is. At six months it's quite nice. So at about a year it would be really nice. I don't like it too strong.

Other cheeses? Well there's the soft, spreadable cheese. I've got a semi-hard goats' cheese, the Fiesta, the hard cheese, then the smoked goat. I don't like over-smoked cheese. Bridfish do some smoking for me, but I have got a little kiln and I do a few cheeses at a time. If I get into a rhythm I can do quite a few a day.

The day's routine with cheese making. Ok. The hard cheese is the main one that's made. So I usually get in at about six o'clock and get the pasteuriser going, because we pasteurise all the milk. Then that goes into the big vat and it's warmed up and a starter is added, and that will help give it flavour. Once it's at the right temperature, we then add rennet, and we leave it to coagulate, about 45 minutes. Once it's set it's like a big blancmange in the vat and we use the curd cutters then to cut it into little cubes.

We do a criss cross with the knives so that it cuts it into cubes. And it's stirred and heated and that's to help reduce the particle size and expel the whey from the curd. And that goes on for about half an hour. Then you let it pitch, which is to let all the curd settle at the bottom of the vat and the whey sits on top. And once that's settled, about half an hour, you can drain off the whey and you're left with a mass of curd at the bottom. Once you've got this curd, you then go through the process of cutting it into squares and stacking it to the side of the vat. It is quite physical and can be wearing. And you continue that process, every 20 minutes, cutting it into blocks and stacking it. When you pull the cows' milk apart it goes like chicken breasts when it's ready. Whereas with the goats it's a much finer milk and the curd is much softer. You do get layers but nothing like the cheddar. The first time I ever made cows' milk cheese I was so shocked at how robust the milk was because goats' milk is so fragile. It's very delicate. Whereas cows you could bash it around and it really didn't harm it, or it didn't break the curd.

Goats' milk is so delicate, it's lovely to work with. But once you've got the right acidity and texture, then the curd is milled and that breaks it up into little particles. Then add salt and put it into moulds. And then it goes into the presses, which are Victorian, and it's pressed for 36 hours. When they're ready to come out, they're taken out of the cheesecloth, trimmed, and then they go into store where they're left to mature, and they're turned frequently.

During the summer we're actually vacuum packing, because otherwise the cheeses are drying out so much we actually lose a lot of weight. Problems with hot weather? Yes, I found the cheeses were really cracking badly. And it's the first year that we've flooded the cheese store floor to keep it moist and the humidity up.

Farmers' Markets? Poundbury, Bridport, which is our best one. Bridport is a really good market, it's so well supported. There's so many regulars plus I think it gets the holiday people. Taunton, that's weekly, Weymouth, Verwood and also Penhill. So we do 13 or 14 a month and cover quite a biggish area.

Supermarkets? Well actually they approached me, which was very good. Waitrose came first and the cheese went into about three stores. It then went into about eight stores last year, and at the beginning of this year, they said to me "Could you cope with 65?" Well the farmer Chris needs to grow and I had been making more cheese so it worked out really well. Sainsbury's phoned me a bit later and it now goes into about 30 outlets.

You don't know who is actually looking at you when you go to a Farmers' Market. I think it was at the Bath and West, where they held a special Farmers' Market, and that was where Sainsbury's found me. The buyer actually came up and tasted the cheeses, and I didn't know that she was the buyer. And it was afterwards that this fella came up and said "Oh that's Rachel from Sainsbury's, and we'll be in touch." And I thought 'Oh well,

yes,' But they did get in touch and were very interested. But it took two years for Sainsbury's to go through all the rigmarole and auditing and everything else, from them saying "Yes we like it, we want it," to actually getting it on a shelf in their deli.

Now I want to build up more direct sales. I really enjoy the shows. We went to Plymouth festival. We did the Exeter festival which was really good, it's fantastic now. And those sort of things are great because they get the celebrity chefs doing the demos and that brings in so many people.

The cheese is on quite a few cheese boards. I meet people at the Farmers' Market and they say "Oh I had that last night at so and so restaurant." Chefs do all sorts of things with it. I really ought to write it down as soon as people tell me what they've had. But it's used in cooking as well as on cheese boards, which is great. I do the agricultural shows like Dorchester, Honiton, Gillingham and Shaftesbury. A lot of those are very good because there's a lot of local support. At those sort of places you meet lots of trade buyers as well.

The yield of goat's milk is about three litres a day. The lactation is the same as a cow really. Ten months on and two months off. Goats. They are great creatures. Obviously after kidding they'll produce a lot of milk, so you'll get a peak and then it'll sort of tail off.

A lot of people that have tried the hard goat cheese have said it's very much like the manchego, and I thought well that's strange. I think I must have had some ancestors somewhere that made cheese. I think it is my Spanish side that is the farming side. Definitely. Well they would be amazed.

Over the years I've been making cheese I've never taken huge leaps, I'm very cautious and I've grown very steadily. I may have lost business because of it. Perhaps I could have grown quicker. But my intention is to keep slowly growing. My son is also interested in the business. When I actually started with the goats he didn't want to know. He was involved a little while, and he said no, too much like hard work. He went off to get a degree in computing and is working in London. He's now finding that he loves coming out to Dorset, and he also would like to escape the rat race. And he has said to me "Mum, don't ever get rid of the business because I would like to continue it."

He is getting more involved. He comes and does Farmers' Markets. He's helped me make cheese. What he needs to do is set himself up with his house first, make sure he's got enough money behind him, and then eventually he can come and take over. So it's great for me because it makes it all worthwhile.

My reward is seeing people enjoy eating the cheese, and to see it turn up where I least expect it, which is good. I mean it's great that in London it goes to Neal's Yard, and Jamie Oliver has written about it. It was in the Sunday Telegraph, and I thought fantastic if he's using it. We've got James Martin using it, Lesley Waters and Hugh Fearnley-Whittingstall, so there's quite a few that have found it, so it is rewarding.

It's the fat that gives it the flavour. And when it's really high in fat that is the best tasting cheese. It really is good, so the cheeses that are made, that are eaten round about July-August, are from the spring kidding, so they're the best cheeses.

Prizes? I mean the most prestigious one was the wooden platter which I got at the British Cheese Awards. It was the Cheese Lover's Trophy, it was chosen as the best cheese that year, 2001. I've won other prizes since then, I've got the silver plate and the trophy up there, that was 2004, at the Bath and West. It was the best goat cheese in class, and the best in show, so that was fantastic. I was absolutely amazed. It never ceases to amaze me. I've got two this year at the Taste of the West for the smoked cheese, a silver for that and also my cheddar, I got a bronze. It's the first time my cheddar has ever won anything. I've got something in the British Cheese Awards but I don't know what that is yet. They're not letting on. But I know I've got something for the hard goat and something for the smoked goat. I am going to the Awards, to meet all the cheesy people.

11. Daphne Jackson – Elwell Fruit Farm, Waytown, Bridport. Born 1931.

Coming here I loved it. I loved the peace, the open spaces, the greenery all around me…It has a very good apple climate. We've been here 50 years.

I was born Daphne Ridley in Prestwich near Manchester, spent all my early life in India, South Africa, Pakistan. India. Mostly in the Sind desert, but also a chunk in Bombay. Father was in the government. ICS (Indian Civil Service). His father worked in a bank. The other side of the family worked on a farm in the Lake District. Arnside on Morecambe Bay, mixed farming. Mother went out to marry my father in Karachi on the day the ship landed. She had never been out of England before and it was the most tremendous culture shock to get off the ship, to see the young man whom she hadn't met for years and marry him, all on the same day. They married in 1929 and I think it was 1955 when they eventually came back to England. After '47. Yes, both India and Pakistan asked for him to go back, but because he'd spent time in Sind, he chose Pakistan.

We were in Quetta. My father came up and he felt very concerned. He said he could hear the earth moving and he brought us down early from the hills and there was that horrendous earthquake, in May 1935. Many thousands died including children of friends of theirs. But otherwise I think we had one other leave in Kashmir, which was great. I went to 15 schools altogether and if there wasn't a school, there would be a governess, so I still can't add up but I learnt so much more about the world than if I'd just been stuck in a classroom. A different sort of education.

In 1943 my mother became seriously ill and was sent home.

They said she wouldn't survive if she stayed in India. So they found passages for my mother, myself and two younger sisters and we came home on a troop ship. The Stratheden and I remember as we zigzagged through the Med, looking back at all these ships which were doing the zigzags to avoid the mines and torpedoes. I hated coming back to this cold, grey country. Everybody wore dark coloured clothes. I did miss the bright colours and the sunshine so much.

So I had four years at school in England and then went out again. I worked in the passport office in Karachi. Loved it and they paid me for doing it as well. The High Commission was near the docks. I met Peter when I was 17 and we were married when I was 20 and we were posted down to Ceylon. He worked in a bank and our two older children were born in Ceylon, then we were posted to Bombay where Peter had been born in 1926 and then we came back home in '56.

We found Elwell in the personal column in The Times. It was a newly planted orchard. It was seven years old. These two gentlemen had planted it up in 1947-48. One had been in the Indian police, and the other had been a fruit grower in Essex, whose orchard had been bulldozed to make way for an American landing strip. They found this south-facing slope and planted up the orchard. Originally they asked for people with a degree to come and work as a labourer here, but they offered nothing other than a labourer's wage, and four families came here but could see no future in it, so when we came they eventually offered a partnership, so we stayed.

Only 30 acres to begin with. There were 38 varieties then. In those days trees didn't behave as well as they do now. Everything picked by hand, well it still is, but graded by hand into the boxes which you lined with paper first. It was very labour intensive. Wooden boxes to begin with. And we picked into bushel boxes.

Daphne and Caroline Jackson with apple boxes, Elwell Fruit Farm

Somebody had to go round and put the bushel boxes under the apple trees in the long lines and they all had to be picked up, fully laden and put on the tractor and trailer and brought down. We didn't have a pack shed then, we graded them in a Nissen hut.

Prior to being an orchard it was a dairy farm. Elwell is a hamlet. It's a Celtic word for healing spring and even during the drought of '77 it did not dry up. But it did a few years back when we had no rain, and I'm wondering what it's going to do this year. Coming here I loved it. I loved the peace, the open spaces, the greenery all around me, I just loved being able to live here as a family. William was born in the farmhouse and his younger sister Lucy, they had a marvellous childhood, the freedom to run around with no shoes on and loads of pets, it was a very happy childhood. We were the first commercial eating apple orchard down here.

The men who first planted the orchard were Mr Douglas and Mr Russell. Mr Russell is of an old Beaminster family. Mrs Douglas is his cousin, that was the connection, but he was from an Essex family. Pears. Yes. Two or three varieties. Conference definitely and I think Packham's Triumph was the pollinator, planted every seventh tree. And then sometimes for another pollinator they would graft another tree, just a branch.

To begin with the apples went to Weymouth. AJ Digby was the firm. Four local ladies who would come in and do everything, hoe the strawberries, because we used to send strawberry plants to Europe and all around the country. It wasn't until the terrible frost that we had which made us lose all the apples that we realised maybe people could come in and pick their own strawberries. It would be an April, May frost. And I looked out of the upstairs windows and I could see the orchard, the bottom of which had been all pink the previous day, was brown this morning. Halfway up it was brown and pink, above there it was pink. We walked round to have a look at this, and the following day it was brown right up to the top. We'd lost the lot. You can almost see the frost rolling down. That's why you have rows like that, so the frost can go through. We lost everything. So we put a postcard in a post office window, come and pick a few strawberries and were almost knocked over in the rush, so we did Pick Your Own thereafter.

It was the beginning of Pick Your Own. We then planted raspberries, blackcurrants and redcurrants and we had some whitecurrants, tayberries, loganberries, tummel berries, it is such good soil. I think only two per cent of England is on grade A. We're on it. The top soil goes down and down and down and is reasonably sheltered.

Thirty years of Pick Your Own. It was very popular to begin with, but after a while, when the supermarkets became so powerful and they could fly strawberries in from God knows where, people lost their interest in coming out to pick. People's lives changed. When I was here with small children, women would come out, this is the time to earn some money, and the baby would be brought and put in a bushel box at the end of the row and mothers would happily pick up and down. Blackcurrants was a very exciting time of the year, and we sent blackcurrants to Robertson's jam people and we arranged for a coach to go to Beaminster square and pick up these mothers and little ones and unaccompanied children, we said no one under the age of 11 to come picking, I don't honestly think the coach driver asked how old these small-sized people were as they clambered on, he drove them all here, stopped in the top field over there, they all bounced up and he turned round and belted off, so we had got a bunch of little rogues as well as the good sensible pickers. First of all we picked into those old chip baskets, but after a while it became those gallon plastic buckets. And there were some very quick, clever, careful pickers.

They were paid piecework by the weight of their bucket. And there were those rather older rogues, who, when Mrs Bloggs wasn't looking, pinched her full bucket from the end of the row and so this wretched person would be paid for Mrs Bloggs' bucket and we found buckets with stones in, not many stones because this is not very stony land, but all sorts of dodges were used, but I think that happened on every farm.

I think it would be in about '61 that we built the pack shed there and had to start packing and get in these proper graders, I think '61. Digby would drive the fruit to all these little grocers' shops but when he grew older he gave up the business he was feeling the pinch because so many of these little grocers had gone out of business. The supermarkets just weren't interested in all the little varieties. They were planted so that we would have a succession of picking, starting in August. We started with one with a very pink flesh. We went down to 18 varieties from 38, but William has been planting more and says that we now have 37 varieties so we're getting back.

In the early years we got a reasonable price, yes, but after the supermarkets came in it was a struggle for everyone, and I think that 65 per cent of England's orchards have been bulldozed in the last decade. It's staggering. Sheer economics and supermarkets. So many of these foreign countries do not have a minimum wage and workers' safety security and all the rest of it, and we are tied by this red tape, we're almost strangled by the red tape.

We were going for bush trees because they're easier to pick and you don't have to stagger around with a big ladder which is what we had to do. Modern planting is very close, and there are four rows in a track and then a grass alleyway either side.

Picking is quite difficult because you have to wriggle through with your picking barrel.

Long Ashton Research Station, some years ago, predicted that the orchard of the future would be spindles six inches apart, acres of them, that would be picked mechanically which would cut this little tree off, down to six inches high and then that would be left to grow next year because this lot would be fruiting. It didn't sound like an orchard that I'd like to sit in. We would consult Long Ashton on absolutely everything but I think the Government closed them down.

Pruning lasts for six months of the year and it can be quite a lonely, cold job. William does nearly all of it on his own, so I think he's had RSI and now has a pruner that is charged over lunchtime, battery charged. A vital part of the operation and it lasts six cold months of the year. The deer have taken to nibbling his grafts off so badly that he's stopped grafting now. So we put a replacement tree in rather than graft.

The Brit valley in early May. Lovely. Just lovely. It has a very good apple climate. William is finding at the Farmers' Markets that people are asking for the older varieties. He cuts them, hands them to people to taste and finds that they will ask for certain varieties again and again. He will plant more trees of those. I think we're the last commercial orchard in Dorset. When we first came here there was a lovely old cider press which Douglas and Russell dismantled and threw out, and that became the ladies' lunch room, and they put a washbasin and loo in there and that's where they lunched. People still need apples. We're mad at the supermarkets because they've cut down the choice that people used to have.

We've been here 50 years next month.

12. Caroline Jackson – Elwell Fruit farm, Bridport. Born Bradpole 1961.

If we could sell everything we grew direct to the person who was going to eat it, I wouldn't be sitting here talking to you, I'd be on a cruise ship somewhere.

My maiden name was Franklin and I was born in '61 in Bradpole, so I haven't actually gone very far, unlike my mother-in-law! My father was in the building trade, he was born in South Wales, but both his sets of grandparents, so my great grandparents came to South Wales from the Wincanton area and the Somerset levels to go into coal. So they were coal miners a couple of generations back.

Then my father's father and his wife came back to Somerset to take on the running of a pub in Chard, The Live and Let Live, I'm sure it was that, and then they moved to Bridport and took on what is now the Lord Nelson, it was the King of Prussia. Mum's father worked in the rope making, net making industry in the town, in North Mills and Pymore, and my mother's father's father had been a coastguard so he had lived and worked all along the Devon and Dorset coast, Wyke Regis, Dawlish, Salcombe.

Bradpole in the 1960s? There were orchards at the top. On one of the new estates at Gore Cross the road is called Bath Orchard. I was the clerk to the parish council at Bradpole for about 11 years when that latest development was going on and names were being chosen.

When I left Colfox School I went to work for Lloyds Bank in Bridport, where I stayed for 19 years. Then William and I moved in here, when Daphne moved in with her father just down the road. I changed my hours to part time so that I could help run the farm shop through the winter. We still did Pick Your Own soft fruit in the summer, so I shared the shop duties with Daphne and Peter.

I married into the orchard lifestyle. Our daughter was born in '96 and so I left the bank completely then, and haven't looked back. Now we have two children. Life is all around you. It's very peaceful most of the time but sometimes I think it would be very nice to have a neighbour, occasionally, because you can sit here for days on end and not see anybody, which is a contrast to when I first came here when soft fruit was reasonably busy and you had people looking over the hedge.

The heyday of Pick Your Own was way before my time, and the whole length of the pear orchard would be stacked with cars, parking anywhere that they could get their vehicle in. Time. I think that's the main reason for its decline. I think people's time is at a premium now, and you can buy produce all year round, albeit not as fresh and not as tasty as when you've picked it.

People have no idea about apples. They phone up in February and they want some apples and you say 'We don't have them at this time of year.' I think people have lost seasonality, thanks to the availability of imported fruit. One of the very common comments that you get at Farmers' Markets, people taste apples and they say "Gosh, that takes me back to my childhood."

We started doing Farmers' Markets in '99. Since we started that we have planted varieties that William had previously grafted over or grubbed out and replaced with the common ones. We've planted things like Blenheim Orange, Ashmead's Kernel, Ellison's Orange, Kidd's Orange Red, Charles Ross. People come along to the stall and see them and they're absolutely ecstatic. "Oh no I don't need to taste it, I know what it's like, I just want to buy some, I haven't seen it for years, why can't you buy it anywhere else?" And they're really thrilled.

Selling direct to an appreciative public is extremely satisfying. A lot is said about local produce, and you're just not sure about how much is really meant. Because if we can sell them, why can't other people sell them? The large multiples say they sell what the customer wants, but I've never been in a supermarket and been asked what I want. And if it's not on the shelf I can't buy it so how do they know what I want?

Main varieties: Cox, Bramleys for the cookers, Red Pippin is very popular, Jonagold, we grow various Gala clones, Elstar, Early Windsor has gone down really well, Braeburn we now grow. People come round to the market stall and say "But that's New Zealand," Doesn't have to be. I've researched a lot of the history of varieties to put on cards next to the fruit on the stall because I think some people are interested in that sort of thing.

Farmers' Markets: what we're doing today is working out which markets we're doing this season, but we're definitely doing Bridport, Poundbury, Sherborne, Blandford, Verwood, Weymouth and I think Broadstone, which is a new one. So that's quite a commitment. But 95 per cent of our fruit goes to Wye Fruit at Ledbury, it's only five per cent that we store here in the cold stores that gets sold at Farmers' Markets or goes to a couple of local greengrocers. So we're talking very small amounts comparative to what we grow here. But if we could sell everything we grew direct to the person who was going to eat it, I wouldn't be sitting here talking to you, I'd be on a cruise ship somewhere!

The apples to Ledbury go off straight from the trees. Pickers pick into a picking bag which they wear across their shoulders and on their front, they pick into that, when their bag's full they empty it out of the bottom into a bulk bin which is a four foot square wooden bin, and those bins get put on articulated lorries and go up the next day to Wye. Wye store it, they grade it, they pack it, they deal with the marketing and it ends up on the supermarket shelves.

The last two years they've been contracted solely to Asda. It will be traceable back with codes, we have to code each bulk bin which goes off now, we have to keep a record of which orchard it's come from and when it was picked, and then Wye Fruit have to code when it's in their stores, so you could go to a bag of apples and theoretically you could trace it all the way back but you'd have to go through the right channels to do it. We have sold in the local supermarket in Bridport, but only when it's suited them, when they phoned us up one day and they were in a bit of a pickle, it was prime English Coxes season and they had failed to order, so they were very grateful to us running round in circles. We drove down there and got some of their green packing boxes and we brought them up here and we worked silly hours to get them down there the next day. We did that for a couple of weeks until they got their orders right, and we were never required again. The nearest our apples could possibly be now is Weymouth or Yeovil because there's no Asda in Bridport.

I think a lot depends on southern hemisphere fruit. If there is an overhang then southern hemisphere fruit is going to be going very, very cheaply and that can have a knock-on effect on how much of the new season English fruit is required and more importantly what price you get. I don't think enough is made of seasonality of all fruits and vegetables.

The Pick Your Own soft fruit we phased out. We finished it in the summer of 2004, but over the previous five years we reduced the quantity and the number of varieties. We stopped strawberries I think in '99, they were the most labour intensive. If you have a couple of wet days the whole strawberry patch is gone, because we don't grow it under cover.

All the soft fruit finished in 2004. We used to have a sign at the end of the road with little boards that we hooked up, we'd have a whole list of things at soft fruit time, and now we just have 'Closed,' Financially it did bring money in prior to harvest, which is our most expensive time of the year, when we have wages to pay out, but I was talking with William and he said "Do you know, I really don't miss the soft fruit." It was an awful lot of work for not a great return. It was a bit of a 24-hour thing. We don't miss the phone calls.

Well you would get families come back and three or four children would have very red fingers and very red mouths and red down the front of their T-shirt and they'd come round with this little quarter pound punnet and say "We couldn't find very many." We needed a weighbridge to weigh people before they went out and again when they came back.

We have eight foreign students most years. Not so many from Poland now. I think since Poland joined the EU, Polish workers can now come over here and work in any industry, they're not tied to the SAWS, the Seasonal Agricultural Workers Scheme. So more often now the workers we have are from the non-EU countries. We're getting more Ukrainians, we've got four Slovaks coming this year, who are European Union, so they can come without coming through Concordia. One of them, this is his fourth year, and he's come back and brought friends with him. We're now wondering how we'll manage when he stops coming when he graduates. I hope he never graduates, I hope he fails every year for the next 20 years so he still wants to come and brings a group every year, because he is absolutely invaluable to us now. He's more of a friend than anything else.

I think their expectations are a lot higher now. This year we've put in wireless broadband to the house so that it will reach the caravans so that they'll bring their laptops with them so they don't have to cycle into the library in Bridport every evening to send messages home. And I think they're much more picky now about which farm they go to, looking at the facilities that are listed as being on offer on that farm. It's also great for our children. They have a whale of a time with them, so they love having the students staying here. One year, one girl said she had earned enough working here for five weeks so that when she went home she didn't have to take on a part-time job to do her next year of university. She could concentrate on her studies.

William was at Ledbury yesterday for the pre-harvest meeting when they give you the dates, because they now give you windows in which you have to pick the different varieties, between this date and that date. Now you have to get each variety picked within a time window. If your orchard is functioning slightly out of that window, you have to make a lot of fuss, and you have to beg. Because once they've closed the big cold store they don't want to open it again to put some more bins in. He was up there yesterday getting the dates and he said he noticed a lot of signs in the packing warehouse there were written in Chinese as they employ a lot of foreign packhouse staff there.

We started the apple juice shortly after we started the Farmers' Markets, but we don't press it here. The nearest fruit farm to us is Jonathan over at North Perrott, and he's on the board at Wye, so we send some of our fruit over to him. The lorries very often come round half a load of our fruit and then they go round to Jonathan and put that on, so that makes good economic sense. We often put on a few bins which just get dropped off over there, and then he presses it and bottles it for us and we buy it back from him, which we did yesterday on the way back from the meeting. So we sell that at Farmers' Markets, and this year we are hoping, to start doing apple sauces at markets and possibly collaborating with Bridport Gourmet Pies to do apple pies and crumbles.

One year you make money, the next year it's an absolute disaster. You pick in September, but we don't get the full money through from Wye until July, so you're nearly ready to pick again, before you actually really know whether last year's crop has made you any money or not. We also pay the transport as well. At one time we had a baby food contract to Nutricia in Wells. We were there from '97 to 2003, when they moved to the Czech Republic.

Jonagold, Golden Delicious and Conference pears. For baby food they need blandish sweet apples. The Conference pears are the same trees as the ones when Daphne and Peter moved here. The only thing with the baby food was that it was good money for the varieties but of course we invested money in planting more shortly before they left. When they folded at Wells we had to convert some of the newly grafted trees back to Cox. We have more rabbits than we know what to do with, we have deer that can be a bit of a nuisance, badgers can be a bit of a pest too.

We don't have irrigation systems but if things are looking really bad William will spray water onto the trees with the old sprayer. He had to do that this year, mainly with the young trees but the older ones, their root systems are such that they should be alright in a hot summer.

Ideally we will replant an orchard each year, about 2,500 trees, and you have to order the trees about 18 months before you want them. We have 55 acres. Pruning never seems to end. When you finish winter pruning you start summer pruning, then you harvest. I'm just pushing paper all day.

I'm quite good at pushing paper around, I push it around quicker than William does. Paperwork is not his department. I do the accounts, the books, the returns, the assessments, the regulations and dealing with the students, with booking them, and sometimes they might need National Insurance numbers obtained and that means a trip to Weymouth and an appointment booked via an answerphone at Bournemouth, so that sort of thing is getting much more complicated.

The main problem for fruit growers is the possibility of hail, you can have hail on the whole farm, or it can just be one corner of an orchard, so when there's bad weather we look at the forecasts, we sit here chewing our fingernails looking up and listening for hail, and if there's a hail storm you go out and you look over the whole farm and see if you can find anything, because that can wipe a farm out. A lot of farms have gone out of business if they've had a series of hail storms over a number of years. You may be able to recover from one, but if you're hit often enough, it can finish you.

Blossom time is critical and also at fruitlet size. We had a hail storm here in '93, which was the first year that William and I had moved into the farmhouse, and we could not sell the crop through the cooperative to the supermarkets, the whole crop. Sometimes if it happens early it can grow itself out and it's fine, but later on it's much worse. There's nothing actually wrong, it's not going to do you any harm to eat it, but there's just going to be this brown spot that's going to go right through the flesh of the apple, so now we have to insure against it, which will cover part of it. But the interesting thing that we found is that in '93, when we had the hail, almost all of the crop went for juice. We still sold a little from here, we just reduced the price. But the price that we got per tonne for the hailed fruit to go for juice then, mainly it went to the makers of Merrydown Cider in Sussex, was the same as last year's juice fruit price. So we're talking 13 years and the price was the same.

We like to think that if we can get £100 a bin for Coxes, we'll be ok. The indication for this year is the juice price is going to go up, because there's a resurgence in cider because of the Irish advertisements. So this year we've already been given a price as a cooperative for juice fruit, and that's the first time we've known that happen, and it's a good price, it's £110 a tonne. Well we certainly weren't getting that back in '93.

The juice could well be going into Magners. The other problem with the juice price is all the apple concentrate coming in from China and because it's turned into cider over here it's marketed as 'Ye Olde English Cider,' China could create problems for the future. Who knows? Sometimes I think the English take their rules and regulations far too seriously.

All the grading is done at Wye, and it's so technical, there's a lot of machinery, a lot of cameras, percentage of colour for different varieties and different stages of when the fruit has been picked, you couldn't possibly grade by hand to that specification now, but it does beg the question, does it really need to be like that?

When we grade here for the two or three local shops that we supply, we still grade by hand and it's very time consuming, horrendous job. There's a minimum size and a maximum size, and within each box it's a mixture of sizes, and we find that's what people want, because on the Farmers' Market stall, customer number one comes up and says "Can I have some of those big lovely Coxes," the next person says "I don't want them as big as that because they're for lunch boxes."

We're going to be positive, otherwise we would have sold up yesterday. Supplying Lloyds Bank staff with apple juice? I think they need something stronger than that if they still work there now!

13. Sadie James – Biodynamic stockman & ferret handler, Melplash. Born 1973.

I did the Bath and West for the very first time this year… I thought 'That's really mixing it with the big boys,' but Murray was breed champion there as well. It's my year…

I was born in Weymouth in December 1973. My father was a farm labourer, mum was a housewife and barmaid. My grandfather on my dad's side was in farming and my grandma was a housewife. She later became a post lady. That was my father's parents. My earliest memories of them were when they lived at Mere in Wiltshire. My mother's parents were up in Cheltenham. I think my grandpa was in the services.

I started school in Dorchester. We moved around a fair bit. We lived in Weymouth, Dorchester, then we moved to Tolpuddle. Then from Tolpuddle to Thorncombe, Thorncombe to Bridport, Bridport to Beaminster and now I live at Melplash. Unfortunately my parents divorced. My mother remarried and her second husband moved to Thorncombe. My father stayed in Tolpuddle and also remarried.

When I left school I did a YTS in farming at Kingston Maurward College, but the farm that I was working on, they had problems and I couldn't stay there, and I couldn't find another farm to continue the studies, so my placement kind of dried up and I left the college.

Odd jobs. A little bit of relief milking. After that I did a short course in visual arts at Weymouth College, art and photography, that was good fun, but unfortunately again I had to leave the course early and didn't complete it. And then I got a part time job at a cattery in Beaminster, assisted the manager in the day to day running of the cattery. On average there would be between 20 and 30 cats, I think 39 was the maximum the cattery would hold. Some were RSPCA cases, others were just people going on holiday. The lady that owned it has now retired and it's no longer going.

I was still relief milking and I also helped a lady called Daphne Crook, she had a small flock of pedigree Jacob sheep. That's where I first got interested in sheep. She was at Colley farm at Dottery. I helped them part time. It's a super place, and she let me go to Melplash show and show her sheep 'cause she was getting quite elderly by then, and that's when the bug first bit me. I had a working arrangement with her that I could buy a couple of her sheep. These were two horned, and that's how I got my first sheep. We rented a paddock in Netherbury, and the chap there had horses previously and they had made a dreadful mess, so when we suggested sheep he was very keen on the idea. Unfortunately it's going the other way now, it's getting a bit sheep sick so I've got to look for somewhere else.

A friend of mine kept Grey Face Dartmoors, and when I first saw them I fell in love with them. In 1998 my husband, Bernie, decided to get me my first Dartmoor sheep as a surprise. It was an in lamb ewe called Barley, and she lambed the following February and had a lovely little ewe lamb, and once I started showing them I found the difference between the Dartmoors and the Jacobs was immense. Temperement, the Jacobs were so scatty, nervous and jumpy, and the Dartmoors were so laid back, quiet and placid, so I made the decision to sell the Jacobs and concentrate on Dartmoors.

The wool's very different. They always say you wear a Jacob and walk on a Dartmoor. I go to a lot of shows. A tremendous amount of shows, a lot of the Devon shows as well as the Dorset shows.

Sadie James with Murray at the Melplash Show

Shaftesbury and Gillingham. Yes, Murray the ram was breed champion there, which was very pleasing, and I had the reserve champion group of three sheep as well. Today at the Melplash Show we had a second with Murray the ram, and a third with the group of three, which is very pleasing given the size of classes. There's a lot of different breeds. I did the Royal Bath and West for the very first time this year. Never been before, it's such a big show, it fazed me. I thought 'That's really mixing it with the big boys', but Murray was breed champion there as well. It's my year.

We started with the Bath and West, then there was a break until the middle of July, then there was the Mid Devon show, I had the champion Dartmoor there with a ewe lamb, which is very unusual, then the following day I went to the Singleton Show in Sussex, they hold Dartmoor classes, and Murray was breed champion there. He was a winner last year as well. He's three years old. He's a good stock ram, he's my main stock ram.

I've got 15 breeding ewes and 24 lambs at the moment. I've got a full time job as well. I work at a little place called Shedbush Farm, it's on the Golden Cap Estate near Lyme Regis and it's a mixed farm, cattle, pigs, sheep and poultry, and I do all the usual farm tasks, stock husbandry. It's a biodynamic farm. Basically the principle of biodynamics is to work with the rhythm of the cycles of the heavens and the influences that it has upon the ground, which has influences upon the plants which have influences upon the animals that eat the plants, and then ultimately on the people who eat the animals. It's regarded as being quite whacky. It's very complicated.

Certainly with apples and things, you pick those on a fruit day and they're supposed to be at their best. You plant things on a root day or a seed day and again they're supposed to be at their best. They've got Aberdeen Angus and Beef Shorthorn cattle,

Portland sheep, Tamworth pigs and Black Rock hens and a few Aylesbury ducks. They do mail order meat. The farm is just a little bit in from the coast. It's a very pleasant place

Ferrets: I had my first ferret when I went to the Rousdon Game Fair in 1993, and there was this chap there with a box. 'Ferrets for sale, five pounds', and I looked in this box and that was it. I had to have one. I pestered and pestered and pestered Bernie all day, kept on and on and on and in the end he relented. "Alright, you can have a ferret, what are you going to do with it? You haven't got a hutch, you haven't got anything." So I went and bought a book, read a quick bit about ferrets, thought 'Yes, this is for me', crossed the chap's palm with a five pound note and came home with a ferret called Ferris. I had a cardboard box with the ferret in, and as luck would have it I had a rabbit hutch at home so he moved into there.

That took off. It did. At the same show I bought myself ten purse nets and within a week I'd taken him out on his first ferreting forays, caught one rabbit, which was quite interesting, and the following year some friends of ours at Mapperton were asked to do a bit of ferret racing. They had some old carpet tubes and things to make up the racing, but they didn't have quite enough ferrets. They only had four ferrets, so I added mine as well and a lad came with his couple, and between us we had enough to do this little event. It's certainly taking off now. That was the Powerstock fete, and then the following year the primary school in Bridport got wind of us and wanted us to do some ferret racing, which we did, and the Stoke Abbott street fair as well, we've been doing that nearly every year since.

During the winter I tend to get a bit frisky and think 'It's time I went out and caught some rabbits.' It's quite an efficient way to catch rabbits, it's certainly very environmentally friendly. I eat rabbit and I feed the rabbits occasionally, so I tend to stockpile them in the freezer and use them to feed the ferrets the rest of the year. I've got round about 40 ferrets. They eat a complete dry diet as well, it's a good standby. And also in the summertime when you've got lots of flies around…

I show them as well. We're actually retiring from the ferret racing because it is a lot of hard work, and the sheep are taking more time and I've also got far too many ferrets. I do a little bit of fishing, more of a hobby than a profession. I feed eels to the ferrets. I go out shooting as well, shoot rabbits and pigeons, the usual. And I go out beating on the Forde Abbey estate. I've got a Springer Spaniel dog as well that I work. I do a little bit of drawing as well, again, more of a hobby than anything else.

Full time on the land. Yes, very much so.

Melplash. There's a good atmosphere here. It's known locally as The Friendly Show. People do buy ferrets from me. I've actually got to supply some to Kingston Maurward College. They use them in the animal care courses. I went back there after leaving Weymouth College and I did a National Certificate in Animal Care, and after that I did a National Diploma in Animal Care, and I saw those courses through.

Animal welfare's very important. It is. If an animal's not well it's not going to perform and that's it. You've got to keep them well. I do use some homeopathic cures, I also use some conventional treatments. With my sheep, they're worth a lot of money. I bought Murray for 150 guineas, at the sheep sale in 2004. Probably now he'd be worth 300. Some rams, the record price I think is nearer 600. The white faced Dartmoor is a smaller sheep, it's got a slightly more lustrous fleece, and obviously a White Face, and they're horned. The wool of the Grey Face Dartmoor is used for making carpets, traditionally Axminster carpets, it's very coarse and hard wearing, the breed society was formed in 1909, so in a couple of years we'll be celebrating the centenary, which is nice. It's a minority breed now, it moved out of the rare breeds section of the watch list this year. There are an awful lot of Dartmoor sheep breeders around, some of them show but most of them keep them just because they're nice sheep.

I hand shear Murray, otherwise all the rest are done by machine. He's a big chap, it takes about three quarters of an hour and you can't sit him up and do it, I tie him up to a hurdle, start with his back, then down one side, down the other side, then sit him up and do his tummy. He's so placid, he just stands there. He's quite relieved really.

Our flock is called The Hazelwood flock. The whole flock is registered, every year the breed society have what they call studding, where ram lambs are inspected by two association inspectors, and if they fulfil the criteria of the breed points they get their stud as it's known. The ewe lambs are self registered, so whatever you like you can tag and they're officially registered. In the whole country I would imagine it's somewhere between one and a half, two thousand Dartmoor sheep.

I'm hoping to buy another ram at the breed sale this year which is at Exeter market. They have breeders come from all over the country. There's a ram in the catalogue that comes from Shropshire, his credentials look very good, so I'm hoping that he's a good as he looks on paper, and that he's not too expensive.

I don't have a farm. I manage with lots of sweet smiles and offers of half a lamb here, there and everywhere. A couple of patches of ground we rent for money but most people are quite happy to have half a lamb for the freezer. It's all little parcels, which is a nightmare with the paperwork, so every time I move from one place to another I've got to do a four copy form and send it off.

Six days I have to wait,. Unless you've got an isolation

facility, which I have, so my show team live the whole summer in the isolation facility, and that means you can move between shows if they're even one day after the next, as long as you stand still for six days before your first show and six days after your last show. And you can move as often as you like in between.

Yes, I've got an old cider orchard in the middle of Netherbury where the ram lambs graze. They don't take much notice of the apples, but now the grass has got down they're starting to raise the odd eyebrow at them. I find a few with chomp marks in them, but on the whole they tend to leave the apples alone.

Some lambs will be fit to go by November, my dad's second wife works in the House of Dorchester chocolate factory, she puts the word around whenever I've got lambs available and the orders come flooding in.

I've got a handful of hens at home, there's only ten hens, they're Heinz 57 varieties, couple of Blue Bells, and a Maran, and Rhode Island Red, the usual suspects – and I've got some brown eggs, some cream eggs, and the contents of a hen's egg entered today as well as a couple of pictures and some photography. This is my local show and I really like to support it as much as I can.

To move the sheep around I've got an old AA pickup, and it's been converted in the back so all what were little cubby holes and cupboards have been ripped out, and the back has come off and a grille's been put on and they move around in there. It's also known as the Yellow Peril and the Banana locally.

14. Abby Bunyard – Farrier, Shillingstone. Born 1975.

It was horrendous because I was 17 and tiny, I was about seven and a half stone, I couldn't wield a hammer for love nor money. There were 45 on the course, and I was one girl. That was it.

I was christened Abigail, but nobody ever uses it unless I'm in trouble. I was born in Weymouth. My father was in the Navy, he's an engineer. He's retired now and works a couple of days a week at Westlands. My mother works in the office at a large warehouse Hansons, in Sturminster. My father spends most of his time wind surfing at the moment between Weymouth and Portland, much to my mum's disgust.

My father's father was in the Merchant Navy, and my mother's father was a grain merchant, a feed merchant salesman. They were all Welsh. My father's father came out of the Navy and owned fish and chip shops. That was in London. I was christened in the HMS Ark Royal bell, they turned it upside down. My father was Chief Petty Officer and he was also Chief Diving Instructor. My mother's mother was a Green, you know the boiled sweets, years ago, they were the owners of the hard boiled sweet factory.

I grew up in Stalbridge and started working when I was 13 at the Southhill Veterinary group in Wincanton. I was a Saturday girl. I'll never forget having a dog on the table and the intestines everywhere, thinking 'Oh my God!' but it was so interesting. It was brilliant there, character building. It was get in there, get on with it. I thought I'd be a real dogsbody, but they treated me impeccably. I was very lucky. I was desperate to work with animals, and so I wrote them a letter, and there was this lovely,

lovely man called Mr Giles, he's a vet. He answered my letter and said basically because I'd had the balls to write this letter, come in and we'll give you a try, and they gave me a job. He was such a nice man, and it turned out that he was the vet on the Committee of Farriers examining board. It was all connected in a bizarre way.

I'd ridden from about five, so Sundays I was out competing in pony shows. I left school at the age of 17 and went straight into my apprenticeship. I said to my farrier when I was about seven or eight that I wanted to be a farrier or a blacksmith and he laughed at me and said "Yeah, when you're big enough," because I was tiny, "come back and ask me." He continued to shoe my ponies and forgot all about it. When it came to work experience I rang up our farrier and said 'Look, I'm really sorry, but I'm coming for a couple of weeks because I've told the school that you'll do it,' and he just laughed down the phone, he's like Captain Pugwash, and said "That's no problem, I'll do it." I had a brilliant time, he just gave me a good insight into everything. My science teacher came out and we had a laminitic called Applejack, a high class show pony, and a couple of hunters, one was called Abby, she had a day-old foal. This teacher was only supposed to be there half an hour. Two hours later she finally left the yard. She had a fantastic time. And when I'd finished the work experience, the farrier said "If you're really serious about this you've got to get on and write letters. You'll be hard pushed to find an apprenticeship being a girl."

I think at that time there were five qualified women farriers in the country but they were a lot older. I worked with him for the whole summer holidays as a gofer. I wasn't allowed to shoe, so I was just cleaning the van, picking up tools, brushing the yard, getting water, shoving shoes in the fire, anything that didn't involve working on the horses, and by the end of the summer

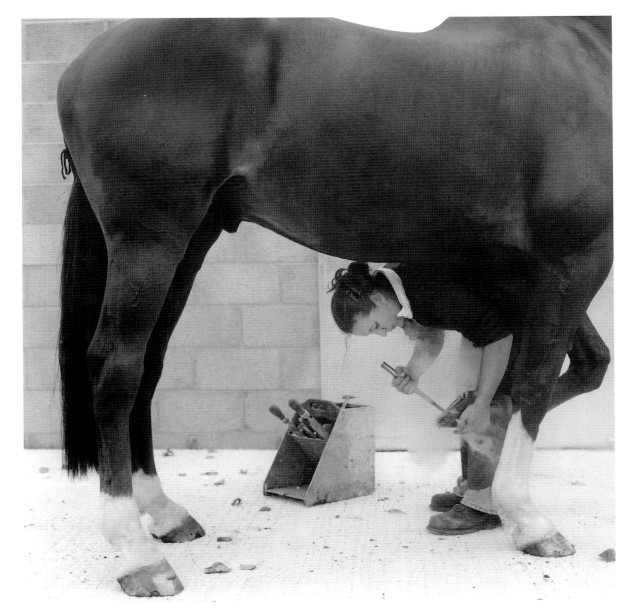

Abby Bunyard, shoeing Chester

holidays he said "Right, we've worked pretty hard, and if you really are serious about this I'll give you an apprenticeship."

I was so lucky but I had absolutely bust a gut that summer. I was up every morning, I would never be late. It was so hard to get an apprenticeship, I was determined. I loved working with horses but I wasn't going to shit shovel for anybody. I wasn't even going to try and be a stable hand. I knew I wasn't clever enough to do veterinary, but I knew that in farriery you can make a difference. You can make a substantial difference, you really can.

It's physically a hard apprenticeship. God yeah. You've got four years' book work, but it's on one animal. Four years two months, and you know about those two months, you really do. The first few months, he had a big forge which had a huge canopy and two fires, so you'd work from either side, and then he had his mobile forge. When I first started you had to find your master farrier, which was Richard, and then in the two months that you're there you have to do these test pieces, so when you went up to the college for an interview, this was Hereford, you had to take these test pieces up. I'll always remember I hated him because he left me in this forge to make these test pieces and for ages he made me work on these and I couldn't see any point in it.

It was horrendous because I was 17 and tiny, I was about seven and a half stone, I couldn't wield a hammer for love nor money. You just build up slowly, so I developed in the right way for the job. When I got to the college these test pieces were good and I got accepted. But after that he continued to make me work in the forge as much as possible, I just thought he didn't want me in the truck, but when I got to college the first thing they made us do was a replica of these test pieces, and because I'd been left in the forge and the other guys had been out sweeping the yards and clenching up to make life easier for their bosses, I was that

little bit ahead. He had huge logic. I was not going into college unprepared.

When I got into college and lifted the boot of the car, the car park went silent, because they realised it wasn't the secretary, and I had to lift this tool box out of the boot of the car, which I couldn't lift because it was so heavy. It was just brute force and ignorance, you will lift the tool box and it will get to the bench and it will be fine. I don't know how I did it. I don't know if I could lift it now, to be honest. There were 45 on the course, and I was one girl. That was it. Oh and a Spanish girl called Monica for a short time.

The first day in the car park was horrendous because you did feel like you had four heads and a tail, and after a couple of days doing these forging exercises the chap next to me decided that he might actually speak to me, that was good. He realised that I was quiet and not cocky, and actually that the work was good. Every time he went to go and cut off a piece of metal he cut mine off, never said anything, just did it, because they'd have creamed him. The guillotine was a very old fashioned one with a huge long handle and I couldn't reach the top to pull it down and I wasn't heavy enough to put my weight behind it, so he was my saviour for the first week.

The tutors were very hands off, they were good. There was a wonderful man called Slim Simons and his first ever lesson was just brilliant, "Whatever you do, if you ever get involved with anyone make sure that you get your money first," and that was his law to run by. He was kind of cool. And we had Mr Sutton, who was from up north, and he used to specialise in heavy horses, and he makes me look tall and I'm five foot two. When you learn shoeing, you learn to nail on dead legs, that are chopped off at the knee, and you've got to learn to make a shoe to fit these feet. First you've got to take this shoe off that the last pupil's nailed on. You get the dead legs from the freezer. If they thaw out we used to have races up the forge because if you pull the sinews at the top you can make the feet tap. It's got to be done!

You were trained with business studies, anatomy, practical shoe making and blacksmithing. In the second year they started bringing in real horses. They'd have about 20 in a group so they'd split you in half, you'd have about ten fires in one room but they were double-sided like my boss's, all coke, it'd be an electric fan and coke on top, but you'd have a long line with fires down the back wall, then in the middle you'd have horses tethered. You could walk straight through to the back which had another ten or 12 fires on, so you would have 24 fires going at a time, some would be shoeing and some would be shoe making. Quite a lot of noise.

To make a shoe you measure your foot from toe to heel, then measure the widest part of the foot. Depending on the length you want in heel, you add on a certain measurement, if you want it just to come to the heel or slightly further round or if you're doing a remedial shoe, or a bar shoe which is joined at the back, it's all different measurements you add on. So you chop off your steel, you find your centre point. The first thing you do is make your toe bend, so you get the middle of your steel hot, then you'd forge one half of the shoe, so you'd get one half of the metal hot, make your heels, round your heels off, then make the quarter of your shoe. I would stamp my nail holes, and then you do the other side and stamp that side. Some people would make the shoe and then stamp the holes, then you put a clip on depending on whether it's front or hind, front, you'd have a toe clip, hind you'd have two quarter clips, and there you go, job done.

All your shoeing is done by eye. There is something to be said for a hand-made shoe, you know the pitch of the nail holes,

you know where you want them, it's made for that foot for that particular day. It makes a difference.

So you start to learn trimming and nailing. I was taking shoes off and then clenching up, you make the job faster for your boss, that's the gofer jobs, then you start learning to trim and clients looking over you with beady brows, "Does she know what she's doing? And she's a woman! Oh my God!" It's really funny.

A lot of owners are women. Horses that take the Michael out of a female owner are going to do the same to you. You walk, you're doing a job and you're assertive. You're not going to win if you're faffing around. It's a very hard trade to learn. My first year was about 40 quid a week. My third year, when we were going out and shoeing, I was still earning about 70 quid a week. A pittance really.

Working from home I did have the best of both worlds. I get on with my parents really well. They're quite modern parents, so they were "Ok, if you're going to go in wholeheartedly then we'll back you." My friends were just "Oh yeah, great, cool, off you go," they couldn't think of a better job for me. My God, if I was in an office I'd kill someone I think, you couldn't put me inside, I don't know what I'd do, I'd be horrendous. I couldn't sit still that long.

In the fourth year you had two weeks' worth of exams. You had an anatomy paper, a business studies paper, there were several other papers, you had veterinary oral and farriery oral, there was one particular oral where you had X-rays and you had to say what was going on and what you'd shoe for that condition. There was a vet there examining you, a couple actually, you had several orals and then you had a forging exam on paper and then you had to make specimen shoes and put them on horses, front and hind and then you had a veterinary practical, they were trotting them and you had to assess them, were they sound? How would you shoe them?

I'd never cut myself with a knife and I'd never been shat on, and this bloody practical, I made the front shoe, really chuffed with it, burnt it on, and sometimes you get this little tiny ridge where you've burnt it on and you hold the front foot between your legs with your hand round the toe and usually you tuck your thumb down the side of the foot, and I don't know what I did but obviously nerves, and I'd just eased the sole with the knife, just to take this ridge out, and I took the skin straight off my thumb. Ends of fingers bleed, it wasn't bad, it just peed with blood, blood everywhere, up the inside of my arm. It was fine, because when you're in that line of work you smash yourself regularly and your pain barrier must be higher, anyway, so I was giggling about that and Mr Simons got me a plaster and each time we wrapped it up it just soaked it. I got the front foot done, and I was just nailing on the back foot, and this horse just shitted everywhere, and it's never happened to me before, so when I got out of this exam room I was red down one side and green down the other, it was hysterical. Also, because I'd been in the forges and it's dry heat I was just caked, just green and red, it was so funny. But I passed.

A lot of apprentices fall out with their bosses, because it's four years and you're one to one, but I got on with my boss very well. He said "Right, how do you want to do it?" And I said 'I want to set up on my own.' He said "Right, you work x amount of days for me, and the rest of the week you find your own work." So I worked four days for him, so he was fab.

I refused to advertise, I wanted my work to speak for itself. My ambition was to make up a full round, just me, no adverts at all. My boss had always said "Your work speaks for itself, and you will always be busy, always arrive five minutes before the time you should be there," and he was right. I then went on to a chap called Paul Gibbons in Newbury who specialised in polo, so I would then do a day for Paul, a day for Richard and a day for myself. I'd been shoeing around the county with Richard, so anything that was out of his area. You weren't allowed to pick up work within a five-mile radius.

This polo chap, he'd have a team, so they'd line up between ten and 25 horses in one yard. So an apprentice would take all the front shoes off, and I'd follow, trimming all the front feet and Paul would follow fitting all the front shoes. And once he'd finished the last front he'd start down the back, taking all the backs off, I'd follow after trimming and Paul would follow fitting, and by the time we got to the first horse again I'd nail all the front shoes on, the apprentice would follow me clenching them up and then we'd go down the back lines, and once a horse was done a new one was replaced. I think the best we did was in two days we shod 50 horses. It didn't matter if I didn't work a full week because in those two days I'd earned, I think it was about ten pounds a horse, so if you'd cleared 50 horses you were alright.

So I built up my round. Yeah, I didn't advertise, it was just word of mouth. Occasionally, you'd get a phone call saying "My horse doesn't like men," that's rubbish, it just doesn't like being shod, you know, it's never it doesn't like men, usually you're going to get a kicking to be honest, or it just needs to be told to behave.

With a perennial kicker you just get on with it. There's always a way. There's modern methods of dope, but there's old-fashioned methods as well, you've got twitching, some people feed them. I don't really agree with that, they've got to learn to stand there and accept it, but if they're trained properly as a youngster you don't usually have a problem. The main problem you have is when horses come over from Ireland, I think I don't speak the right language. Usually if they've just come off a ferry they're a bit wild, but they usually come round, slowly.

I started when I was 17, I qualified when I was 21, so I started my own business when I was 21 and I'm 31 next week, so ten years. Plenty to keep me busy.

If anything, the hunting ban, some of my clients have got extra horses. My theory behind it is the drag hunting, because you're not stopping, or not drawing a cover, the animals are moving more, doing a lot more work, there's less standing still, and they're more knackered, so it seems to me that they've got more horses, so I'm shoeing extra. Now they're flat out from point to point. I hope it doesn't affect me. I know one fanatical hunting lady who this year isn't interested in going out, but she'll snap out of it.

I've got an eventer, I wouldn't hunt that, he's special. But some clients ring up and say "Do you want a day?" So I pop out on theirs. I'm not a hunting person, I go out for a bit of fun, a bit of a social, but I wouldn't want to do it regularly because you've got people out there you shoe for, and it's not quite a day off, busman's holiday type thing.

Yeah, I have a mobile forge in the red van. And as for backache, when I first started at the age of 17 my boss said "Find a back person, and preventative rather than cure," and that's a lady called Lorraine, down in Poole, and so I went down and met her, and she's just made sure that my back's straight ever since.

Hundreds of memorable incidents and they're all so funny. My boss was hysterical. When I was training we were down at a place, I can't say the name, but they always had bastard hunters. I got sent in to put a pair of hinds on this mare, and I was only a fourth year apprentice and this bloody woman bolted the top door, and at the time my boss wanted me to make it because he'd invested a lot of time, and I can't really remember what happened, it didn't kick me but it did try and I was on the end of its back leg, and all I can remember is sitting in the yard looking at the arse end of this horse, and then looking down and seeing this stable bolt on the floor, thinking 'Jesus,' and I still had the hammer and the nails in my hand, and thinking 'God, that's going to hurt,' and I couldn't cry so I just sat there for a second and my boss came across the yard and he bent down and said in my ear "Are you going to bloody shoe that horse or are you going to play with it?" and marched off again. So I stood up and I shod it. I don't think we spoke for about a day. I never said a word. But it was that moment when you either were going to be a farrier or you weren't. But it was quite funny. We laughed about that.

Horses come in all shapes and sizes. I go miles and miles, I go to the edge of Studland, and I go to West Bexington. Right out to West Knoyle, there's a polo team there and all round. The further afield the bigger the yard because you don't really want to be travelling for one.

Shoeing takes about 40 minutes. I take off a front and a hind, and then I put four shoes in the fire, so when I've taken off the next hind and front they're ready to go. And then you have a cup of tea, and then you move on. You get your shoeing tools as you do your apprenticeship, and then the main layout when you start on your own is your van, but the only thing that you do really need then is your forge and your anvil, because the rest you've been working with for the last four years, unless your boss is going to take them back.

I used to play rugby for North Dorset, but I did that whilst I was an apprentice, and then my boss sat me down and said "Right, you're going out in the world, and nobody's going to support you, therefore you give up these games," in a nice way, "How can you work on a Monday if you go out and play on a

Saturday?" He was right. I loved playing, I had a fantastic time. I event, I shoot, pheasants, partridge, and I do a little rough shoot in Warmwell, that's a nice shoot.

With farriery, you're a vital part of other people's lives. You see your regulars every four to eight weeks, you book in their next appointment when you get there. At the end of the day, you're messing with their pride and joy, you're enhancing their life. It's a lovely feeling when you walk away and you know you've made 100 per cent difference.

Self-sufficient. Yeah, totally. Probably sometimes too much, but it comes with walking into a room with 45 blokes. You have to get on with it.

15. Liz Duke – Falconer, Maiden Newton. Born 1983.

I had a little Harris Hawk called Dante who was the first bird I ever trained, and he was absolutely cracking, he was gorgeous. You couldn't fault him in anything.

I was born in the Old School House in Maiden Newton. My mother was born in Weymouth and my father was born in Dorchester. On my father's side they were auctioneers. Duke's Auctioneers. My father works as a relief sub-postmaster and my mother is a secretary at the Dorset County Museum. He works all over Dorset. He just goes wherever they need holiday cover.

I started off at Greenford School in Maiden Newton, I then went to Cerne Abbas, Dorchester and finally Beaminster, so a fairly eclectic school career. My earliest memories. I remember going down to the river, we used to play in the river all summer, and up on the old railway line we used to make dens. It was great. We certainly did have freedom. From here you can go straight up behind the church and you're in countryside, and again, just across the road by the bakery and then it's just countryside. Lots of friends around. We always had a house jam-packed with animals. Dogs, cats, rabbits, hamsters, guinea pigs, budgies, cockatiels, you name it, fish. I had a little rabbit called Bold, he was a little Netherland Dwarf, such a cutie pie. He was the best rabbit. He used to live up in my bedroom until my mum found out.

After I left school early to be a nanny in Mozambique. I found that very difficult because of the two totally different worlds. I was working for a very rich white family, and they had everything they could possibly want, and then you looked out

the window and saw the rest of it going on. You have to be very strong, I think, to be able to cope with that. I was only there for a summer. I'd love to go back, but not into that sort of situation.

I went straight to Gloucestershire from there, and that's when I started birds of prey. It was a five-day course to teach people to keep their own birds. I've just always loved birds of prey and I wanted to know more about 'em. My dad's got a piece of land up by Hardy's Monument, so I thought it would be nice to have a bird that I could go and fly up there, just tootle round catching food for myself. I just like watching nature really and a bird of prey is the easiest way to get up close and personal to it.

I don't agree with shooting at all. I think it's nicer to use animals because then it's got a chance. It's a natural way of doing it, isn't it? If you're shooting it's indiscriminate. You shoot whether it's healthy or not, whether it's old or young…It's dead or injured. Whereas with a bird of prey or fox hunting, if it's healthy it's going to get away, it's natural selection. I think it's a nicer form of pest control.

The course was at The National Birds of Prey Centre. It's now under new management. The owner moved to America and it's a lot smaller. I went back to learn a bit more about the practical side of it, it's hammered into you day after day. On the course you do basic training, first aid on the birds in the field, husbandry, aviary design, food, equipment making, telemetry. By the end of it your brain feels like it's dribbling, it's that intense. I did really enjoy it but I felt that I needed more practical experience. I went to volunteer for three months and two years later I was still there. I was paid for the last six months, and bits and bobs in between times if I helped out at events. It was very addictive.

I had a little Harris Hawk called Dante who was the first bird I ever trained, and he was absolutely cracking, he was gorgeous.

Liz Duke with falcon Malaki, Maiden Newton

You couldn't fault him in anything. He did belong to them.

I had to leave him behind. That was heartbreaking, but I was given one of that year's babies so I brought her back and hunted over here. She's a Harris Hawk. She's staying with a friend of mine in Portesham. The last job I had I couldn't take her with me because I was working six days a week so I didn't have time to fly. So I gave her to him and she now hunts on my dad's land where she was supposed to hunt, so that's poetic justice.

I've got a big aviary outside in the garden. My dad calls it the bird palace. Because this used to be an old school we converted the outside toilets into a big aviary.

A guy called Mark Parker taught on the initial course and he was fantastic. He has kept birds all his life and he's really good with laws and legislation because he used to be a policeman, so that's perfect. The legal side is a big thing with hunting. Anyone can go out and buy a golden eagle tomorrow, and they could keep it in a big box and that's not illegal, but if you're hunting birds there's lots of laws and legislation about going after quarry. There are certain seasons things can't be hunted in and out of, you have to get landowners' permission, if your bird catches something over somebody else's land then you're in trouble. Obviously once the bird is in the air you've got very little control over what it does or where it goes, so at the end of the day you can't say "Your bird caught this over my land." 'Well I'm sorry, but what can I do about it?' You can do your best to keep on your land.

If my bird was hunting on my land and it caught a pheasant, it might catch it in the air on my land but take it over the border as it's going down, then technically they've caught it on their land. It is difficult to prove on either side. Most people are fine with it, especially if you offer them to have a close look at the bird.

The next bird I had was a little owl. He was a Tropical Screech Owl. I wasn't a big owl fan at that point. They are birds of prey but you can't hunt with them. He only weighs four ounces but he was one of the cute fluffy ones so they did the sob story on me, but I absolutely love him now. He's a little dude, he's a little character all to himself. I fly him in the displays but you can't really hunt him. And then I got a peregrine which was a wild injured one, and he'd got something wrong with his wing, and I nursed him back. He went to one of the vets in the village who keeps birds.

In the last six months I started getting other birds. We've got a buzzard now called Periswana, he's a good boy, if a little dense at times, but he's catching rabbits, albeit small rabbits, and he did catch a twig the other day, and viciously killed it, we've got an eagle owl, Amber, she's a big girl, she weighs about 12 pounds and she's caught rabbits before, she's caught pheasant, she's not technically a hunting bird, she's supposed to be a display bird but she does occasionally catch things.

The difference between a hunting bird and a display bird. It's just how you teach 'em, it's what you bring them up to do. Amber was hand-reared, she was actually rescued from a child's bedroom, part of the Harry Potter craze, you wouldn't believe you'd buy a three-foot eagle owl for your child, would you? She was nursed back to health and we started flying her in the displays. She's a good girl, but occasionally if she spots something that's not moving very fast she says "Ooh, I'll have that." And she's so silent, she can sneak up on anything. She's snuck up on me in the past and you just don't notice it's there until it lands on your glove and you get knocked backwards.

Every bird has their own little personality. The Harris Hawks aren't actually hawks, they're like a cross between a hawk and a buzzard. Hawk temperaments are very manic, very highly strung, nervous. Buzzards are kind of laid back, chilled out, whatever, go with the flow. Harris Hawks have a hawk's flying ability, which is better than a buzzard, and a hawk's catching ability. So that's why they're commonly used in falconry. Peregrines have two speeds, there's flat out and dead, no brakes and no brains. They're total maniacs, but quite sweet. Hamish was very sweet, he had a lovely little character on him. He'd call to you as he was in the air, he'd make this little chipping noise, he never did fly very well. Buzzards are very chilled out, they won't catch a lot, they're half hunters and half scavengers, so if they can get an easy meal they'll go for it, 50 per cent of the time. You'll catch road kill if you take a buzzard out hunting. Periswana's very sweet, he's a good boy but a bit of a maniac. Owls tend to be more chilled out than other birds because a lot of them are hand-reared so they don't have the same respect for humans. Other birds respect you, and you have to respect them or you don't get far. They have big talons! Owls either like you or they don't and it's not good if they don't.

Normally they show their displeasure by grabbing your arms or your hands, and that hurts. We do have a crow. He was hand-reared by a member of the public. We've tried seven times to release him and every time he flies off in the middle of the day and in the evening he's sitting on the top of his aviary going "Open the door!" so we've just given up now. He is a bit of a munchkin. They are very intelligent, crows.

Jemima Parry Jones is one of the best falconers in the UK. She's a very strong character, put it that way. Everybody in the falconry world will know her. At the moment she's in South Carolina, she moved there the year before last with 280 birds, she chartered a flight and took 280 birds and six Labradors and moved over there. There's rumours that she's coming back. She's quite a determined lady, when she decides to do something, that's it.

I went because her centre was the biggest in the UK. I love her to bits, I think she's the most fantastic person in the world. Falconers aren't supposed to be women. I think it's still very much a male-dominated world. If you go to falconry centres they always have the token woman, and she's always blonde, good looking and not much between the ears. Ninety per cent of the display teams in this country are men and then you'll possibly have a female assistant, but there's very few women actually doing it.

The falconry world is very macho, it's always "My goshawk's bigger than your goshawk," all that. You can go to shows, honest to God, and sit in the beer tent "Oh my goshawk caught five rabbits the other day." "Five? That's nothing. My goshawk caught 20" and it goes on and on and on. And what do you say? 'My goshawk caught a spider!' At the end of the day I know what I'm talking about, I know I can train a bird and I can have great fun doing it.

Falconry is the art of catching quarry with birds of prey, hunting with falcons. If you're hunting with hawks you're an austringer, if you're hunting with buzzards you're just a raptor keeper. There's a huge history of falconry in China. In this country it goes back to when written records started, there have always been very strict rules on who flies what, and what they can catch when they fly. Emperors could fly vultures, Christ knows why they'd want to, but they could, and then going right down servants could fly kestrels and everything in between, Lords could fly peregrines but they were only allowed to catch grouse, whereas clergymen could fly peregrines but they were only allowed to catch something else.

I'm really fascinated by it. I've never managed to find out why there were such strict rules on it. The regulations are very odd, and it's a load of rubbish anyway because it says Lords were allowed to fly peregrines, but they never damn well flew peregrines, it was their falconers that did it. Ladies were only supposed to fly merlins, which are tiny little falcons, they only stand four or five inches high, the lady's bird, but actually merlins are the most difficult birds to fly so that's one up for women falconers. They're so speedy and you fly a bird of prey on its weight system. So if it's too fat it won't want to fly and if it's too thin it can't fly, so there's a very small margin and with something as small as a merlin there's such a tiny little margin that it's very difficult to keep a balance. If it's too cold it drops weight, if it flies it drops weight, so they are actually a very difficult bird to fly.

We are constantly weighing our birds, we weigh them every day. If it gets really cold and we've got small birds we'll do twice a day. We'll go up and check everybody in the morning, sometimes we do flying displays in the afternoon so if we're doing that we'll weigh the birds in the morning and sort their food out for them.

They eat day-old cockerels, hatchery waste. We buy them in frozen. They're all shipped over from Holland. They also get rats, mice, quail, pheasant, rabbit, anything they catch they have. They'll also have chicken, beef, just make sure it's a nice varied diet. Vitamin supplements once a week. All raw meat. With all birds of prey apart from owls they've got a crop which is like a hamster's cheek pouches, so they stuff it all into the crop and it takes maybe four hours to digest through. It's just so they can ram as much food in before somebody else comes and steals it. So you have to be a bit careful because they can eat a lot more than they actually need. So that's why we weigh them, to see what weight they should be, and how much food to give them.

We just have a set of kitchen scales with the weights on one side and a perch on the other. Pop them on the perch. We just get the food ready, but we won't feed them until after they've flown. They fly to us for food, that's the way it works, some of them go from the cage, if they're flying in our flying area you just open the aviary door and out they go, they know their little routine, they go back when they're ready. If you're hunting the bird you take them out, sit them on the fist, walk to wherever you're going, loose them off and see what they can find.

We hunt with ferrets as well, so ferrets can go down and flush any animals that might be hiding, and then you just have to be careful that the bird's trained with the ferret and doesn't ever catch the wrong thing. The way you do it is the first few times you put the ferret on the ground and you hold the bird so it can't do anything, and after a few times it knows it can't get that, they tend to learn fairly quick. The first time they ever catch something they have the whole thing, so they understand it's a good thing. After a few times you give it some of it, so if it's a rabbit you take a leg off and you keep the rest so they still get a reward.

The rest of the rabbit we either eat it ourselves or we dice it up for the other animals or it goes in the freezer. It depends what they've caught. We've got 12 birds now so it saves on food bills.

We do displays at the centre where we are, we also travel. Last week I was in Tunbridge Wells, that was a static display. We tether the birds out and we talk to people about the animals, answer their questions. We're thinking about the Dorchester Show next year. We used to go when we were kids.

The bird's got permanent jesses on its legs, permanent anklets on its legs, they're called jesses, it's then got straps which are also called jesses just to confuse matters, it's got flying straps, basically the anklets go round the legs, the jesses go through the anklets, that's to hold it on to the fist, then through the jesses you have a swivel, and that attaches to a leash so you can tether it to a bose. With falcons you've also got a hood, and that tricks them into thinking it's night. Falcons tend to be quite skittish, but if they can't see it they can't freak out. Other people use bells and telemetry. I don't tend to use bells because it's not very easy to use bells when they're hunting, because they make noise. If a bird lands in a tree, nine times out of ten you can't see it but you can hear it. Telemetry is a little transmitter device that clips either to the leg or the tail, and that transmits an electrical signal. You can pick it up and track it like you would a tracking device. I've got one, but I don't think it's got any batteries.

We have gloves and it's a left hand glove so you can do everything with your right hand, unless of course you're left - handed, and a falconry bag to keep all your food in, because it does tend to leak a bit and it's not very pleasant. You'd also need a creance which is a long piece of string tied to a stick, the same as taking a puppy out on a lead, it gives the bird a bit of confidence. It tends to be up to 50 feet long, so they can have a bit of exercise. With falcons you'd start off training them with a lure which is again a piece of string tied to a stick, and we'd use a leather pad tied to the other end with a piece of food tied to it, and that simulates a bird in flight. You just swing it round and snatch it away from the bird as it comes in. Everyone says that's mean but basically if a falcon's chasing a pigeon, the pigeon's not just going to go "OK, catch me," so you're just trying to tell the falcon that it just has to keep trying and it'll get it in the end, but the first couple of times it's going to miss, so that's how you teach a falcon.

It's certainly not a cheap sport. The aviary to keep them in costs probably more than the bird does. Harrises are round about £300 at the moment, goshawks a bit more, falcons, anywhere, lanners are £450 at the moment, snakers are £350, it depends, barn owls are ridiculous at the moment, they're £30 each.

The ideal age with hawks, anywhere between four and five months, with falcons, maybe three months. You want them to be what's called hard down or hard pen which is when their proper adult feathers have come through. They have juvenile plumage, but they won't be fluffy babies. Training you'd expect to do that from scratch. The bird has to learn your commands and movements, especially if you're hunting. With an older bird, it's very easy to train them, but it's not easy to retrain them.

Harrises live together naturally, they live in family groups of anything up to 30, and they'd hunt together like a pack of wolves would. As far as I know they're the only birds of prey that will live together. Kites will fly together, vultures will fly together, buzzards will occasionally. I like going off on my own, it's my time. I love flying my falcon at the moment, that's my favourite occupation. It's just so nice to be able to see him so close and he's getting there, we've only had him for about four weeks, and he's just beginning to work things out. They're very sneaky falcons, they'll go right behind the tree line and then wick over, or they'll fly into the sun so you can't see them, and he's just beginning to think "Oh if I go round there she won't be able to see me." It's really nice to watch them developing. He's seven now and he's been kept in an aviary all his life so he's never been flown before, so it's really nice to watch him developing from this falcon that would just sit on a perch and stare at the wall all day. They are such amazing creatures and so few of them reach their absolute peak. They're so happy when they work something out or manage to catch something.

At the moment we run a wildlife sanctuary in Staffordshire. We take on any injured wildlife or orphaned babies, most orphaned babies aren't orphaned, but don't get me started on that! We do try and most of them go back to the wild, but it's just a long tedious process. My fiancé, Mark Palmer, he set up the sanctuary four years ago. We just opened to the public this year, but it's only six acres that we've got at the moment so we're looking to move back to Dorset and get a bigger place. We're upwards of 80 animals now, so it's a little chaotic.

Hunting from horseback it's something I've always wanted to do. I've got my own little pony now, well, big fat cob, and she's stunning and she tolerates everything. I'd love to come back down to Dorset because the land's a lot better for falconry, and Mark wants to come down to Dorset because it's closer to London and that's where most of his jobs are. We're just looking for a place, but we'd really like to be in this area really. On my dad's land there's a piece at the bottom which would be perfect, but unfortunately it's on a lifetime lease to a farmer who does nothing with it.

I'd like to have some eagles and some bigger birds because that's what people want to see, and I'd like to have a few more falcons, and possibly a goshawk that can hunt properly. To be honest I'd like to fly vultures. I've hand-reared a few and they're cracking little characters.

16. Sophy Burleigh – Supply teacher and cider maker. Monkton Wyld. Born 1963.

Cider has been made in this valley forever. It is an unbroken tradition…

I was born in Reading but I never lived there. I first remember being in Farnham Surrey, then we went to Derbyshire. After two years up there my father got a job near Winchester. He is an electronics engineer and has worked in Italy and now has his own business down here. His grandfather worked for Marconi and his father, my grandfather, worked on the development of radar during the war. He also worked in Cambridge for a long time. I don't remember my great-grandfather but my great-grandmother was a fearsome lady with a hooked nose and very blue eyes who played the violin. She wasn't a professional violinist but she could have been. She used to make me play my violin to her, which was a really terrifying experience.

My mother's father was a GP, and his father. They were architects, vicars or doctors on her side of the family. Mother started to train as an architect and then gave up and had all of us instead. I have three younger brothers. The connection with Wootton Fitzpaine is through my father's mother's family, so my grandmother's family. My great-great-grandfather was an industrialist in Bristol doing lead smelting and he basically decided he would like to become landed gentry so he bought the Wootton estate, as you do, in 1895. He only lived for ten more years so my great-grandfather then inherited it, and my grandmother and her four sisters were born in Wootton manor.

I have been coming down to Wootton since I was born, to stay at the manor while my great-grandparents were alive and then down in the village. When my great-grandfather died, the estate

was sold off, that was in 1969-70, around that time, my father's generation inherited it, they had the option to either take land or money and my parents kept a bit of land, two farms, and we now live in one of the farm cottages, Greenlands. We went to Italy from Winchester in 1977 and I went to school out there for three years, at the European School in the north of Italy. I was in the German section, one brother was in the French section, another brother was in the English section and another brother was in the Italian section. And then after three years because I was a very lazy student I was sent home to sixth form and so I spent two years at boarding school in Wiltshire and I ended up studying languages at Cardiff University. I loved Cardiff. Then I went to help out a friend, an old matron from school, she was teaching at a Steiner school near Wimborne and they wanted somebody to teach languages to six-year-olds, mainly German and so having sworn blind that I would never go into teaching, that teaching languages would be my worst nightmare, I ended up teaching German to six year olds for two terms and just loving it, absolutely loving it. I have come to the conclusion that teachers fall into two categories, those who like young children and those who like adolescents. Although I like working with adolescents, I help with the Somerset County Youth Choir, I teach young children best, it is young children that I have the best links with. I met Dave my husband when I was teaching at the Steiner school. He was born and brought up at Shapwick, near Wimborne, a farming family, they farmed on the Kingston Lacy Estate. We met at a party. He was at university in London doing geology.

I went off and nannied for six months in Tuscany, we kept in touch and so when I came back I moved to London where he still had his final year to do and I worked in Miss Selfridge in Oxford Street. Then I got into teacher training college in Winchester. We

Sophy Burleigh in her cider house, Monkton Wyld

moved back to Dorset and I got my first job in Parkstone at a Catholic school, as "an acceptable non-Catholic." It is very difficult finding teaching jobs in Dorset because everybody wants to live here. This was September 1989. So I got a year's teaching in Parkstone with a wonderful head called Sister Angela from Ireland. She really supported me through my first year of teaching and then passed me on to a Catholic school in Boscombe to cover for somebody's maternity leave, by which time I was married and also pregnant so those poor children must have thought that all Year Three teachers were always pregnant. We had our son Jo. We were then living in a farm cottage just outside Wimborne and my husband was working one day a week on the farm to pay the rent. This was another branch of Dave's family who farmed north of Wimborne. When we got married we happened to mention to Uncle John that we had nowhere to live, we were living with Dave's mum and dad, and he said "If you can spare some time on the farm feeding the calves and driving tractors…" It was out on the downs between High Hall and Badbury Rings, right up on the downs, it was a lovely place to live, next door to the dairyman's daughter. We had a great time there, we were there for seven years.

I got a job, teaching full-time at Wimborne St Giles, on the Shaftesbury estate, which was a two-class school at the time, so we had 40-45 children in the school and the head, myself and a part-time teacher and we got on like a dream. I taught there for six years and then the opportunity to come west happened. Basically the house that we live in now was tenanted by an old lady, she and her husband had farmed here in Monkton Wyld, they had handed the farm over to their son and moved into the cottage. When her husband died, she carried on for another year or so, she was 87 and it was too much for her. The house is all up and down steps, and only has a solid fuel rayburn, no other form of heating. So she gave up the tenancy and we took it on. We have our own water, it is very reliable, it has never run out completely. Most of the village is on spring water but the house opposite has mains water as he didn't trust the spring water and he had mains put in at great expense. He asked everybody around if they wanted mains, but they all said "No thank you very much we like our own water." It is by far the nicest water in the county.

We have a cow that my husband milks most days, I milk when he gets fed up, and her two calves. We have ten sheep but they are down at my grandmother's in Wootton at the moment at their summer grazing. We have very poor, unimproved pasture, beautiful wild flowers, but because we have only four acres of pasture we have not got really enough to keep the cow and all the sheep going at the same time. My grandmother who is now 93 is down stocking and has a few fields she isn't using and so we have the summer pastures down there. She still keeps Jacob sheep, she has about 15, her mother kept them, my great-grandmother, and so they have had sheep down at Knapp Farm for 40-odd years. Ours are Jacobs as well but some are crossed with an 'all spare parts' ram. We have them as grass cutters and because we want to know where our meat comes from. It is part of the way we live, we have four acres of pasture and you can't let it go rank, it has to be managed, it is part of living in the countryside. The Jacobs are lovely, easy to handle, relatively tame and lovely wool as well. I don't spin the wool up, I don't have enough hours in the day however a friend of mine has just started spinning so she has spun me up some and I am in the process of knitting it for my husband. We have bantams who are the most unproductive bantams in the world. It is our fault because we don't keep track of them and they go off and hide a nest away and all of a sudden come out with 12 chicks. They are completely free range, we don't clip their wings and so generally they are fairly good when the foxes come…they fly.

But we had a sparrowhawk take one of the chicks the other day which was quite exciting. It came down, flew off with the chick and all of a sudden there were nine instead of ten. We grow some of our own vegetables but not that many because just down the road we have a friend who has seven acres of organic vegetables. He runs a box scheme, he comes and borrows the shower and uses the car occasionally, we help him out when we can and he gives us vegetables. A local, mutual support system really.

Well I taught for six years up in east Dorset and then the opportunity came to come and live down here, the house became free, so I handed my notice in and instantly fell pregnant, seven years after having the last one. So that was a bit of a shock and when we came down here we decided that it was time for me to be at home. When I was teaching full-time Dave had stayed at home and had been a house-husband , so he had been house-husband for six years. He had gone off to Bournemouth university to study stonework conservation and so his job now is working on historic buildings and monuments and timber framing. As we have the animals, land and woodland to manage and with no central heating there is the firewood to be collected, it is a lot of work, so we decided that both of us would work part-time. I was at home for two years with Anna who is now eight and then I started singing.

I started singing with a 'Sing in the bath? Come along and have a go' group, which was brilliant fun, I loved it and I also started singing with a four-piece a cappella, I met a teacher at the singing group and she said "You can't just give up teaching, you're not allowed to, I need a supply teacher who thinks the same way as I do. Somebody who likes children." And so she got

me back into teaching and I have been doing supply ever since, and I love it. I love supply teaching. I generally work in the same few schools, Winsham and Avishayes in Chard, and then Parrett and Axe school in Mosterton, Charmouth and then in Devon I do Kilmington school where my good friend Caroline works and also Shute. Apart from Avishayes they are small country schools, primary schools.

There are some aspects of Steiner teaching which I think are very compatible with good teaching practice in state schools, some aspects which are just plain wacky but that's where I think the Steiner system hasn't moved forward from the 1920s and I think Steiner would be completely horrified if he saw what was being done in his name now, he was a very progressive, forward-thinking man.

As a supply teacher you have a great deal of licence, you go in and teach what you are asked to teach if it's a pre-booked session, but if you don't understand what the teacher has left you, which not infrequently happens, you can make it up as you go along, as long as you are teaching the children something. If they are working and excited and enjoying what they are doing they are learning and to me that's what teaching is about. Teaching children to explore the outside world and the inside world, just to explore and open their minds and teaching them to read. And I think as a supply teacher I have much more licence to do that because nobody is going to fuss if I don't follow the National Curriculum exactly.

I have a lot of pre-booked supply, this teacher has to go on a course or that teacher has a doctor's appointment. Some heads even give their teachers time to write reports. A lot of my teaching is pre-booked so I know in advance that I will be working in that school on that Tuesday. I have a modicum of planning and preparation for those schools where I am doing my own deal. When I leave the school at the end of the day that's it. I don't have to worry about it.

Secondary school supply teaching from what I have heard seems like a complete mug's game. The primary children are the age of children that I enjoy teaching. We can talk to one another and understand one another and we have fun, and I hope they get a lot out of it. I certainly get a lot out of it.

It helps put bread on the table, literally, it helps pay the community charge and the rent and all those sorts of things but then my husband works part-time, so we both share.

The cider world happened because our neighbouring farmer, Winston Chapman, originally from Hereford, has been making cider in the valley for 25 years, more than that I should think. In fact he is continuing the tradition in this valley, cider has been made in this valley forever. It is an unbroken tradition. He has a beautiful orchard and he got the press from up the road, because I think the press at his farm, Stubbs, had gone already. He is our local parish councillor and when we met him and he and my husband, our family and his family hit it off straight away. Dave was down there like a shot making cider, we all were, it is a real family tradition, everybody joins in and the kids are all there, up to all hours and that was it, we were smitten, cider making is a way of life for us from the end of September to December. We make cider nearly every weekend.

We started helping Winston down at his and then, about five years ago we found a press, it came from Ryall by Whitchurch Canonicorum, from another farm. They had gone over there to see a tractor or something and Dave was poking around in the barn as is his wont and came across this cider press and said to the old chap "This cider press, if you are ever interested in selling it, I would be interested in buying it!" And the man said "No. No. No. I couldn't possibly, it is all worm eaten." So Dave wrote

him a postcard when he got back saying "If you do ever think of selling it to get in contact" and so he did get back to us and said "You can have it if you want it." Now we have a cider press, Winston has a cider press, another friend Tratty has a cider press in a barn near Winston's. We have never yet managed to have a three-pressing Sunday, two pressings is our limit. It is not the time spent pressing that is the problem, it is the alcohol drunk whilst pressing and two pressings-worth of alcohol is more than most people can cope with.

The press is in the barn, there are two floors, a hay loft, which is where the apples get stored with a hole cut in the floor and the apples go down through into a mill, a scratter, which is basically a glorified mangle, slighty looser than a mangle so you chop up the apples, not into a fine pulp but into a loose pulp. We had a hand mill for a while but it broke, but now we have Mew's beautiful mill which we fit up to the PTO on the tractor. So the tractor gets fired up, the belts start clattering, the dogs run riot, we have to put barriers up to make sure nobody does themselves too much of an injury and everything starts clattering. The apples start coming down through the mill the pulp comes out and it is shovelled into square former on the press, between layer upon layer of straw. We try to use organic straw, we have used wheat, barley and oats, it depends what you can get hold of to be honest. It is not terribly easy, it is not a great arable area and so you have to go quite far afield to find what you need, so long as it is clean, good clean straw. We have no slats, just the straw, the wooden former which goes up layer by layer, peg it in with hazel pegs and then put another layer of straw and a pile of pulp on top then press it down good and firm so that it forms a cheese. Keep going till you run out of apples which is normally 23 bags, animal feed bags, 25 kilo bags of apples to a good pressing. It takes only about three-quarter of an hour at most, it depends on the skill of the builders. I am normally chucking the apples down though I do help build occasionally.

We had an all-girl pressing down at Winston's last winter and it was fascinating, although we were quite capable and built a beautiful cheese, could we stop the men from interfering? We could not. They kept coming in and kept saying, "Oh, I think we need more... I think this needs to go a bit faster..." "Taint zuant! taint zuant that cheese!" It wasn't falling down at all, it was perfectly all right! The juice all comes out into a big pot underneath the press and we drink it straight away because it is sweet and delicious that juice. But you have to drink it that first night because if you drink it any later it just goes straight through you. It starts working incredibly quickly. It goes into a settling tank and it stays there for a couple of days. It just depends how organised we are and how many barrels we have got cleaned out. It is only at weekends, very rarely have we done a mid-week pressing, you can't get the staff. There needs to be at least five of you, it is a real hands-on job, building the cheese takes a good two or three people and somebody has got to push the apples down and somebody rattles the scratter to make sure the apples don't get stuck and somebody else is shovelling them out. And somebody has to sit around and make stupid comments to tell them they are not doing it right, I mean it is obligatory to have people like that so it takes at least five people. Normally there are about ten or 15 people, plus all the children and the dogs running round and we often have visitors just to come and see how we do it.

Yes so the juice gets put into a barrel and after about three weeks the top froths up. All oak barrels, we get them from different sources, we buy them from Vigo, they tend to have rum in them but they are lethal. Good, clean barrels, we pour the rum out, we don't leave it in, it makes a cider which is just far too strong. We had a barrel this year with a little bit of rum in it, most of it was poured out and Dave measured it with a hydrometer and it came out at ten per cent freshly opened. That was a bit of a risk really. We just drank it in very small glasses, we don't do pint glasses any more we just go for small glasses. It is more like a wine, it is certainly wine strength, but it tastes like delicious apple juice, it doesn't taste strong. Natural yeasts. The juice just comes out of the press into the barrel, occasionally the barrel gets topped up, you lose a bit with the frothing in the three weeks before you tap it down, you maybe add a bit of water or maybe with next week's juice until is right full up at the top and tap it down and leave it. We get at least one barrel from a pressing. We know which barrel is which, we write on them in chalk which orchard the apples have come from. The apples are very mixed. We never use cooking apples. We have made one or two single variety ciders but the best ciders we have had, have been from the blended ones that we don't even know what the apples are. The majority of the apples in each pressing are cider apples. We planted a small orchard here when we moved down eight years ago, that was one of the first things we started doing and every year we have planted more trees. It used to be an orchard but it was grubbed out in the '50s and the neighbouring farmer, John Ody, remembers it happening. We have planted all sorts, so it is a real selection of different things, cookers as well eaters and cider apples, but we have got Dabinett, Yarlington Mill, Tom Putt, there's a wonderful one called Winston.

It really is its own microclimate here. Up here we have two inches of snow and down the valley they have nothing at all, and down the valley thick mist and up here brilliant sunshine. And the south west hillside means we don't ever get strong winds, whereas everybody else gets strong south-westerlies. It is a good sheltered place for an orchard. We get the frosts, the frosts stay hard for longer but I don't think that does any harm as it doesn't thaw out so quickly which does the damage. When we have had snow in the area, which happens every year, our snow is still here three days later whereas everybody else's has gone by the same afternoon. So it is a funny little microclimate.

We put in standards and they were mostly 13 -14 ft high by the time we got them so they have taken a long time to get established, they do take that much extra when they are so big. It should be a good year this year, last year was a very poor year. It is already biennial. Fascinating.

Cider is just such a wonderful way of life and you really keep in with the seasons. Cider is the autumn season, a time when actually the other harvesting is finished, you get on with the cider apples. You are picking them up in all weathers on the Saturday and then on the Sunday you are pressing them and reaping the benefits. No other way to store the apples, you need something dry and cold and we haven't got that down here. We make about 1,000 gallons between the three presses, about 1,000 gallons a year and we don't sell any of it, we drink it all. If you make lots of cider like this you have lots of parties and so it is ideal. The wine merchants do lose out. I can't remember the last time I went to the pub, there is no need. We have one here. The Powerstock Festival is meeting other people who make cider a different way or the same way. They come from all over Dorset and Devon, quite a few mad Devon friends. Devon is only a spitting distance, under a mile a way, and there are Hawkchurch cider makers who come down and help us. Tays still make cider. Tim Chichester's is a cider making experience, donkey-drawn cider making, a menagerie of animals, more terriers than you can shake a stick at eating rats in front of you, tame deer, that was interesting.

Dorset cider isn't well known, people don't know that Dorset makes cider at all. The orchards that we are picking our apples from have been there for years and years, they are not new and if you look at the old ordnance survey maps and the tithe maps it is all mapped out. It didn't go commercial in Dorset, it was purely for personal usage and that is what you drank, you drank cider when you were out haymaking and it is still what you drink. If you're out bale hauling within your own farm you still drink the cider, maybe watered down, just like they water Chianti down in Tuscany if they are working during the day, watered down with ice cubes.

My husband and I have decided that we are international peasants. We go off in November and visit our friends in Tuscany he goes every year and I go every year I can, we go and help with the olive harvest in November, miss a week's worth of cider making and come back with fresh olive oil. International peasantry.

17. Penny Whatmoor – Mill House Cider Museum & nursery, Owermoigne. Born Dorchester 1982.

I had to go live abroad for a while to appreciate living in Dorset, the cider museum is now my baby.

I was born in Dorchester. I have got two sisters both older than me, there is a two year gap between each of us. I was brought up in the same house I live in now. My father originally did his National Service in the Army then he went over to Nigeria and worked with the Ministry of Agriculture over there for about three years and then he got into farming and came to Dorset in 1962. They moved into this house with his parents, bought the nursery and have been running the nursery in lots of different ways over the years and started the cider museum about 20 years ago. My grandfather worked for the Bank of England in London and he retired in the '60s. The mill stopped working early in the twentieth century and they diverted the river. Really sad, I would love to have it working now. Water-powered cider making. That would be very exciting.

My mother was born in Dorchester and when she was younger she trained to be a dental hygienist and then she came back, fell in love with my dad, they got married and have been working together on the site ever since. A family affair. She was from the village. My gran still lives up the road. Her father was a gardener and went round all the villages doing the hedges and lots of gardening. When he retired he helped in our veggie garden and helped out. My mother has always been interested in growing things, she loves her veggie garden and she is the main one who does it here.

January 4th it kicks off every year and then it is absolutely mad getting busier and busier till May. We ordered our seed potatoes last month and they will be delivered some time over Christmas. Last year we had over 90 varieties…I am not going to quote every single one. We have a bit of everything. You get the old boys, they have been coming in every year they won't try anything new, they will have the same ones every time and then you get people who will say "What have you got new this year?" and they will have a look round. So there is probably half who like really old ones and half who like to try all the new ones.

The tomatoes, my father used to grow on a really large scale and sell them wholesale. Cucumbers, red cabbage… you name it we just start them off in the seed trays and that is much easier for people to try all the different varieties. We have two really big greenhouses, two polytunnels and then whatever space we can find outside. They did lettuces and cabbages on a really large scale as well and again when the cider museum started about 20 years ago they moved over to the beddings, the geraniums and fuschias…The tomatoes went to a wholesaler in Weymouth. We are doing a lot on a small area of land. We certainly make the most of it. The river goes behind the trees, we have two lakes there so it runs inbetween the lakes a tributary of the Frome.

The cider presses: it happened about 25 years ago. My dad has always been collecting antiques, glass, clocks, pretty much anything, and one of his antique dealer friends said "I have got a cider press and a cider crusher." I don't know why they were even talking about it but it just came up in conversation and so he said "Oh yeah I will try that" him and his brothers, and they got them just for ornaments and when they got it they thought we can actually try and use this. And they just got a few apples, because there were a lot more orchards around then, and made a little bit of cider and it all took off from there really.

They made more and more cider on that equipment and the

Penny, Mary and Laura Whatmoor with scratter, Owermoigne

shop got so busy then. It was a much smaller shop then, and so they wanted to get the brown and white road signs up, and in those days you had to be a museum to be considered for that, and all those rules, so they went on a mission and in the space of a few years collected as much as they could possibly and put it all together from that. The presses and crushers came mostly from Somerset including Mark and Henstridge, Devon – Okehampton, Shute, Dalwood and Sidmouth – with some from Dorset, and a few from Glastonbury, Gloucester and Wiltshire.

My older sister Laura she has been working in the nursery for the last seven, eight years. She is much more into the plants and makes up hanging baskets and she wants to do something for her own so she has just finished training as a driving instructor. She has just got one more exam to take and she is giving lessons. But also that's flexible so she can still come back and do the hanging baskets in the season. My other sister, Mazzii, is a midwife up in Bristol.

We make small amounts of cider now. We are just starting to plan the open day for October about a ton of apples and use the really old equipment to show people how it is all made in the school half term. All the locals love to see it being made. They come in and help. There is definitely a cider tradition around here. The locals come in with their containers to get them filled up. This summer has been absolutely mad. Cider sales have gone up, everyone has been talking about it, and this August has been the busiest August we have ever had in numbers and the amount we have been taking.

We have got 15 different varieties of cider, a few of Julian Temperley's farm ciders and sparkling cider, some from Perry's because they do the single variety ones, and I have got some from West Monkton in Somerset, Rampant Rosie and Bonking Billy, just for the tourists, they like that, one from Lyme Regis

Jack Rat 7.4 per cent and the Ashridge from Devon, the posh looking sparkling ones, one with blackberry liqueur in as well. I try to get something for everyone. I am responsible for the Cider Museum, the shop is pretty much my baby now. Draught farm cider sells best, that is what we offer for people to taste, so they taste it and then buy it most of the time.

Once a year, just before the cider open day we go round with our little wire brushes and oil and make the presses a bit more presentable. Apart from that they really don't need much care, they are all under cover and indoors.

The nursery, loads of vegetables, including tomatoes and peppers. We like to have loads of different and unusual varieties. Squashes, I spent six months in South Africa, squashes there were just fantastic so when I came back I said 'Yeah let's try some' and in our normal grower magazine you just find so many sorts. This year we tried growing okra. We didn't know very much about that, Lady's Finger, but it did really well. Still not sure how to cook it. There are so many different names for it. Melons, they have done very well. Sweetcorn, my dad loves his sweetcorn, then all the lettuces and brassicas, asparagus, we have been selling asparagus crowns and getting people to start their own beds. We have got a lot of regulars who come every year. And the potatoes because we sell them in open trays people can pick only one of each potato if they want just to try the different varieties. Pink Fir Apple is one of the most popular and we had one called Anya this year which is Pink Fir crossed with Desire and so that is similar, looks like Pink Fir but not quite as nobbly. So it is just a little bit easier for the chefs. We do get a few chefs coming in from the hotels in Weymouth and Hugh Fearnley-Whittingstall he comes in and gets his tomatoes and squashes.

We have had runner beans, dwarf french beans, stringless

beans. This year we had some purple potatoes, we wanted to try them because my mum had them in Peru. It wasn't Blue Edzell but it was a similar type of thing. I think we will have a few next year as well.

All this area has connections with Thomas Hardy. Our mill house was featured in his story The Distracted Preacher, where Owermoigne was 'Nethermoynton' and the miller was a central character. In The Woodlanders one of the main characters was a travelling cider maker, visiting the farms that didn't have their own equipment.

The clocks, there's over 30 long case in the museum. We have six turret clocks, one from Dorchester prison. This time of year every visitor gets a guided tour by Derek. Just reading notices about them can be boring, you need someone to tell you to bring it to life. There is just so much information about each one and the apprentices, how each was apprenticed to the next. A family tradition again.

When I finished college I worked up on the nuclear site at Winfrith on the decommissioning team for a year just to get some money together and then I went travelling round the world backpacking, America, Fiji, New Zealand, Australia then Indonesia, just exploring really. In Australia I worked for Amnesty International, really fun, mostly going round door to door talking to people, so you get a lot of abuse. But then again that was quite funny. It was just giving information about Amnesty International. Leaflets. not trying to get money from them so much as just ' Talk to me. Talk to me about political prisoners etc.'

The first time I was there I was just in their records department so going through old paperwork that they have just stored and stored, sorting out the papers and also the other bit was going through all the old photos and that was really fun, so all the photos from 1950s, 1960s. going back to the early building. Sorting them into albums and getting them onto computers. It was very interesting working there but after a year I had just had enough of the whole nine to five office thing really.

I went travelling that first time for a year and went back to Winfrith for another year, they enticed me back again with good money to work as admin and then I went to travel around South Africa for six months then I came back here. I had to go live abroad for a while to appreciate living in Dorset, So that was May, two and a half years ago. We will have our big cider making day in October then really November and December we are quiet just tidying up really. So I shall try and get away then. Not for as long this time as I am being a bit more responsible now.

Just fun. You never know how many are going to come or who's going to come. And again you meet such a wide range of locals and tourists. The Museums are open all the year round. We build up to our open days in October. December is busy getting ready for Christmas, everyone's buying their brandy and their aperitifs. We try to be the hub of the cider world in this end of Dorset. That is the idea.

We have definitely inspired a lot of people to make cider. Especially after they come round and see the open day demonstrations. They say "Oh we can make it at home?" And we give out the Vigo leaflets, to buy the equipment and they are fantastic. They do not realise how simple it is. They think it is magic, chemicals or something. But when they come and see that it is just apple juice fermented, they say "Wow we can do that." So it is nice that you can show people how to do it, and how they can make use of the apples which they usually just leave and don't do anything with.

So the nursery starts off in January and then manic through

till June then it switches over, July is busy then August to October is the cider museum. We have had loads this August. We don't count the children as they are free.

It never stops here that is just why I have to try and get away in the winter. There is always something to do. Some of my friends they just play on the internet and computer games and I am just 'How do you have time to do that?' I hardly ever have time to play a computer game or anything like that. Wouldn't really want to.

My partner works in a motorbike shop in Dorchester but he helps with the cider making. We went to Italy on the back of his motorbike last summer. A BMW. Four days there, a week riding round, then back again. We did a day's falconry for my partner's birthday in the New Forest and it was absolutely fantastic. I'd love to get a falcon one day. Definitely.

18. Caroline Fowler — Feed mills, motorbikes and computer troubleshooting. Westford, Thorncombe. Born 1966.

I have no interest in a computer that doesn't have a problem. I prefer people without problems. Computers are easier than people. They'll tell you what's wrong. They won't go into a corner and sit in a sulk and not speak to you.

I was born January 18th 1966 in Taunton. My mother had moved down from Newcastle to marry my father. He worked in a feed mill. Westford's down a no-through road, you end up in a farmyard or a river, you can go no further. Beyond the milk factory, beyond the pallets, beyond the quarry where it says 'No through road.' We celebrated 125 years before we sold it, so it's been a mill a long time.

Apparently the monks stayed there when Forde Abbey was built, there was an old legend that there was a tunnel from Westford to Forde Abbey. We think it was a double hedge. Great-grandfather was a baker in Hawkchurch. Again it's family legend, the bakery burnt down and he built it back up again. He had three sons and he had enough money to buy each son a mill, two in Bridport and one at Westford. We stopped flour in the 1950s and went to animal feed. Grandfather died in '74. He was bedridden most of the time that I remember. My father ran it. I never saw him, he was working all hours. We lived in the house attached to the mill. We owned it, 2000 it was sold. And he was running the feed mill up till then.

Memories. Oh it was a wonderful playground. Glorious. It was a water mill so the river ran underneath it. We used to climb on the roofs. It didn't occur to you as a child that you were

mortal. We used to be hauled out of the river covered in mud, the very old part of the mill that was brick was dark, it was cold, it was scary and we used to dare each other. 'Go in, pick up that pile of sacks' because there might have been a rat's nest underneath. In the '50s they had a Perkins engine put in and then after that it was electric.

I wasn't frightened of water. Well we had a weir. We had two weirs and the weir gates used to be raised or lowered to divert the water. We used to go sliding up and down the weir. Water was never a problem. I've got a younger brother, so I was a bit of a tomboy. You had to be, you couldn't be a girlie, there was no such thing. We had tree houses and freshwater leeches and you get used to it. You can't run around in a dress in that kind of environment.

I had a fantastic upbringing. Idyllic. Absolutely wonderful. We had orchards, apples, nuts, it was a farm, we did have a farm at one stage but we stopped that. The farm was down past one field, we had pigs for a long time and that teaches you a respect for pigs. They're intelligent and they're also very bolshy. Indoors. Except for one big boar who was kept in an outside pen. That was absolutely terrifying.

My dad was in the Navy and they met on a blind date. Dad being a country boy and Mum being a city girl she showed him around the city and they kind of lost touch for about seven years and then she sent him a birthday card out of the blue and she got this huge great letter back and it went from there, but Mum's people were all railway folk. Newcastle LNER. Mum was born on Tyneside. No countryside, nothing. The countryside down here always amazed her. The first time she came down here in her winkle pickers with metal tips and Dad took her for a walk she ruined three pairs of shoes. She said "I was such a city girl, I wouldn't know where to buy Wellington boots in Newcastle." No

Caroline Fowler on the mend, Thorncombe

idea. She was a fish out of water. Especially with the accent, it wasn't harsh, it had more of an Irish lilt to it…

The blind date, this was in Newcastle. Dad's ship docked and they got given the freedom of the city and she showed him around the city, and she took him home, she took a sailor in uniform home, which you didn't do. Not on Tyneside, not unless you were a certain type, but she took him home. This was in the early '50s. So in fact I am half Geordie. Her father was a guard. He was a carriage guard. Scotland, London, yeah he was very well travelled. But he always insisted that the children had an education. They all had training, apprenticeships. My mother was working for the Dean of Newcastle University on house acquisitions, buying up houses for the student digs. Yes. The education paid off. She always said "You can't go wrong with shorthand and typing" and so she ended up with a sailor in the country. I don't think she realised how hard it was going to be.

When she first moved down they were living in Seaton and Mum was earning more than my dad. Secretarial work. She was a couple of years older and used to call him 'my toy boy,'

Mum had a lot of style being in the city. I think Dad was proud to have her on his arm. Women were kept away from the mill. Yeah. Very old school. Even from the accounting side. He didn't make use of her skills. He could have done but the accounting was still done in a ledger with a red ink pen and a black or blue ink pen and two bottles of Quink. Red and blue. Dad did all that. Just him and my uncle. I only helped if there was maybe sickness or once I got older. The Fowlers are an old-style family. The men do the business work and the women marry a wealthy farmer.

The Axe flooding? Oh Lord, we had swans in the kitchen because the house was actually lower than the river and when it flooded we had swans on the veranda, it was fun. We just decamped, the house was maybe on three levels, we had the kitchen and maybe a front room going out into the garden, and then up again was a living room and another room and a walk-in larder, and then up again was upstairs, so we just used to decamp into another level.

We had flagstones in there, so you just swept it out afterwards. Father controlled the hatches. Oh he'd go up in absolutely appalling weather to try and lift the hatches. Very dangerous. A weir somewhere up river went a few years ago and there was a wall of water came down the river and we had railway sleepers as the flooring and it looked like a hand had punched the floor up, that was incredible.

We didn't have a mill pond. The river came off at two points, one was in the upper meadow, there was a weir where you could divert it down, and then further on down just before the mill the river would split and come together behind the mill. So the mill was on an island.

The Axe moves about quite a bit. I've seen oxbow lakes come and go and land appear where there wasn't any, and then land disappears. It's quite gravelly in places. There's quite a band of flint down there and a few fossils.

The orchard? I remember the smell and the wasps. I know we had a Victoria plum and a strange orangey blood red apple, we used to eat those. There were a lot of eaters and cookers. I think it was just a spare bit of land that they didn't know what else to do with. And then we would go fishing once in a while. A lot of eels. We used to have an eel trap and the eel man would come down with a hessian sack and take them on.

That would be in the autumn. And then there were elvers. Oh all the time, you used to call them nine eyes. You'd put your hand in the water and they'd all be stuck on your hand. It was just fun, miller's thumbs, minnows…trout mainly. Dad used to feed trout round the back of the mill, corn-fed trout and he wouldn't let anybody fish there. There were salmon in the Axe. A few years ago the water board did actually put a salmon pass in there because they were concerned that there weren't enough making it up river. There used to be a pike, whether that was just told to scare us I don't know. We had a mink problem. They were killing just about everything on the river. I don't know how Dad dealt with it but I have a feeling he used rat traps, water rat traps, drowned them. Otters up there? There is now, from the milk factory down apparently there's otter tracks. We had cockatiels from Cricket, Dad saw a flight of cockatiels, we've had lemurs. They're very cute. They're just not the kind of thing you expect to see in your garden on the bird table. They've gone now, but that was a bit of fun.

As far as the mill was concerned we dealt direct with the farmers, independent. We'd buy in whatever was needed and if say a herd didn't have enough copper we were small enough to be able to make a tonne and a half with a bit of extra that was needed where the bigger merchants couldn't.

They could come down and buy a bag. We had the whole range. Sow, weaners, pig nuts, every type of cattle feed, we used to feed the big old bulls out at Horlicks a special mixture when they were doing the AI up there, chicken, duck, pig, sheep, cattle. We had to be careful with the levels of minerals because what would be fine for one animal could kill another.

We had all the recipes and all the different mixtures. You had to know exactly because if you killed anything then you are dealing with other peoples' livelihoods so you've got to be very careful. Inspectors came down and sampled the feed all the time.

We never abstracted water, it was just a straight flow through. It depends what they called the course of the river. The actual course was straight under the mill and we diverted a bit

off the side if there was too much or whether the actual course was round the back of the mill and we were diverting it. We've had the river turning pure white when the Milk Marketing Board flushed the tanks out by accident, the slurry tanks somewhere upriver burst and killed everything but the eels. That stank. And then the river disappeared. About ten years ago. They actually called the rivers authority and said "The river's disappeared." Somebody was extracting it and there was nothing. I think it was the milk factory. There was nothing. And they were like "What do you mean, the river's disappeared?" "It's gone." There's still milk churns in the river, the huge flood about 20 years, we were still pulling milk churns out, they just came banging and clonking down the river.

The working day was long and hard. My father, I don't remember seeing him much as a child. There's always dust. Stones, I remember two big ones. The machinery? A lot of it was sold off when we closed. For my mother it was a constant battle to keep everything clean. We used to lie in bed when we were living at the mill house and you could hear rats running around. It was a constant battle for her to keep things dust free. The mill was actually attached to the mill house and yes it did vibrate. They would just carry on until it was done. Uncle he lived up in Tatworth. It was dangerous yeah. I've got great-uncles that lost fingers, on a chain hoist, he got his finger caught in a bag and the bag went up. During the war milling was an exempt occupation, apparently. He's got all sorts of stories.

Mother was a housewife and 'cause she couldn't drive, she was so short-sighted, she was literally stuck there. She decorated that place from top to bottom. And then when we moved up to Valley View, which had been Grandfather's house, she decorated that again. She was very isolated most of the time. We didn't actually take holidays until I think my brother and I were at school and then it was a day trip. We'd chug off in the Riley at 23 miles per hour somewhere, hold up the traffic all the way there and then hold up the traffic all the way back.

Milling was full time. And then we started growing nuts. It was unused land. Couple of fields and they put nuts in. Cobnuts. We were the biggest grower outside Kent at one stage. The whole family would get out there with their hooked sticks and, whole weekend we'd do nothing but pick sodding nuts! And then we'd drag 'em all into the old stables and we had these boxes. You'd make up the boxes, and a pair of big old scales and you'd weigh them up into ten kilos, 12 kilos, something like that, stick them on the back of the truck to go out on Monday morning up to Bristol. It was literally a month of doing nothing by picking nuts. The squirrels were a menace. The back row of the cobnuts was left for the squirrels, 'cause if you left them the back row they wouldn't go any further. They were Kent cob. We had them coming down from the South Coast because they were organic. We sold them in the shell. There was a printed label that we used to staple onto the box.

During the war Granddad flew pigeon messages. We had a huge, 40, 50 foot long shed that was built by Italian or German prisoners of war for Granddad and his pigeons. He was breeding them and then during the war they were used to fly messages. They'd come back to him. Even from France they would come back. The War Office built a pill box down the bottom of the garden. We have one in the field and we used to have one in the garden and the one in the garden was disguised to look like a shed and when the war was over they came and demolished it so we don't know what was going on in there. During the war when petrol was rationed, Granddad always had petrol. Grandma was a Cockney! We're not a family for inbreeding!

As for school I went to primary school in Axminster, because Mum was Catholic, we went to Catholic school and then on to Woodroffe until about 16. I kind of got very worried that my whole life was laid out in front of me, and I was to go to secretarial college, it was what Mother wanted, she was happy with it, but oh, we used to have dreadful battles. So I went completely off the rails. I kind of bummed around for a while.

I wasn't exactly expelled. You had a choice, "You can either leave now under a cloud and please don't expect the school to give you a reference, or we will make you leave." So I kind of left home and school on the same day. The day before my seventeenth birthday. I was a horrible, horrible teenager and the family had never had anything like it and didn't know how to deal with it. I was awful. I rebelled against everything. I'm surprised sometimes I'm alive. Mum and Dad had to come and pick me up from hospital after a bike accident, face stitched up. You were not the norm if you didn't run away from home.

I had a lot of motorcycles registered to me, ridden by other people. I learnt to ride. Anything from a CZ to Ducatti Panther. Everything from rat to racer. I love it. Yeah, I think it was the whole rebellious ethos, the men, the black leather. Studs? Definitely studs. Tattoos? Yeah, the mankier the leathers the happier I was. You never get out of it. There's still that thing there, especially in the summer when a bike goes screaming past I think 'Oh you lucky sod.' It's the speed, the freedom, it's different to driving a car. You're not as protected and there's always that 'If I just push this a little bit faster round that corner what's going to happen?' The sense of danger… It's not just the men, it's the bikes. It's 'Will this do 125 up the motorway without anybody being killed?'

I did get arrested once and the police turned up with a summons, and again it was nothing the family had ever dealt with before and they didn't know what to do. I was 17, I was still juvenile so I didn't actually get in as much trouble as I could have done.

Inbetween I'd been working in Chard for six years, Action Aid. Third World child sponsorship, and again it's this thing, every six or seven years I have to deconstruct everything and start again. I was working in the IT department running a computer system when I was into bikes. The earliest IBM computer would cost you about £15,000. Never seen one before. So I got my hands on one…'86, '87? I just wanted to know how it worked, how that wire made all that appear. It's the same with a bike. Everything with a wiring diagram, I love. Well, I suppose I've always wanted to know how things work. Feed mill to computers. It's not so much of a quantum leap, it's still everything working together. Except with a computer you don't get an end product.

I taught myself computing. Literally by taking everything apart and putting it back together. But then Mum always used to say when I was a child she had this thing, this book by Dr Spock, said 'Put a ticking clock by the child's cot,' so she did and I took it apart. The freedom gave me time to explore.

Yes. I think a lot of the time it's peer pressure, it's which group of friends you're in, and are you popular enough, and that's never bothered me. So I've always followed my own course. After Action Aid I took off for Germany with a suitcase and £140 to sell encyclopaedias to American servicemen, which was a complete and utter disaster. Absolute disaster. I was paid by results. Hello starvation!

I took a plane out there, and then I met an American biker. I was working for an English company who stuck me on this army base in Bavaria, where I met this blonde, leather-clad, Harley Davidson American, and I thought 'I don't want to go home yet' and found myself a couple of part-time jobs.

Easy Rider. It was for a while until I realised the guy was completely psychotic. He'd married a German and decided to stay in Germany and got divorced and then I met him. Regular grunt. Infantry. Bored shitless in Germany? Just about, yeah. Four years, four and a half years. He was a prospect in a bike club. Hells Angels. That was interesting. It was fun. It was a lot of fun. I was old enough at this point to say 'Oh no, this is just bull' or 'I don't want to do that,'

I worked in a Country and Western bar, right opposite the base. Luckily I didn't have to wear Country and Western gear, thank God, no, but I got to the point were if some bugger put 'England Swings' on the juke box one more time I was going to kill somebody. 'England don't swing like a pendulum do,' I'm sorry! And I worked road crew for bands that were playing big venues. Some friends worked road crew and they said, you know, "If you want to come along you get a backstage pass and all the rest of it, and you can speak German, you can speak English," My German was rocky, but when you've got stoned road crew all you do is just shout at them in English. I could count to three and say 'No garlic please.'

I had more German friends than American. I suppose when you go abroad you become very patriotic. I was never a patriot before but I used to hang a flag out on the Queen's birthday, just to let everybody know, but the Americans were like that permanently. I celebrated the Queen's birthday and my German and American friends used to come and celebrate with me. I celebrated the Fourth of July, I celebrated German Reunification Day, it was just a party.

The motorbike gangs they were a mixture of ex-pat Americans, Germans tend to embrace a lifestyle to the max, so they took all the worst parts of the American bike culture and embraced it with fervour. Travelled through a lot of Germany.

Yeah. Austria, Germany. I see Europe with the point of view that what the politicians in the EU say is not what the people in the EU want. They want their own countries back. They don't want to be a United States of Europe. The Germans want to be German, the French want to be French, the Italians want to be Italian. They don't want a mass European mishmash.

Five years in Germany. Encyclopaedias lasted about five weeks. I then worked in a fast food shop, big two foot-long French bread sandwiches. I got very good at doing that and not slicing my hands up at the same time. Roadcrew. It was fun. I used to get a backstage pass. We were playing German venues. Most of it was heavy metal.

I'm still compos mentis. I didn't overdo it in any way. Experimented with various substances. Everybody does. You give me somebody my age that hasn't and they're either lying or they really are a scared person.

My parents? I was always told "No matter what you do, no matter what trouble you get into, this is always your home. We'll yell, we'll shout, we'll tear seven strips of skin off you, but this is always your home, you can always come back." I used to call home every other week or so.

I came back about '96. I didn't want to stay in Europe for the rest of my life, so I came home, back to Westford. I'd lost contact with everybody. I had that gap in my work history that nobody could check, didn't know what the hell I was going to do. And I took a series of waitressing jobs, bar jobs and then I did a computer course, programming, a home study course, passed the exam, and it's having that little bit of paper that says you know what you're doing, gives you that confidence.

I hadn't done programming so I started doing that. I thought 'I like this. There's a logic to it. It may look twisted but there is a logic.' So I was writing computer programmes. And went on from

there to think 'Well once it's written, how does the hardware deal with it, where does the colour come from, where does the sound come from?' And then I gradually got into the hardware. So apart from the course. Yeah. All self-taught I could take computers apart and put them back together.

You see I used to take motorbikes apart. Piston rings. I hate changing piston rings. The worst thing you can have with a computer is a spark coming out of somewhere. A little wisp of smoke!

Computers? It's amazing how all those separate parts are going to work. I can see how they all do and I know how they all do, but you just change one little thing and you can watch the whole thing collapse. If there's one fault, computers only have binary, yes or no, black or white. If you put a grey in there, they can't deal with it.

I'm not exactly an engineer, I'm not a consultant. Fixer, repairer. It doesn't sound right. Troubleshooter maybe. PC. Macs are too specialised. I have no interest in a computer that doesn't have a problem. I prefer people without problems. Computers are easier than people. They'll tell you what's wrong. They won't go into a corner and sit in a sulk and not speak to you. Individual computers have got their own habits, their own quirks, things that a user has not set them up to do but they do anyway.

Motorbikes have their own personalities. Some of them will electric start on the third turn, some you've got to prime it then kick it. Every mill would have had its own personality.

Computer troubleshooting. I didn't think it would take off, I was still working in a pub at the time because I thought 'I'll never support myself doing this,' and I found myself stood behind the bar one Sunday night, earning £3.20 an hour when I knew damn well that Monday I had two calls booked in at £20 an hour. I thought 'I'm a mug.'

The name helps because people say "Oh you're Fowler, is that Westford Fowlers?" So it does help. Oh yes. I'm working for families whose grandfather dealt with my grandfather. It's nice to have that sense of history.

Mum, oh, she was proud. She was very proud. In fact she was a better PA than my dad. In Mum's eyes, making it means that you've got enough to support yourself and you're happy doing what you're doing.

The best advice I can give anybody is 'Do not trust your computer. Don't trust it to hold your data safely.' It will, at some stage have a serious problem, and if you're not prepared for it… Computers have mental breakdowns. They have overloads, they have a funny five minutes, they'll go completely off the rails like people do. People put crystals on them, I talk to them. I talk to them, say 'You're struggling there, what's wrong with you?' It's putting it back on the straight and narrow.

I am a firm believer that generations coming behind me are not going to be able to use body language, they're not going to be aware in social situations of potential pitfalls. They can't read expressions, sarcasm is something that's now lost. Interpersonal skills are dying. The written word, reading, writing, I know some teenagers who literally write the way they use their text phones.

It's not a dumbing down, it's a rape of the English language. It's just the fact that it's computer and you don't have to use a capital letter after a full stop and it's dying.

We are literally in the corner of three counties. Dad definitely classes himself as Dorset. Technically our postcode is Somerset. It's actually Westford, South Chard, Somerset, but we are Dorset for everything else.

Cider always was a big part. During haymaking it used to be jugs of cider. Though why in the heat you're going to drink cider I'll never know. You always know good cider, you have to strain it through your teeth before you can swallow it. I know we used to get farmhouse cider, I never knew where it came from but it used to come in the big old gallon containers, no label on it, funny murky misty concoction. I always remember it as being, when you're a kid and you're allowed to drink it, it's a big deal. And I could never understand why people would voluntarily drink it. I drink it now but I would never drink fizzy cider. If it's sparklingly clear with bubbles in it, take it away. It's not actually cider.

I've seen the end of a family tradition. I've seen the end of nearly 200 years of history, but I'm creating my own history now.

19. Val Crabb – Publican, Hope and Anchor, Bridport. Born 1940.

I've always loved ragtime or boogie woogie like Ben Waters plays, that sort of stuff that makes you want to, grab you by the feet.

It starts with a pub called The Quiet Woman in Halstock. I was born 5/9/40. So I'm 66 next month. My mother and her sister moved to London and my aunt got married in London, married a man called Jimmy Doyle, who'd been in the Navy, worked in a bank, and then they decided they were going to take a pub. So they came down and they took The Quiet Woman. My mother was from Chard anyhow so she was local. My mother met my father in Halstock and the rest, as they say, is history. So it was through The Quiet Woman really that I came into being and I've got two sisters younger than me, Lorraine and Madonna, and my family still own the bakery in Halstock, they still cook with coal fires, my two cousins are still running that. Father worked on a farm in Halstock for the Holloways, then we moved about a bit as farm labourers did in those days and we ended up at Lower Wraxall. My first school was Rampisham.

So we stayed at Rampisham and then we moved back to Halstock. My uncle and aunt still had The Quiet Woman and I went to Evershot school. Then we lived near Coombe St Nicholas at The Eagle Tavern then we moved to Cricket St Thomas for a time, I went to Winsham school, then Chard school. Then we came back to Halstock. I left Evershot school when I was 14, we'd moved to Corscombe by then, that's right, 1953, and I went to work at Ewan's farm, West Chelborough. I was there for three years and then I worked with horses at Prince's Place, near Melbury Bubb. Horses in the winter, hotels in the summer.

I went to Osmington Mills, then I went up to North Devon in a holiday camp and worked there in 1962. Waitressing, chambermaid. Eventually I did cooking.

Oh God, I remember The Quiet Woman, my formative years were spent there. My uncle took it in 1939 and he was there till 1959. I didn't live in it but I was always visiting, you know? Eventually, Dad died at 52, he was ill with emphysema, he ended up working in Westlands and Mother was working in Westlands as well, though she did run The Fox at Corscombe for about two years. The Quiet Woman was the biggest influence I suppose. There was always a piano and singing round the piano. I used to sing in the church choir but only because everyone just went there, and Dad used to sing in the pub, like singalong stuff, so I've always loved music.

Mother always said she was hatched at Hatch Beauchamp, which is near Taunton. When she was about two they moved to Chard, 'cause my grandfather, her father, was a ganger on the railway, he lived on the railway line and Dad's family had always lived in Halstock. In fact I think my great-grandfather was probably born in Melplash. Crabbs, yeah, if I go to the church now, 'cause Mum's buried in Halstock I can go down there and there's Mum, Dad, Gran, Granddad, aunties, uncles, you know, from Dad's side.

And Mrs Doyle, when they moved out of The Quiet Woman they moved into Yeovil which was the bad winter of '63 which is when I was on Exmoor looking after horses. It was very severe to say the least. We were the last road, I think, to be opened in the country, the Lynton-Lynmouth-Porlock road, 'cause it's very high up there. We were digging out the roads and that, trying to get the horses out exercised, we lost a lovely dog, he was poisoned, somebody put strychnine in a sheep's head, to kill foxes I suppose and the dog picked it up and he was killed.

Val Crabb with some of her regulars — The Wild West of Dorset

Helicopters dropped us food. Even in those days the old helicopters were about. My boss Mr Seel wanted to get back to London, so we had to ride horses from Oare Manor, which is where Lorna Doone was supposedly killed or married or whatever, down to Porlock, and it was the easiest time I've ever gone down Porlock Hill because it was in the snow, the electric wires were down and you were going over rivers and fences you didn't even know what was underneath you 'cause it was so, so high and I've got photographs of it, you know, old black and white ones, and I stayed there until 1964. And then I had my son at the end of '64, September '64.

I'd come back to Dorset and then I worked in a hotel in Seaton called The Golden Lion. lived in with him, I should have written all this down because I've lived rather a chequered life! I've worked on Lundy Island as well, back in 1975. You only stay there for the summer because only about 12 people live on Lundy in the winter. When I came back I got a job at the police training college at Chantmarle until it closed, about 1990.

Well The Quiet Woman. I've been known to be behind the bar at 12 and I always remember being very upset when a man came in "You're not serving me," he said, "you're not old enough." And I was so hurt, he was right, I realise this, I do understand. I was supposed to be 18 you see, and this is going back to the 1950s. Mr Lombard, I always remember him. I just enjoyed it because they had the piano in there and life was life in those days. It was just a nice pub.

The songs? Oh well it was the old standards I suppose, Show Me the Way to go Home, You Made Me Love You, Sunny Side of the Street, 'cause I've always loved ragtime or boogie woogie like Ben Waters plays, that sort of stuff that makes you want to, grabs you by the feet. A couple of brother-in-laws that used to come out from Stoford, one of them was a train driver, and I think the other one used to work in Westlands. But whenever they came people used to say "Oh play the piano, play the piano for us" you know! There was never bands about in them days in pubs, we used to go off to, like, Sydling for local hops or Evershot Hall, farmers' dances, maybe the occasional hunt ball.

My dad's mother was Irish, I think my mother's family were all Somerset. No, I've always had itchy feet. I've never been one of these that stuck anywhere very long actually. My grandmother used to do the school dinners. She was the school dinner lady. I am from a long line of cooks. I cooked before I bought the pub, after I'd finished at the Police College, I was living at the house I bought in Yeovil, I worked at Chilton Cantelo, private school at Mudford, cooking there for five years until I bought the Hope and Anchor, the pub next door.

My first job was, well, as a kid I used to go out with my granddad on the farm, with the shire horses, turning hay and dragging in hay, the farmer would give you two bob. It seemed like quite a lot of money. Yes it did to us, 'cause I was only 12, probably spent it on sweets. We never had a lot of money 'cause when you worked on a farm, money was pretty tight. Our gran was good to us, and my auntie and uncle in The Quiet Woman, we always used to spend Christmas Eve there. So really Halstock has been sort of my home, and when I came back from Lundy I lived in Halstock for 14 years working for Mrs Smith, just for the cottage, and that's just next door to the bakery. April Cottage. I used to go in there and clean for them, mow the lawns, chop up the wood, you know.

And then I bought the house in Yeovil. I was driving out to the Police College then I was at Chilton. I've still got the house there. It's a huge Victorian house with cellars, I ought to let it really 'cause it's in the park, in Sydney gardens where the art college used to be. 'Cause Polly (Harvey) was there for a time, wasn't she? You know, before she decided on a career in music as opposed to art. We bought that in 1990.

Chantmarle. To be quite honest, when I first went there it was Home Office was doing the catering. Yes, you belonged to Home Office. I could see that we were over-staffed. Then dear Margaret, in her wisdom in about the early 80s, Maggie Thatcher decided to privatise it. I was one of the head cooks. We were cut right to the bone and everything came in frozen, even omelettes. It's extraordinary. I sometimes wonder if it really is any cheaper. Loads of people were just chucked out. We had quite a lot of parties there. They were good fun. They used to have parties the sergeants did, I used to go down there sometimes to the sergeants' bar, to the inspectors' bar. Wild? It depended on who the commandant happened to be at the time...

As for food I've never been a burger fan, 'cause I'm vegetarian, and coke, I've never drunk a can of coke. I like my cider. I also ran bars at gigs. I used to put on the gigs. It started on my fortieth birthday. 1980. I wanted a band for my birthday and I tried to get a jazz band from Sherborne but they were booked up. So I said to Eva, I said 'The one I want's booked up!' She said "There's a band coming down to play in West Allington," a lovely old hotel there called the West Mead. "We've got this band coming down called Diz and the Doormen." That was in the October, see. She said "I think you'd like them." I said 'Well if you like them, Eva, I will,' 'cause we've got the same sort of taste in music, and she said "Right, I'll ring him up." I didn't know what the hell I was going to have, I'd booked this band, I'd booked Evershot village hall, I'd done the bread and cheese, invited people, and met up with the band up at the Acorn in Evershot. It was a huge man with a huge amount of hair, there was another miserable looking thing with a cap on and glasses, and then there was this other funny little chap with a hat on with

a beard down to here and little glasses. The big bloke was Diz, the other miserable looking one was Craig, brilliant musician, absolutely fantastic, keyboard and guitar, and the other little one was Kieran, he was the drummer, he was brilliant. He died before he was 40. He was wonderful. They were great. They went down a storm.

The next time I saw them, I said 'Would you like to come out and do Evershot hall again?' you see, and Pete Thomas said "Oh yes, such and such a price." I said 'No, you'll have what money we take on the door once expenses have been taken out,' 'cause I'd never done this sort of thing before, you see. He said "You're a hard woman." I said 'Well, maybe.' And so they decided that they would come and do Evershot Hall again. I don't know if that's when we started doing the Bell Inn at Ash, to make it worth their while coming down. So I became their promoter.

It started off with Diz and the Doormen. Yes. Then it was Juice on the Loose, then it was the Balham Alligators, then we had Dr John at the Bell Inn at Ash once, then there was a band from Wales called the Blues Bunch, they were brilliant, then we had Bobby Valentino with his band, then there was the other bloke that looks like him and plays keyboard, Big Town Playboys, and Robyn Hitchcock came to Rampisham one year. I did the bar then, we ran out of beer by half past nine, ten o'clock. I loved putting on these gigs. Craig is still in touch, he spent Christmas with us in 2005. Diz often comes down this way playing in various pubs. Not bad after 26 years.

The next step was buying The Hope and Anchor. I always wanted this pub with the piano you see, this was always my ambition 'cause I was brought up with that sort of thing, and when I was at Chilton Cantelo, even when I was at Chantmarle I was looking at pubs. I went to look at one or two others then this one came on the market, it was in The Publican or one of the pub papers and it said 'Pub in Bridport,' well I've always loved Bridport 'cause I used to come down here with the Harveys down to West Bay in the late 50s early 60s, it was always parties and music. And so I saw this one advertised, so I rang up this company which deals in pubs and I said 'Oh I see you've got a pub in Bridport for sale,' "Oh" they said, "it's more or less sold." I said 'Oh really?' They said "We've got one in Honiton." I said 'I don't want to go to Honiton' I said 'I love Bridport, you see.' He said "Well" he said "No, it's going through at the moment." I said 'Oh yeah.' So he said "Well I'll take your name and address and phone number" and this was in the March, I think it was, anyhow, it was the May Bank Holiday weekend coming up and we were in Yeovil, stood in the kitchen and the phone went and I said to my son 'You answer that' so he answered it and he said "Oh it's for you Mother" it was about five o'clock. I always remember it was the May Bank Holiday, it's whenever Roger Bastable had his steam rally, that's how I remember it. And so I answered the phone I said 'Hello?' "Oh" he said, "you showed an interest in a pub called The Hope and Anchor in Bridport." I said 'Yeah?,' "Don't sound too enthusiastic," he said "well it's come back on the market again." I said 'Oh really?' he said "But what I suggest you do" he said, "is go down and see it." I said 'Fair enough.' "Go and have a drink" he said. To cut a long story short I bought the street for 70 grand. That was ten years ago. I'm no business woman whatsoever, but unless you try these things, you never know!

Well of course I did introduce music into The Hope and Anchor, 'cause it was doing nothing when I took it over. I didn't do food in there, I lived on the fact that I did good real ale, good cider, 'cause we did have the CAMRA pub of the year about two years after I started, only for the Westcountry. And then I had a couple of beer festivals and introduced this Cheddar Valley red

cider, wish I'd never done it to the town, but never mind, they've got it now. I just had a barrel at beer festival and it just took off. But I've always liked proper cider. Dorset and Somerset is such a home for cider, so many pubs don't do it, they think it's below them. But I mean it's a local drink. Dorset and especially Somerset, it's such a cider-orientated county, it just amazes me, you go into a pub 'Do you do cider?' "Well we do blackthorn." I say 'No, that's not cider.' I don't like this fizzy stuff, I like it when it looks cloudy almost.

The Hope and Anchor could open at nine o'clock in the morning, every morning, 'cause that was the market pub. Then usually the George and then down to West Bay. Oh and of course the Packhorse, I remember the Packhorse. The Bull we used to go to for music and then the Eype's Mouth Hotel when Nick Forbes used to have it, Nick's Dive, Custer's Last Blues Band and that, they all used to play down there in bits and pieces, Johnny Spencer, they have the John Spencer memorial gig every year.

Teenagers? Well, they've always drunk, haven't they? I suppose youngsters now have got more money than they did in our day. When I lived at Corscombe I used to walk to The Quiet Woman and walk back at about 12 o'clock at night, which is about two miles. I think the thing is drink has got so much nasty stuff in it these days, beer and proper cider, there's not the additives in it. But you get Stella. I don't drink it but I can see what it does to people on the other side of the bar. I always said I'd rather handle somebody that's had four pints of red cider than I would somebody that's had four pints of Stella.

Women? Used to be Babycham, port and lemon, occasionally gin and tonics, Ponies... They were horrible little bottles, I wonder if I've still got any... No Cherry B, that's what it was. Cherry wine. I drink cider, a lot of women I know drink cider. Cider and Guinness mix, lovely with a spot of blackcurrant.

Violence? Yes. I suppose everybody has it. The first one I ever had, it was a Monday evening, it always seems to be Mondays when things kick off. Vern and I had gone upstairs to have something to eat, it was quiet and this chap came in and he'd been on the cider, and his uncle was working behind the bar and his uncle wouldn't serve him. "You've had too much." And 'course being family it's very difficult to handle these things, but anyhow, he said "You're not having any." And he kicked off and said "I'm having a drink." And he started to smash the place up. So he caught his uncle down the side of the face, he's still got a scar to this day, it must have been about seven, eight years ago now, and so they called me down from upstairs, said "Oh Val can you come down, you'd better call the police." So eventually we called the police, he smashed up the fruit machine, he used to box and you've got to be pretty tough to do that. He put his fist through the fruit machine and the fountain that was on the Carlsberg, he smashed that as well. The police came, the ambulance came 'cause he'd cut his hand, and it took three or four policemen to hold him down and the ambulance guys. So they got him off to hospital, he had to have stitches and all that and he came in a couple of days later all sorry, sorry, so I thought I'd give him another chance, but that was the only chance I gave him, he did it again.

I don't suppose we called the police more than three times in seven years. Other people may have called them but I didn't. It was like a family pub in there because everybody looked after everybody. Alright, we did have some that come in and I'd know they could be a bit difficult so I'd go up to them, the boys, the big chaps and say 'Come on, give us a hand out in the cellar, you know, move some barrels around, get rid of your energy that way.'

Why did I stop in the end? George. Great friend of mine, used to come in and he died at 52. I was 62 and I thought 'What the hell am I doing, still doing this?' I'd done it for seven years, I was only going to do it for two or three. And I think I'd reached my peak. And then everybody else started to do music, nobody was doing music when I came here, and then you get somebody, you know, Ropemakers started doing it, Hardy's started doing it, different people started to do it and I thought I'd had the best so now's the time to get out. And I'd worked since I was 14 and I'd brought my son up on my own, so that's why I decided to get out really. I know a lot of people say 'You should have stayed' and sometimes I think perhaps I should, but then I saw the grief they had in there the other Monday night and I'm glad I didn't.

The pub is important socially for the people who don't have family or anywhere else to go. Yes, because I used to open up on Christmas night, there's so many lonely people on their own. Especially men, we didn't do it just because it was men, men or women could come in, and you'd be surprised how well I did on Christmas nights. And then other pubs started to open then. I always opened on Christmas lunchtime anyhow, I always used to give my customers a drink for being good to me over the rest of the year, and also on New Year's Eve, where some pubs were charging people to go in, I would put out, just a little gesture like sausage rolls and mince pies, just after I got there I used to do cider punch, heat it up, cut up apples, oranges and lemons, chuck whatever you've got going in it, usually put mixed spice in it, and stir it all up, sometimes I'd put in a bit of sugar if it was too tart, or a drop of wine, just throw it all in and ladle it out in glasses and people used to love that. Especially in the winter it gives you a lovely warm glow. I've always loved my cider anyhow, I was weaned on it when I was about two years old I think!

So I sold the pub and kept the cottage. Well I didn't want it to go to a local brewery. I don't like the way they treat their tenants. So I made a clause that they were never to buy it. I think I would have preferred it to have gone completely free but it didn't happen.

The future. I never do plan very much. It never pays to plan. I've got my bit of land at Corscombe, we've taken the willowy trees down that was choking everything, and I've planted about 500 hedge trees, blackthorn, spindle, hazel and all that sort of thing along there, and I'm going to get a digger down and dig out what was there, nothing's been done to it for about 20 years, 'cause that land belonged to somebody that used to have a pub, the old Tiger's Head at Rampisham.

The lucky thing about Dorset is that we haven't got a motorway through it which is a blessing. Because people do tend to bypass it. How The Quiet Woman was allowed to be shut I really don't know. It's on the market now but it's a bed and breakfast and they've built in the back, you'd never be able to turn it back into a pub.

Beaminster? There was the Red Lion, the Greyhound now. Pickwick's, the Knapp at the other end, the Eight Bells, the Sun, the Royal Oak, then there was the one down past the fish and chip shop, Mr Wakely used to run it, old man Wakely. I remember that as a pub. There used to be two pubs in Halstock when my uncle was there, there was the New Inn. I remember that being a pub. I think there was only one in Corscombe and one in Rampisham, 'cause they were estate pubs. The Fox used to belong to the Benville estate, because when I knew it, it was only a six-day licence. Didn't open on a Sunday, 'cause my mum ran that for a bit in the late 50s. The local pubs, it's the same with everything, I mean I suppose Halstock is lucky, they've got the golf course and there's a bar up there, and still got the bakery and the shop in Halstock.

My land at Corscombe? I did my straw bale building course in Winsham, the organic farm there. You see straw bale houses are so eco-friendly. I'd like to have a turbine thing out there if possible, away from certain trees and that, there are some beautiful oak trees on my bit of land, it's only a scrubby damp land. Solar panels? Yeah, but I've got to get planning permission to rebuild the barn, you see, whether I'll be able to build it as a house, but it's falling down but somebody said "Don't pull it down until you've got planning permission." 'Cause once you've pulled it down they'll say it was never there. Well we've got a photograph to prove that it is there, but I must make an appointment to go up there and see the council. I'd like to dig my own well there too. There obviously is water there because it's boggy land. I need to get a diviner. Colin Browning used to do it, apparently. 'Course he wouldn't be able to do it now, would he? Vern reckons his dad used to be able to do it, he worked on the Wessex Water Board and he could do it.

I've got a partner called Vern who I've been with for 17 years now I suppose, we knew each other when we were 17 and we went our separate ways and had our tough bits in life, but we're now back together. People get things off their chest to me. I'm a social worker. I was before I took the pub. We'd be out somewhere and Vern would say "Here comes somebody with a sad story" and they come over, probably a complete stranger, and I'd have to hear them out. But you never tell yours to anybody, do you?

People don't need much really to be quite honest. I think we live in far too much of a throwaway, must have, must have world when you think about what other parts of the world are like. That's what really gets to me. And cruelty to animals.

20. Rachel Jackson – Stone carver and letter cutter, Shaftesbury. Born 1965.

I like to be doing physical work as long as it's interesting. I like being outside, I love working outside…Portlanders are really, really lovely people. They were really enthusiastic about passing on their knowledge.

I was born in a little village two miles north of Chelmsford. Both sets of grandparents lived at the bottom of the road. In about 1950 after completing National Service, Dad got an apprenticeship as a draughtsman at Marconi's. He moved down with his parents from Yorkshire and then worked for Plessey's and Ford's. His parents then ran the little wool shop with haberdashery, absolutely jam-packed like Cordery's was in Shaftesbury.

In about 1964 Grandpa persuaded Dad that he could do well selling wool. His wage was mostly made up on commission so it was not always lucrative. He then went back to engineering and worked on the design for the new Boeing 747 baggage handling equipment, flight re-fuelling, moveable staircases etc.

I was there till I was four and then we moved to Rayleigh near Southend in 1969 just after they walked on the moon. So Dad was going into London working as a design engineer in the Barbican, projects to do with Concorde and Alice Chalmers tractors. In the early seventies he had nine months out of work which was very dicey and he even held art exhibitions in Rayleigh Mill selling his paintings. Eventually he got a job at Plessey's Marine at Templecombe and so that was really quite exciting because it changed everything for the whole family. We came to Shaftesbury. Jan 6th 1976.

We lived in Enmore Green, so I have been here 31 years, 1975 we moved. I've been away and then to come back, and live right in the village again, it's really nice. I went to the village primary school and then to the high school in Shaftesbury. That was quite entertaining, like going to St Trinians really!…Lots of trooping round town because it was built on three different sites. The uniform was quite smart, navy blue, red braiding, silver and red tie. Yes we were very naughty, and it was great fun being at this very old-fashioned establishment. When I finished the sixth form that was the end of the school, they built the new upper school. So it was the end of an era.

I then went off to Bournemouth to do an art foundation course, which again was great fun, best of both worlds. Then I went off to Farnham and studied textiles. I didn't finish the course, but I carried on with textiles when I came back to Shaftesbury and wove a little bit.

I decided that I wanted to go travelling and worked in a pub, then went apple picking in Somerset, which was great, near Huish Episcopi. I went off with a friend, we camped in the orchard, and it poured with rain. But that was fantastic, being in the orchards joining with the local ladies, all full of very rude gossip... The harvest is such a lovely thing to do 'cause you've got to get it in, it's hard work but it's celebratory almost. They were all eaters. They had some really nice big, old, mature trees. So you'd have to get up those very long, funny ladders with a sort of pointy stick on the back. And that's lovely to be in the top of the tree. You can't see anybody but you can hear these voices all nattering away! We didn't know the area so we didn't know the local gossip, but we could pick up quite a lot of juicy information. And then we did cider apples at the end of the season, which again was bloody hard work and you're grovelling around on your hands and knees. You've got waterproofs from

Rachel Jackson in her workshop, Cottage Green, Shaftesbury

toe to top of your head, with rubberised suit and wellies, trying to keep dry, and scrabbling up all these apples, but it was still fun. We'd do this really long day and then walk across the fields to South Petherton, do some shopping, come back and then walk off to the pub and have half a pint of beer and feel absolutely addled 'cause you'd just worked so hard that it really goes to your head.

Then I spent some time off with a girlfriend travelling in Europe, hitchhiking and catching trains, boats, walking. We went through France, into Italy, then down through Yugoslavia into Greece, to various different islands and eventually ended up in eastern Turkey. Yeah, yeah it was great. Slightly dodgy, there were still bandits around but it was worth going. Right up to the Iranian border and then we hitchhiked our way back from a lorry park in Istanbul through Switzerland via Yugoslavia.

Then I went off to work in the Holland, the Bollenstreek, which is the bulb strip where they produce all the bulbs. And they've got all these huge packing places and factories that sell plants and there's lots of Brits, Irish and Scottish. Loads of young people working there, trying to sort of earn a buck to travel, quite often. The first job I got I went with this girl that I didn't know particularly well, and we sort of struck up friendship. It was quite interesting because I was quite puritanical and she turned out to be a complete alky. We bought this trailer together and she had one end with crates and crates of beer and I had the other end with little pots of tulips. We went and worked at this orchid nursery, which was absolutely fantastic, for three brothers. They didn't speak any English at all. But that was lovely, working in these huge greenhouses heated and really humid. So, you know, the most fantastic sub-tropical environment with really big plants. They're great floor to ceiling vines trained up bits of wire to sell stems of blooms. The stem would grow with the flowers on, and then you had to train that up other wires so that you got a straight length of bloom. Intensive, specialised horticulture.

They were so sweet to us, they would bring us, I presume because we were English, they'd bring us these tea trays with sort of bone china tea cups, the whole thing, a little milk jug and everything!... It was absolutely bizarre, and they were just very, very nice to us. I worked a season at the orchid nursery and then we moved on, we got a job at a distribution centre. A big company that sold plants all over Europe. Mail order and they've got it absolutely sussed. It was jolly good fun as well, because we could work in Holland and then we'd say 'let's see what Portugal's like.' So we'd save a bit of money, go off...

At that period I started going to a place in France, grape picking, with my partner Chris. We loved this place in the south of France, it was close to Perpignan, in the foothills of the Pyrenees, between the Pyrenees and Corbieres, a fantastic area, stunning scenery. There was constant work, maintaining the vineyards through the winter. So we did that for a couple of years, and that was really interesting. We learned how to prune the vines and spray them with loads of chemicals, which we tried to avoid – 'Oh no we want to go away for two weeks whilst you're doing that, you can do that bit.' They were quite blasé about it. It's a very good way to see Europe, working like that, much better than going off on holiday. I like to be doing physical work as long as it's interesting. I like being outside, I love working outside.

They'd got a particularly good wine co-operative, they'd won quite a few awards for their rosé and their Muscat. Their Muscat was very good because it was natural, so all of the sugar in the Muscat was from the grape, generally it's enhanced with added sugar. So it's a very rich, fruity drink.

Then we came back to Shaftesbury. That was '95. I knew lots of people that had been to Weymouth to do the stonemasonry course and all of them had enjoyed themselves, and they'd all got interesting work from it at the end. So I had a go at some stone carving with a friend and just thought 'Yep, that's good and I can go and live by the seaside and have a go at that.' That was a very good move because it was great fun and I learned heaps. It was a very practical course. Ninety-nine per cent mature students. People that had done all sorts of different things. Fine art to building. The course lasted two years. You're learning architectural carving, masonry and lettering, some building skills, geology and quite a lot of geometry. Which is absolutely imperative if you're going to draw, set out and make something that's going to fit into a building.

To start with we learnt about Roman lettering because that's your starting point for modern lettering. So the shapes of the Roman letter are dictated by either a chisel-shaped brush which you would have been writing the letters with, or a squared-ended chisel, with which you'd have been carving the letters. The serifs are ways in and out of those, of getting your chisel in and out of the surface of the stone. So that's what we were studying to start with and then we went on to look at various other letter forms. But that's your starting point that you go back to.

Tools are pretty basic really. A dummy, which is your hammer, I think it's malleable iron with an ash handle. It's got weight but you don't do great bashing with lettering. It's very fine tapping. And then lettering chisels, you've got a steel shaft and then an inset of tungsten, which obviously can be sharpened to a finer edge than steel. You need an incredibly sharp edge for, for lettering. I've just got a diamond sharpening pad that I use. Different stones will blunt the chisels quicker and obviously if you're using a very fine stone it will show if you haven't got it

absolutely sharp. So you need to keep it sharp all the time.

We did a Portland Quarry visit. It's just very hands-on. I mean I'm absolutely stunned that they got us carving stone on the first day. You're right in there, I think probably all the tutors were local blokes that had been in the industry, worked on Portland as masons or they'd worked other places as fixers. It's a very rich heritage, the stone industry particularly related to Portland and Purbeck. It's got quite a reputation but Portlanders are really, really lovely people they were really enthusiastic about passing on their knowledge. Such a good atmosphere. Yeah, thousands of years of knowledge isn't it? I've found now that one of the best things is showing somebody else how to do it and seeing their satisfaction in getting a carving out of a lump of stone. It's really quite exciting. So I can see why the tutors were enthusiastic. We all wanted to be there and we were all mature and had done other things.

Architectural carving is all the twiddly bits in churches where you've got foliage or whatever. I mean it could be anything. It could be figurative. We had various projects where we'd have to make a capital. It might be a Corinthian cap or a Doric. Still rooted in that classical tradition. All of that is just as relevant, anything that isn't modern architecture, it's all taking its lead from those classical orders. So you're learning something that people have been doing for a long time, and it's interesting because it's still taught.

Air tools are used a lot in the industry, you have a chisel but instead of you bashing it with your mallet, you've got compressed air which keeps hitting up against the end of your chisel and pushes it along. So that makes it much quicker. White finger that's the main thing that stops me wanting to use air tools. It's fine to use them now and again, but I would hate to be in a big commercial workshop using them all the time. The compressed air, the chisel gets really cold as well. So the cold and the vibration is the thing that screws up your nerve endings… You mustn't hold your chisels, or your mallet too tightly or you end up with this arthritic feeling in your hand. You want to hold it quite lightly. And the same with the mallet you've got it balanced, and you're not forcing it down on to your chisel, you're just letting your bicep pick it up and then letting it fall on its own almost. I'm sure they must've been singing away, like people rowing or doing anything repetitive. I'm sure the old masons would've been, beating out a rhythm.

Obviously for lettering I've got to do some drawing for that. And if you're doing architectural carving then the more drawings and the more research you can do, the better the carving's going to be unless you're some sort of kind of genius that just has it all in your head. There are people, you know. But generally masonry is a set thing, it has to be absolutely precise and you're working with a tolerance of a millimetre, plus or minus a millimetre. That's the idea, so you're aiming for perfection. Masonry is an incredibly clever thing to be doing.

Imagine making a rose window with all these different geometric forms and you've got to get those absolutely spot on, otherwise, if they're all a millimetre out and you've 20 things all in a row, by the time you get to the other end you're two centimetres out and there's a bloody great gap. It's a very precise and complicated thing actually.

At college we made a rose window between a whole load of us. I think the medieval masons were revered because they had this amazing knowledge and it was almost magical too. When the great cathedrals were built the mason was the architect as well. And there probably weren't drawings, it was just in their heads. OK, they'd set everything out, full size on the floor, but yeah it's magic definitely.

So I started doing lettering jobs for people whilst I was still at college and then, in the summer between the two courses I worked at Longleat, doing conservation work on the house. So that was a useful learning experience. When I left they offered me a job at Longleat. Each year they were trying to do one side of the house. That was a fantastic place to work. It wasn't the best job in terms of money but to be up on the side of this house, right up against the medieval stonework, and then the roofscape at Longleat is fantastic. It's covered in statutes, lots of little turret things where different staircases come out, strange little dogs holding up Bath family coats of arms, and peculiar bits and pieces just dotted all over the roof. It was like Gormenghast!

So I loved that and you'd go to the estate at eight in the morning, and be up on the roof and you'd get swans flying past just amazing. Obviously in the summer it's pretty busy there but you're up above all of that…And also you got to see inside the guts of the house as well, all the places that the public don't go to. The house has been changed again and again. So you've got mullion windows the full height of the building, there's a courtyard on the inside. In the inside courtyard there's mullions that have then been bricked up but with a big gap in between, and you can climb up these mullion windows. And there's rooms where they've lowered the ceiling height, so you can go up through a hatchway and get into the top of a room, which is eight foot high again. Interesting to see bits of original wallpaper. Really amazing. There were certain nooks and crannies where only I was small enough to get into, when we were trying to knock out wall ties. Sometimes you had to be on the inside, just underneath the roof, so it was like mining.

Then I started getting more and more commissions. So once the work at Longleat had stopped I just carried on with headstones, bits of poetry for people's gardens. Sometimes I exhibit at Roche Court, at Winterslow near Salisbury. And then bits of carving for churches. I usually get some beefy bloke to help me with the fixing because even if something looks quite light and delicate, it's not, you know, it weighs a ton. And you've got to have help.

I tend to use quite a lot of local stone. Headstones you want something quite fine. I wouldn't use a Shaftesbury greenstone because it's a building material really. It doesn't take fine carving and it doesn't weather fantastically. Although having said that there's bits around town from Shaftesbury Abbey still. Sometimes I use Chilmark stone, that's not bad, takes carving ok. Salisbury Cathedral is Chilmark stone. It's a very peculiar stone. You can order a load, various different blocks, one block will be as soft as butter and another bit will be like concrete. Underground quarries at Chilmark they're like caverns, quite an interesting place actually. The RAF had all sorts of goodies stashed away there and it wasn't on the map, And then obviously Portland and Purbeck. I'm really lucky here actually because you've got Bath stone as well. I wouldn't use Bath stone for a headstone, I'd probably use Portland or Purbeck.

I do like Welsh slate, so that's really it, Welsh and Cumbrian slate so that's something that I use. They aren't local, but they have such a lovely effect. They've such a fine texture. You can cut a beautiful clear letter into them and they've got a very good contrast. When you cut into the slate you get a light greyey colour and then you've got the dark surface. The contrast between the two makes a really good letter.

You can oil the surface of the slate. so that darkens the surface and makes that contrast bigger. You can leave the cut letter. If people put their greasy fingers in, it will gradually darken up. If you paint the letter in, the same as the cut letter it's very difficult to tell that it's been painted.

I've got a workshop in St James that I'm using at the moment, at Cottage Green, which is opposite St James' church. Just in an old outbuilding, what was a calf shed. But that's been a perfect space to work in apart from the access.

The Wessex Ridgeway project is to put pieces of sculpture along the Ridgeway, with the poetry on. The first piece is going to be this stone bench at Ashmore overlooking the pond, which I think will be very nice. There's a balance between what it's going to look like, what it's going to say and practically how it's going to work.

I've also been working with two London charities, kids' charities. One is arts-based called Rise Phoenix and the other one is environmental-based, called Global Generation. I got involved because they'd been coming down to Pertwood Farm, near Longbridge Deverill, just over into Wiltshire…It's an organic farm. And at Pertwood there's a small bit of waste ground in terms of agricultural use, up on the top of the downs, fantastic views all around, right in the middle of the organic farm. And it's an area that's covered with lots of gorse and hawthorn and various trees, but basically it's a wilderness. And the charity have cleared little areas and they've made a sort of wilderness camp ground, which is lovely, it's fantastic. The charity bring down groups of children to do environmental or arts-based projects. The main purpose really is to give them an experience of being in the country.

They're all from around Camden, Kings Cross area. And I've got involved with them to start doing stone carving workshops. We started making little carvings of various leaves that we'd found on different trees, and naming the trees and so forth, which has been fun. And the kids just respond. It's such fun teaching children. They absolutely love it and once they've started you can't stop them. Some of them, they'll have been working ten hours on their stone carving. You say 'Well really you should have something to eat.' So it's like slave labour!...And that's evolved into me going up to London and doing projects up there with them. One project I did was at Kings Cross, it was a rooftop habitat garden that they've created. The children carved images of endangered species that hopefully will make their home on the roof.

The last project, which I spent a lot of last winter doing, was a heritage walk that was being created around Kings Cross, Summerstown, St Pancras area creating waymarker stones to go round this heritage trail. So the kids got really involved in creating something for their own environment, for their own community. They were all based on natural history because the heritage trail was linking green spaces. Some of the images that were on the stones were trees or plants or creatures living in those green spaces, and then some of the stones were inset into paving along the way. So those were all historical references.

So that project has been fantastic on loads of levels. It was very hard, very demanding, but actually great. For them to make something so permanent in such a throwaway society is quite unusual really. Nine-year-old kids have this ability that no-one expects them to have and actually it's completely untapped.

In Enmore Green my allotment's close to my heart, because there's part of me that would just love to be still working outside all the time. So the allotment fills that need. Yeah, it's right behind the house. There's a bit of shrubbery and a bit of lawn, and lots of raised beds and a priceless view over the Blackmore Vale towards King Alfred's Tower. It's a very well kept allotment because we formed a society that runs it, as opposed to the council running it. We have some quite strong-headed chairmen usually, who will throw you off if you've got too many weeds or you're not really taking it seriously...Every patch now is used, which is quite unusual. Our soil's very good here. It's just on the edge of the greenstone, it's above the clay, so it's fantastic, very free draining so you need to keep putting lots of nutrient back into it, but very easy to work.

Yes there is a waiting list.

21. Eva Harvey — Letter cutter, Corscombe. Born 1940.

Hamstone. I think it is the most beautiful of all of them.

I was born in February 1940 at Weymouth, beginning of the war. I have a photograph of my mother on the buses, when I was eight months old, so goodness knows where I was then - the neighbour perhaps? We were living in Wyke Road and it was quite dramatic. The tanks used to come down there to Portland and I remember seeing the tarmac on fire. I've said that to a lot of people and they say "Oh no" but I saw it. And my sister and I used to sit on the wall and call out 'Give us some gum chum' which they used to throw us, chewing gum and sugar. American troops. I suppose they were, yes. And I remember fetching coal in the dolly's pram, and I remember those big balloons being blown up, you know, barrage balloons.

There were several raids. We had this sort of table cage thing, which we were supposed to go in, but we didn't. We used to sleep under the stairs. But Mother used to take us out to peek at things, when those doodlebugs were coming over for example. And lots of houses around us were bombed and you'd see a lot of damaged cats you know, with eyes hanging out and awful things like that because of all these bombed houses around us.

I didn't really see damaged people, but I saw damaged cats. I remember running down the road to air raid shelters. Quite dramatic. I was there until four and a half to five, so it was like all the war years. I don't even remember going to the beach while I was there. The bomb damage. Yes, one or two houses round us I can still kind of picture, you know how the chimney always seemed to stay up. But that was about it really.

My father was in the Army, Mother was on the buses, and she ended up with a bus driver and apparently my father was rather brutal and rough with her, and used to beat her up, and get drunk. Anyway, I ended up with a bus driver father, who was a very, very nice…Stepfather, yes. And he was always a very good man, so I never really bothered to look for my other father, and he didn't bother to look for me.

Mother was from Wareham and Father was from Weymouth, but his mum and dad were living at Chideock in my young years, because I used to go there and stay with them, right by the church, which used to be lovely.

In Wareham was my mother's family, they had a very successful greengrocer and florist shop, 12 South Street next to the Black Bear, and that was a real treat to go and stay with them. They used to make bouquets and wreaths. Best was their name, it was a very well known firm and it was there till quite recently. My parents were always shifting around. One time we used to live at Corfe Castle, in the middle of a common, then we'd cycle to Wareham, over heathland. I remember raging fires on the heathland.

Father then took a job on a farm. He went from buses to farming. Long Sutton. We lived in a beautiful thatched house which would cost a fortune to buy now, which was just a farmhouse, you know, for the workers, with the privy at the bottom of the garden. I remember the punky nights and I remember this loo at the bottom of the garden which was quite terrifying. It was a two seater and had a long drop down, and at the bottom there was a hole. There was a farmyard behind and you could sort of hear pigs' noses snuffling. Yes, that was Long Sutton. Long Burton, he looked after horses there, just the other side of Sherborne. There's the road sweeps round, there was a big house at the top and he looked after horses there.

Eva and Polly Harvey over stream, Corscombe

Mother was a seamstress, a dressmaker, and she just sat and sewed day, night and we all had to help. Hems, buttonholes, oversewing, even Dad used to have to help. And it was just every day and she'd charge peanuts for it. The house was always littered with pins, cotton, needles, you had to be careful if you walked about barefoot...She did whatever people wanted alterations, shortening, lengthening trousers, that sort of thing...When that Far From the Madding Crowd was being made at Weymouth she did a lot of sewing for that. She had Julie Christie tripping in and out of her little council house, Terence Stamp...My dad thought it was wonderful because there was only like the living room and the kitchen, you know. That was in Weymouth. I was here with Ray by then, but they went back to Weymouth after more moves and that's where they spent their last 20-odd years. That's the longest they were ever in one place I think.

We were living at Pendomer when I passed my scholarship and went to Bishop Fox's School in Taunton and then Yeovil High School as my parents had moved to Yeovil. I went straight from there into the borough surveyor's office, where I was in the drawing office for five years, and then I went to the planning office for five years, doing town plans. In those days everything was done by hand. So I was well into lettering when we drifted into the stone business. I used to watch and criticise stonemasons' lettering. And I thought 'Well I ought to be doing it myself really.'

We drifted into the stone business. It was just accidental. We knocked out a fireplace when Saul was a little boy, so that was about '67, here in Corscombe. It was a horrid brick fireplace. And when we bashed it out there just happened to be two little bits of Hamstone up the sides and we knew somebody who was digging out Hamstone, just through my sister I think, we

thought we'll go and get a little bit of Hamstone to fill it in, and when we got it from him he said "Ooh I'd love to come and see it when it's done." People were just buying his stone for walling and rockeries, that's all. He was quarrying on Ham Hill. He came to look at this fireplace and he said that what he'd always wanted to do was saw it up, but he didn't have anywhere to put a saw. And we said 'Well we've got that bit of land there.' A stone saw. So in no time at all we'd got permission to put a saw there. And so we worked with him. We dressed it here. It was just very lucky at that time they were pushing for industry in rural areas. COSIRA so that was in '67, '68. So we were very lucky really. We had to have three-phase electricity and cost a lot of money. We worked with Richard England, worked with him for quite a long time, bringing his stone here.

And then Richard wanted to do more building houses and then David Phelips who was the last person to be living at Montacute house as a family home, said "Would we like to open his quarry?" It hadn't been quarried for a hundred years when we went there...It'd just been used for storage and some sort of fertiliser. There were also lots of lumps of quartz there, I think some wartime thing. Were there quartz radios or something like that?...Yes there was a lot of crystals there, which I still have a few left, around.

So it was by accident. Ray was a draughtsman, he was at Westlands. But it stood us in good stead because obviously we were used to reading plans, you see, which you need to do for sawing lumps of stone. We were offered a lease on the quarry which we still have. If you're doing a big job you need to dig out a lot of stone to get what you want. Our stone tends to come out in roughly 18 inch beds. Natural beds which the excavator just lifts out. Sometimes we drill, plug and feather. The old way. Real hands on, it's hard work. So it was quite nice for me the workmen all moving up to the hill. You can imagine having workmen here at Corscombe, it would be all day long. "Can't find a hammer," 'can I use the phone?' before mobile phones of course.

I started letter cutting about '84. So I still feel like a beginner. Self-taught. I went a few times to Weymouth College. I've trained one or two people at the quarry to do it, because you know there have been times when it's been more than I can keep up with. But, they're ok as long as I draw it out for them.

The skill is actually in the design, the artistic bit is. They just tend to take it off the computer and those computer letters are pretty horrid. I've still got my little bits of paper with the Roman letter proportions on it, the width to the height and thickness of letter to the height which are from an art lesson at Yeovil.

The business is all the normal window surrounds, the door surrounds, the fireplaces. Plus of course the walling and rockery. But my department is lettering tombstones and house names mostly. Lots of village names, also those girt rocks on Ham Hill.

There's quite a lot about, aren't there, yes. Well I haven't done all of them but I've done quite a lot. Oh yes. The shoes at Odcombe yes…Yes, Thomas Coryates, I think he was the son of the rector. And he was supposed to have walked halfway round the world wearing the same pair of shoes, which I did a bit of research into, and I think in those Elizabethan days they had very fine, kid house slippers, which they would slip into their boots. So it was probably the house slippers. When he came back he's supposed to have hung his boots up in the church, and they were there for years and years, apparently. And they'd only recently disappeared. So that's why they thought they'd have a stone pair.

It is a bit of a treat to do lettering on Portland or Purbeck, but it's not as pleasing in a way. It isn't really. Hamstone, I think it is the most beautiful of all of them. It's a limestone and it's just

bits of iron in it which makes it that colour, and you can see the real lumps of iron in it. That's what gives it the honey colour.

Letter cutting. It's a lovely thing to do, it really is a lovely thing to do, and I like going up to the quarry and if it's a big rock I do it up there. Having your own quarry does help. The geologists say there's enough stone there for another 300 years …that's long enough for us and our children.

Corscombe? It was just chance. My parents were then living in Corscombe, you see they'd lived lots of places, you haven't heard of half the places they've lived in. They happened to be living in Corscombe, they lived in two different houses here, and when we sort of were about to get married, Mother said she'd heard this place was for sale. It was just a wee little house, four rooms it was, and no sort of drainage, there was just a sink with a tap, the loo was where that pampas is. And she said she'd heard it was for sale, and she thought that would be quite good for us. And we came down, some wonderful old boy lived here, he was such a character. House was full of rotting rabbits and all sorts of dogs, bones and things like that…And apparently he'd sold this house before and changed his mind. But we didn't let him change his mind.

The Fox was wonderful. It was very bare, basic. I think some old lady was running it. Val Crabb's mother. Well she wasn't that old then of course, she was here most of her life and of course we did get to know her, called Primrose. But the same time we were buying our house, the Perkins' took over The Fox and they prettied it all up immediately, painted it white. We've had wonderful times there.

Yes, for years and years it was almost just like our private pub, it really was. We've had card schools down there, darts teams…It was not until Martin took it on, Martin and his mother Sally, that it got known for its cooking. It must be the

80s…Ray would remember, he's very good at remembering those things.

The man who was here his nickname was Lord Rampisham, and it was Lord Rampisham you had to say. Studley…I think there's some connection with the Pinneys, there was…Yeah, I think his niece married a Pinney, something like that.

I think we're very lucky to live here, in Dorset. I just love it really. Especially this bit from here to the coast, it's wonderful isn't it? It has got a bit busier since we've been here, the traffic is a bit busier. A lot of the characters have gone, so many characters have. I suppose there will be some more, but oh there were such wonderful characters here.

That was an orchard you know right here opposite us. Because Court Farm was connected to Sherborne Abbey, and that was known as Abbot's Orchard, that field. And there were apple trees in there which were cut down soon after we came here.

When we used to walk down to The Fox you could hear wheezing in these trees which was young owls, very strange sound. I actually was looking at a photograph in The Fox just this last week, which showed then, it was an aerial view that still showed apple trees in there, which must have been about '61 or '62…And our field up here, yes again on the old ordnance survey map, you can see a strip of apple trees. There's still three or four up there, mostly fallen over now. They must be very old mustn't they? And these funny pear trees, you see that, well that's a new one that's grown up but behind it there's two really old ones…They're little tweeny ones, I mean they do taste quite nice. Perry pears. I would think so. Yes, yah I think…That tall one is usually loaded, they're even smaller. Those are slightly bigger, and that's a new young one that's grown up. You see it's loaded at the top. They won't get any bigger than that. There's a cider apple tree just down by the stream there, most of those have fallen off already, that was loaded.

When we came here there was a greengrocer and general store, and a butcher's shop, and the post office. And in fact this house before we bought it, was also a fish shop, plus a general store where you bought your paraffin and stuff. And there was a school of course. The school's gone now. Davis the butcher, now that was up in the village, the butcher. The nearest shop is one at Halstock and they have a bakery.

22. Polly Harvey – Rock musician and song writer, West Dorset. Born 1969.

Really now for the first time on my new album, I'm singing about Dorset, which has never happened before…

Polly Jean Harvey, born October 9th, 1969, Bridport maternity hospital. …My parents run a stone quarrying business and have done for 40 years, quarrying Ham Hill stone from Somerset. When I was younger it was different because they were partners with Richard England, so it was England and Harvey. And we were working from home so the whole of the quarry base was just over the stream. So I was right in the thick of it then.

When I was a small child, all the workmen worked from here. We still brought stones back here to Corscombe. First memories definitely'd be my favourite stonemason whose name was George and he would be carving. There was a carving shop, the sawing area, and the planing area. He is my earliest memory 'cause I sort of fell in love with him about age of three upwards.

I couldn't wait to get up there and watch him carving and he'd always give me half of his sandwiches. I used to love it. He had a metal lunch box with his ham sandwiches, cheese sandwiches, white bread, thick butter. I'd go up there and I'd sit on top of his tool box, which was also a big metal box with all of his hammers and chisels, and sit on top of there and watch him eat his sandwiches, and do puppet plays for him, hand puppets.

I think he was a very kind man with a gentle voice and I felt very safe and loved around him. Of course I did here as well, but it was fascinating to me to watch him. He was from Stoke-sub-Hamdon and used to drive a Morris Minor. I was very sad when he left. He always used to wear blue dungarees and I wore blue dungarees a lot, as well, because George wore blue dungarees.

That's the other thing I used to do. I used to go up there and carve next to him. I think I was fascinated with watching him carving and letter cutting. He'd teach me and I stand by him doing it as well. I used to go up there after school.

I loved English and art, even at that age. Primary school in Evershot. Secondary school, Beaminster Comprehensive. I suddenly felt you were plunged in, small fish… suddenly plunged into a giant school, with loads of people. I was quite shy and so I found that quite difficult. But the work was fine, I still enjoyed the work.

If we ever had an animal die, a cat or a favourite lamb or something, Saul, my brother or I would carve a letterhead for it, and you'll see them scattered around here. There's little carvings that I've done since a kid. When I went to Yeovil Art College to do a foundation I actually did a bit of stone carving then.

At one time we had about 40 sheep. I think we've got six acres total, and there's two small fields. We'd make quite a good living off them, you know off fleeces and selling them at market. We used to call them the Corscombe cross because they were such a mongrel breed. Occasionally we would eat them. We might have one sheep a year and take it to the butcher and just have the whole of the sheep. It used to taste fantastic. And I used to breed bantams. I had a lot of bantams at one time and then the fox would come along and obliterate the lot. But we used to eat those too, and they were very tasty.

Yeovil was a foundation year art course, but I didn't go immediately. I stayed on at Beaminster and took my music O level whilst taking English literature at A level and art A level.

I started learning saxophone when I was 11, and I took up to grade seven on saxophone. Eleven through to about 16. The whole mixture, jazz, rhythm and blues, classical, everything…

When Mum and Dad first started courting, I call it the West Bay days, there was a big group of their friends that would meet at West Bay every weekend, and it was about rock and roll and it was all taking off at that time. Elvis, the Stones, it was all starting to happen. They used to meet there, play a lot of music, play a lot of skiffle. Always been rockers really, rhythm and blues, rock and roll. So I just grew up with it in the house. We joke that we are in the rock business.

My earliest memories are of music playing all day, every day, always has been. The vinyl LPs would just get played all the time and when one of Mum and Dad's favourite bands would release a new album, that album would just get played and played and played. It's very interesting to me, still, that often I don't think I've heard a record of mum and dad's and I might put one on, because they've got such a fantastic vinyl collection, or I might hear something on the radio, and I know every word of it. And I thought I didn't know it. And it's because since I was about two, I'd heard it played incessantly for three months. It's sort of just written inside yourself.

Then I became interested in playing the saxophone probably because a great friend of Mum and Dad's was a man called Ian Stewart, known as the sixth Rolling Stone, but actually was one of the founder members of the Stones. He'd come down and stay a lot, and he was very much part of the family when I was younger. But he had a fantastic band called Rocket 88. And Mum would put on gigs for them in the village halls around these parts, and at the Bell Inn at Ash. So I used to love it because Rocket 88 was a big band. It had a horn section, four people, two tenor saxes and two trombone players and they all used to stay here. And they were lovely, lovely people. I think that was my second love affair because I fell in love with this man called Olaf, who was one of the sax players and he started

teaching me sax. And then Willy, the other sax player, Willy Garnett, I bought a saxophone from, because he dealt in saxophones, he ran a jazz orchestra in London. So that's what started me off, really, playing music.

I started playing recorder when I was four and loved it. Then I started to become more interested in other things, I didn't buy a guitar until I was about 16 or 17 I think, and that just happened. Mum heard of a friend trying to sell a guitar, it was going relatively cheaply and it was almost Mum talked me into buying it. It was an acoustic guitar, still got it. Yamaha FG180, really nice guitar. And Mum said "Well this is a good guitar, shall I get it for you?" And I wasn't that bothered really. And then when we got it I just started writing songs, and it's very natural to me because I think my favourite subject, always, was English and English literature and I wrote stories and poetry as early as I can remember. I think I started writing stories when I was about four. So it was just really natural.

I was creating my own world. Always, definitely. Earliest memories are creating worlds, stories, theatre plays for puppets, always I was writing stories and poems, and always in my imagination playing games in my imagination, becoming somebody else.

I think, I knew I would be performing in some way. I know that performance is a huge element, because when I was a youngster I always wanted people to watch me doing something, whether it was to read something I'd written, whether it was to perform a puppet play, whether it was to hear a song I was going to sing them. But not in a show off, big ego way at all because I was very shy. I think if I hadn't gone into song writing, if music hadn't come along, I definitely would be writing in some capacity, but there'd be a performance element.

When I left school after my A levels, I had a place at

Canterbury College to study English literature. And I was all set to do that but I deferred for a year. And in that year I got together with a girl at Beaminster School. She was called Katherine Garrett, lovely girl, we were the two people that did music so we just naturally started playing together. We formed a little band called the Polkats – it was Polly and Katherine you see – and then later on, she was playing flute, penny whistle and piano and I was playing guitar, and then we had a bass player come and join us, a guy called Gus Mckinley. The three of us, we did local gigs. We played in pubs, we played at the Bell Inn at Ash at intervals, we played at Beaminster Hall at intervals, anything I could find really. And we both were writing songs and we'd both perform each other's songs. And it was lovely.

Then I decided I wanted to go into art instead. I still wasn't thinking music as a career. I think I wanted to explore my art a bit more. During that year at Yeovil College, I had to get my art foundation in order to go on and do a degree. So in that year I sort of lost touch with Katherine and joined a band in Bristol run by John Parish called Automatic Dlamini, and then through that made contact with other musicians and formed my own band.

I was 21. So, well I'm 36 now and it's 2006. Yeah about '91. So while I was doing my art foundation, I put together the three-piece band that I took off with, which was myself, a drummer called Rob Ellis, who was from Sherborne, and a bass player called Steve Vaughan who was from Hardington Mandeville. Well I finished my foundation course. I got a place to study sculpture at St Martin's College, which I really wanted to go to. At this stage I wanted to get out of Dorset. So I got my place in the big city 'I want to go to London'. So, got my place there and then this little three-piece band was doing so well and getting so much attention, really quickly. I think our third gig ever was in London, and I just sent demo tapes around, which was how I got

gigs, I just heard about places. And a very small record label called Too Pure, came to that third gig, said "We love what you're doing, can we give you..." I think they gave us £1,000 to make a better demo.

I think coming out of Yeovil Art College it was a very, very creative time, and it gave me a really great foundation of what I liked and didn't like, artistically. I was very interested in minimalism, my sculpture was very minimalistic, severe almost. And in tandem with this the earliest music was very severe, very minimal rock music, it was guitar, bass, drums, nothing else. It was all about extremely loud and extremely quiet, making these giant extremes all the time.

I was singing, yeah. I was very interested in black and white, it would be shouting or whispering. The music would be so loud or you could hardly hear it. Or the guitar would be all through this part but not at all in this part, and the drums would have to stop here, entirely, and then come back in, in a minute's time.

Well I wrote all the songs. We rehearsed here in my Mum and Dad's top room, they could hear us down at The Fox Inn, we rehearsed there for years and years. Steve and Rob definitely had enormous character in the way they played. And I do think that's why it became very successful, very quickly. It was a very rare combination of ingredients that worked perfectly. You know, I think the three of us just complemented each other.

Well that three-piece started off '91, and fell apart in '94, I think, or late '93... in which time we made two albums. Successful. Very. Like I said, it was the third gig really. And it was just, such a buzz so quickly. I do believe in right time, right place and luck. I think that the climate was right for it. I had the raw energy and the opening, and there were still new voices to be found. I was interested in confronting, shocking, demanding attention from the listener, or the viewer 'cause I was doing it with my artwork too. Surprise. A lot of my artwork was hung from the ceiling, and you wouldn't even, like you'd go into a room and you'd think ooh where is it? And you'd look up and there'd be this giant scary thing on the ceiling. It's all about challenge and confrontation really.

It was the way I was rebelling, it was the way I was. Going back to earliest memories again I think that I always thought in extremes, I always thought there should be more, I was always wanting to push myself to my maximum to find what I was capable of. I don't like complacency at all, makes me really upset and really angry and so I don't want to see it in myself and I don't want it from other people. I was quite tough on myself.

St Martins'? No this is a bit of a myth, people think I went there. I never went there. I deferred for a year, I really wanted to go, I never even began a course. In the early days I made enough to live, just enough to live by. I lived in London for a year. Right after I finished my foundation course, and hated it and moved back to Dorset and never went back to London. So basically I've been based here ever since. I lived in LA for two years and I have an apartment there which I use occasionally, pretty much for sunshine. And it's almost the polar opposite of Dorset. A holiday cottage almost… for the weather. But also I'm still interested in these extremes of what you can find in extremes of life, and I'd say that LA is the opposite extreme to Dorset.

I need that, to go away and then come back, particularly as a writer. It's very good to shake yourself up. My next plan is to go to Russia to write. I think it's really important as a writer to keep forcing new sight. I always listen to new music. I'm terribly disappointed though, I try to find new music but I'm disappointed again and again and again. So I tend to just go back to just old favourites. There's very few contemporary artists that I know I can go out and buy their new thing and I'll love it. I'm very interested in native folk music of all kinds, Greek, Bulgarian, Russian. traditional English, Irish folk music, getting very interested in that.

My career? I feel really pleased and very happy to be where I'm at. It's exactly where I'd want to be, I wouldn't want to be any more successful in terms of being famous. I've been with my manager now for ten years, and I've been with the same record label, now, since '92. Island-Universal. They're based in London.

My life again, is a life of extremes. I'm either at home writing in the beauty of Dorset, or I'm on tour for a year and I'm never at home. You know when I'm at home in Dorset it's a very, very quiet life. I have the friends I've grown up with all my life, a handful of friends. I don't go out much. And then when I'm on tour I'm surrounded by people all the time. It feels like a necessary part of my job but it's not my choice. I mean I'm naturally a person that likes a lot of space and a lot of quiet. And I find it extremely stressful, my job, unfortunately the job part of it. I don't consider writing songs or playing music 'the job.' That's absolute heaven to me, but interviews and the touring and the travel, I find very, very hard and very stressful, and I get easily upset by it. I'm not naturally built to handle that kind of stuff.

I get homesick for Dorset. I get homesick for peace and quiet really. But it's the way it's worked out. When I was younger I wanted to get to the big city. There's a part of me that loves it, there's a part of me that needs to be thrown into turmoil, people noise and traffic. It's the energy. I need that energy. I need that friction almost; I need that fight, you know, it's for my work. I need that stimulation, that over-stimulation.

So actually I have the best of both worlds. I do. I feel, I can't tell you how much I love what I do. And continue to feel like I haven't even begun, I have so many ideas for what I want to do.

Dorset features in my songs more and more as I get older. Definitely, I find more and more memories come up that I hadn't understood before, and it's coming through the song, it's coming through the music, it's coming through the lyrics. Really now for the first time on my new project, my new album, I'm singing about Dorset, which has never happened before… I'm embracing it much more, the older I get.

I've always been the songwriter. I'm very disciplined about it. I think all writers find it differently. I show up and I do my work, and sometimes it's really hard and I get nothing and I might be like that for three months and nothing will come. Or it flows, it just flows through you all the time.

I have a piano, guitars, I have little folk instruments, I have harps and dulcimers, zithers, all manner of things. Anything I can lay my hands on and they're just around me, all the time.

It's very close to sculpture, I find, my music. It's about treating something that's malleable, because music is very malleable, but it's about taking stuff away, or adding a bit. Or no take that away again. It's about finding the smallest amount of ingredients that a song can work on. And I think with stone carving - I know something Mum always used to say to me, and she'd probably had somebody say it to her, an old stone carver or something – it's almost like it's inside the stone already and you just have to take away what isn't needed to reveal what's already there …. It's very much like that with writing, with song writing I think. And then you think there it is, don't touch it any more…

Also I've been performing solo. I've only done three or four shows and again, it's a new thing I've never really done before. And it's opened up a whole new territory of performance, because it's entirely different, you know, and much more fluid… much more frightening, much more malleable, I can change whatever I want to do at the drop of a hat, you don't have to rehearse up a band or anything. And I find it much more expressive, I think because I'm not fighting against too much noise, I can really sing. Much more light and shade. Yeah. It's been fascinating I'm really loving it.

Hay on Wye. That was the second time that I have done a solo performance. The literature festival. Loved it, I loved it. Well for a start I felt really privileged to be there, and the audience they were listeners. It was a literary audience. I just felt so honoured, I thought gosh, people must actually be listening to the words I'm writing. And then again I just played for the Prince and Princess of Denmark at the Royal Opera House. And I just feel like I've been doing this now for what, 15 years or something, but it's only now that I really feel like I'm reaping the fruits of my labour if you like, that people are really listening and really valuing what I do. And it's just the best feeling. I never could have dreamed it would be as wonderful as it has become, you know.

Dorset. It's my home. Always when I've been away. Well first of all I realise how English I am, because when I land at Heathrow, even though you're in stinking Heathrow, but the moment you smell the English air I think ahh, I'm home. I'm very English. And when I start, when you start seeing the hills becoming the shapes of the Dorset hills, which are very distinct. And then you slowly think 'I'm coming home, I'm coming home' and you hit Dorset and the hills change shape and then I feel like yeah, I feel like it's my flesh and bones really.

I live by the sea. The sea, I think, is like part of your conscience. And where I do most of my writing, I'm facing the sea anyway. I've got these giant windows that just look on the sea, and definitely the sky, the shapes of the clouds, the way the sea is behaving that day, the light, it all affects what happens that day in my writing.

Anyway I'm just off to Aunty Val's. Aunty Val Crabb's now, because Arthur Watson, from The Riverside, (I lived above his café for about a year in West Bay before I bought my first place). And when I was there, it used to be his Russian mother's home and she had loads of Russian records, old vinyl records … and I fell in love with her record collection, amongst other things, while I was there. And then I'd been thinking about these records ever since. And I'd see Arthur all the time, so I said 'Can I borrow them?' So he's lent me all these records, mostly of them 78s. I didn't have a 78 player, so I needed to find somebody with a 78 player. Val knows everything, so I got round to asking Val, she knew a friend called Malcolm with a 78 player who recorded all of them for me. So I've got to go and pick up those records from Aunty Val and take the CD to Arthur and the records back… I'm looking forward to hearing those records again.

23. Tracey Copp – Hairdresser and fisherwoman, West Bay. Born 1965.

Sold the hairdressing business to buy Gary the boat. It was really brave, and I must admit, I thought 'What the hell am I doing?'…
I nearly went overboard once, it was scary.

I was born in Bridport Hospital. We were living in Charmouth with my grandparents. My dad at the time was a car mechanic for Gears Garage, my mum was a nanny for the Queen's Arms Hotel in Charmouth, she'd come from Weymouth and we were pretty skint so we had to live with my dad's parents in Charmouth. They'd come from up north, my grandma was from Manchester, my granddad's family died of TB. They were a farming family up there, so he was doing that. All his brothers and sisters got it, he had four brothers. It was rife and he was lucky to survive it. He came down to North Chideock and he worked at a farm there, for the Lyalls. He was just a herdsman there for the Lyalls. Alison, I cut her hair actually, she works for Sidney Gale. So they came down here, then Grandad was ill, so he gave up being a herdsman and got a council house in Charmouth, and my gran used to be a cleaner for Brigadier Buttonshaw, my granddad used to work for Mr De Savary, used to have Duncan Tuckers.

Mother's parents, they were from Liverpool, don't know much about them to be honest, never been that close to them, but they live in Weymouth now, they're both in their 80s. My granddad's just stopped driving and they've moved into a bungalow, my granddad's family up in Liverpool, they've got taxis, and apparently they drive round Liverpool with cages round them in the taxi. My grandfather in Weymouth worked for the tax office, he had quite a good job, unlike my other grandparents.

Charmouth was fun. Yeah, it was really, you don't think so at the time, it seemed boring as a teenager, but looking back it was healthy. It was a good way to live, I look at my daughter who's 13, this holiday she said "Can I walk to town?" And you're like, 'No, you can't,' you just don't feel safe, you really don't. It's strange. When we were kids, my granddad was brilliant, but you didn't realise it at the time, we used to go down to the beach to collect seaweed for the garden, we used to go out to the woods, he made this little cart that we used to tow behind us to get wood, it was idyllic in a way, but at the time you didn't think it was. We didn't have television for the first eight years of my life, we couldn't afford it. I can remember getting cardboard boxes from the village shop and making houses and sticking bits of wallpaper inside, and things like that, we were always doing something, whereas Amy will watch the telly or be on the computer, we just didn't have that. You don't appreciate it at the time, do you, you just think 'God, this is boring.' There was no bypass, it was lovely.

We lived right at the top of Charmouth, looked down over the vale, we spent our time with other kids out at Whitchurch and Wootton Fitzpaine, it was lovely. We had our bikes, we used to take a packed lunch, and we'd come back when it was seven o'clock, usually, we had to be in.

There was a lot of lads fishing, they had their little rowing boats, I was never actually into it. I spent a lot of time on the beach but I wasn't into fishing at all. I don't know what changed my mind.

School was Woodroffe. My dad went there as well when it was a grammar school, he was a boarder and got expelled for being out late and drinking. I was quiet at school actually until I

Tracey Copp with nets and waterproofs, West Bay

was about 14, and then boys got into the equation and I can remember getting on the bus at Charmouth, catching it over to Lyme, getting under the seat at the back, back to Bridport and skiving all day at Lipton's café. I was a bit older and I never got caught.

We always had jobs, my godfather had the beach café, his dad was Barney the Fossil at Barney's Fossil Shop in Charmouth in the main street. It was huge, it was a big thing at the time, so he had that and his son had the beach café down at Charmouth on the front, and from the age of 12, I worked there every summer and we had chores at home to do which were totally boring. Always had to go down and get the paper in the morning, we lived at the top and had to walk right to the bottom. I worked in the White House at Charmouth, waitressing when I was growing up, I was richer then than I am now.

When I left school I went into Boots in Lyme Regis to do a YTS scheme, I lasted there three months, I hated it, and I managed to get another YTS scheme in Bridport, in Andrew Wheatley's, doing hairdressing, he kept me for the six months, gave me an absolutely fantastic report, but wouldn't keep me on because the government were paying the money so he wanted the next person free of charge for six months. But he did me a huge favour, because of that reference I got, I got my job at Style Inn at Lyme Regis to do my apprenticeship, which was a really nice salon. It's still there, it's now up in the main street of Lyme Regis, and I stayed there three years, met my first husband and came to Bridport. Worked in South Street for 12 months in a place called Chantelle's, that's still there. I realised how much money I was taking for the people I was working for, and I was getting paid £60 a week at the age of 22, and thought 'Sod this, I can do a lot better myself,' and that's when I got the shop in West Allington. That was when I was 23. From 23 to 34, 11 years I had

that. I had two girls that worked for me, one girl from Lyme Regis, Angelique, and then she left to go back to Lyme, and Laura worked for me, then Leanne up at the second shop, God it's so long ago, I've a job to remember. I just rented that and it was getting so horrible out there because it was damp and cold and my landlady wouldn't do anything about it, split up with my first husband when I was about 30…

I had sheep with my first husband up at the farm where we live now, so we've had them most of our lives really. Got to 30, split up with my husband, bought my half of the cottage off him, stayed there in Dottery, and we had a mobile home out Broadoak. Amy was a year old I think when we split up, lived out Dottery on my own for a couple of years and hated it because it was so bloody dark and no streetlights, and it petrified the life out of me, even though I'd been born in the country, it was so, so quiet, so I needed to get another business where I could have Amy with me, because of being on my own, because I couldn't afford to send her to nursery. And that shop came up which used to be Brit Stores before that, bought that, mortgaged up to the hilt, but luckily it worked, I was really lucky, and stayed there until we bought the boat. Sold the hairdressing business to buy Gary the boat. It was really brave, and I must admit, I thought 'What the hell am I doing?'

It's a ten-metre potting, netting boat. It's a semi-planing hull, it does about 14 knots and I think it's a really lovely looking boat, and we've had it two years in November. It's the best thing we've ever done, until today, when we get a call from Dave Sales saying that our quota's gone down to 100 kilos of soles a month, which is actually dire. We usually catch that a day. It started off at 750 a month for our boat, then it went down to 500, now it's 100. This is Dover sole, not lemon sole, but what Gary's going to have to do is go over to Poole and fish over there. All around the coast it's different sections, we're in section seven, that's from the Scilly Isles to St Alban's Head. Poole is section eight. So that was a bit of a blow today. But up until today it has been the best thing. We do a few lobster pots, but to be fair we catch more lobsters in the nets. Huge lobsters, they really are. The potting isn't that brilliant and there are so many of them doing it out of here.

We've done wreck netting, and you get a lot of pollock, a few bass if you're lucky, but we're whelking from January to June and that is really boring. It's a horrible little sea snail, basically like a snail you'd pick up in your garden with a harder shell and they are disgusting and I would never touch one, ever. I tried one in Weymouth at Brewer's Quay one day and I just spat it out. We've got strings of 30 pots, we've got about 13, 14 strings, and you bait them with spider crab and some dogfish, the pots go out, onto the bottom, and all the whelks go in there and make you loads and loads of money. They really go well. They go to Ireland to be processed and then go all down through the east, Korea. They must be worth an absolute fortune when they get there. There's one chap from Exeter who buys them all.

The whelking pots are out on the Met ground which is about six, seven miles off. It's such a boring job, that's all you do, pull the pots in over the side of the boat. The wrecks we fish off are the Ailsa Craig, M2, Moidart and the Empress of India. If we didn't have that sounder we'd be lost, because you just mark it all in, where your gear is, set the cursor to it and go straight to it.

The new harbour's got its advantages and its disadvantages. It's got a big advantage for us because we can get out a lot more, and it's a safer harbour, the boat doesn't get chucked around at all, but the bad side of it is we get a lot of boats up from Brixham who are fishing out of here, a lot of scallopers, apparently there were seven out there today and it is bad news for us as an inshore fisherman. If we go inshore you've got the scallopers ruining your gear, if you go out any further than six miles you've got the big beamers taking your gear.

I enjoy fishing. I can't explain it. I get up in the mornings and look at the weather and think 'God, do I have to go?' but when you get out there it's just amazing. To see the coastline from out at sea, and you've just got one another, and we get on really well, we're lucky, and it's just brilliant. I love netting, the whelking I didn't like because you never saw anything other than a whelk, but with nets you never know what's coming in, and it's exciting. He jumps out of his skin sometimes, you get something like a bass coming up, and you're like, 'Wow!' and then you get a huge turbot coming up, 'Watch the hauler!' it is just lovely.

I went out five days a week, weather permitting. I nearly went overboard once, it was scary, I was so lucky, I was leaning over the gunwale, looking down over, and this huge wave hit us sideways on, of course my feet just left the deck, went up and luckily the boat went slamming back down again and knocked me back into the boat, but I was shaking. Honestly. I couldn't do anything for an hour. And they say you're supposed to keep your wellies and oilskins on, but like when I've done sea survival courses, you're not let on the boat unless you've got the tickets, and you do it in a swimming pool, we did ours at Poole with clothes on, and you try and get into a life raft. You do not know how hard that is. It's awful. But like the bloke said, "You're doing it because you've got to. If you thought you were going to die, you'd do it, you really would."

I've done five years fishing, because we had a little boat, Helena, before we bought the big boat. That's how we knew we could make a living out of it. Gary used to go out building four days a week, we used to go out most evenings in the summer doing lobster pots and crab pots, and the last building job he did was at Salwayash for a bloke called Pete Bailey and that was it. He said he wanted a boat and we were going to borrow the money. He doesn't have a day off for months at a time when the weather's good.

We can land wherever we want, but if we do that down to Brixham we've got to pay Clive for the lorry, and what Clive pays is very marginally under what the market price is, so it's just not worth it, so you're better off giving it all to Clive, and it's just up the road, it's so easy. Lyme Regis boys, Barry, a friend of ours, he fishes out of Lyme with the same sort of boat as us, and he has to drive over to Lyme from Bridport every bloody night, and you're catching 100, 200 kilos of fish, you've got to cart those fish boxes, ice them all up, it does take it out of you, it's a very physical job. When there's loads of fish you're not going to get a very good price at all.

The old harbour in a big swell, you never looked behind you, you just kept going. This boat's so different to the little boat, I didn't like it to start off with because it's up in the air, but it's very safe, we've been in a south west six to seven and it's been alright. The only thing that worries me is that because he's done it once and the weather's been atrocious, he'll push it another time. This was out to the nets, we'd left nets out there and we had to go and get them, 'cause we'd lose 'em. And when you've got a couple of grand's worth of gear, you can't afford to lose it just by leaving them out, so you take a chance.

Other women on boats? Yes Nicky, she's at Lyme Regis, they do whelking all year round. Insurance? It's very hefty. It's about thirteen, fourteen hundred pounds a year, but that's your livelihood. You've got 16,000 pounds worth of boat there because you have to buy a licence as well. Our licence was £30,000 pounds, on top of 120. You cannot go fishing without that licence. The quota. We can't buy quota because we're an under ten-metre boat, but the big boats, over ten metres can buy extra quota.

The soles come on this time of year, they disappear in the spring, the whelks come on just after Christmas and that's all we do. If whelking hadn't come on we'd have struggled come the summer months. We did the wreck netting in between, but that depends on the tides over the wrecks. If you've got big tides you just don't catch anything. I don't know what's going to happen. I get really angry. We've got a friend, Pierrot, who lives in Guernsey, he lands everything into Cherbourg and he lands everything. There's no size guide, nothing. So why are we all slaughtered over here? We're supposed to be in this bloody common market crap, it really does get me wound up. 'Cause if we've got spider crabs or lobsters and they're undersized, the lobsters are still alive when we chuck them back in, or the crab, but if you get undersized fish, they're dead. And you're chucking them back in the water. It's just wrong. Completely wrong. But I'm not a politician. You really do feel like going and making a stand and saying 'Look, you try and make a living doing this then.' It's one of the most dangerous occupations there are. It really is. And they're putting bans and quotas and licences, it's bloody expensive.

So I'm setting up a new hairdressing salon. It's quite exciting. I'm looking forward to it. Sheep shearing? I've had a go. Ha ha! There is no comparison. My clients don't kick me or fart on me! Sheep are bloody horrible really. They're so strong, aren't they? When you try and get hold of them it's like having a wrestling match, it really is. We had Dorset Horns. They are beautiful looking sheep, but they are really stubborn. I got really hurt one day by being knocked over by one. I couldn't get on with that sheep shearing at all. Give me a pair of hair clippers and someone's barnet and I'll be fine! Much easier.

I do men's hair as well. Definitely unisex. When I first started I used to be terrified, my hands used to shake, they're always better tippers and they don't take very long, and you can still charge them the same even if they've only got half a head, so we like men. We're going to stay open late two nights a week to do men. I could do fishermen. Yeah, but they stink! Dave Sales is waiting for a haircut. He said "Shall I wear my suit?"

The fishermen get on well. There's a brilliant relationship, there is. They're all so down to earth and hard working. I love West Bay. You just drive down there and you know everybody and everybody's so friendly, I get withdrawal symptoms if I don't go down there now, I go to West Bay, nearly every day, even if I'm not fishing. That's why I'm looking forward to being here. Just walk down with Alfie, 'cause he's coming to work with me. I'm going to get a long chain.

The skills of hairdressing. I love the customers. I love all the gossip that goes with it, it's brilliant, I just love people, I really do. But the hairdressing, I suppose there is a skill, when you know it, it doesn't feel like it, it's so easy to do, but it did take three years to learn, and at the time when you first picked up those scissors, we used to do the Cheshire Homes at Lyme Regis, and those poor kids used to come in, and we were allowed to practise on them, and they didn't pay, and if you had one that had a slightly shaky head, there was a few close misses. I did actually cut a little boy's ear once, and there was blood everywhere. The scissors are very sharp. He screamed, it was awful. But I don't think about being skilful really.

Loads of different types of hair. I think the hardest hair to cut is the fine hair, 'cause it shows every scissor mark. Men are quite fussy, they know what they want, chaps do. But it is a skill. I find talking about hairdressing really boring! I don't know what to say about it. The new salon's going to be called Barnet, 'cause

it's Marsh Barn, and fishing nets. Come here for your fish.

I am pretty lucky. I think if things are meant to be, I remember when I was going to buy the shop out at St Andrew's Road, I actually wanted to buy the newsagent's three doors up from where I was in West Allington. I had the money, and everything that could go wrong went wrong, it was just one thing after another, and I'd sold my house in Dottery so I had to find something, and the people pulled out, they'd sold to a builder to turn it into flats, and I tried and tried and tried to buy that, I was convinced it would work, and then one of my customers told me there was a shop empty with living accommodation up in St Andrew's Road, and I said 'I don't want to go up there, what would I want to go up there for?' Then I told Mum and Dad and they said "Just go and have a look at it, 'cause you've got to have somewhere to live in a minute, you're going to be out on your ear." So I went and had a look at it, and it had parking outside, and I thought 'I've got to give it a go,' and it was fantastic. So I do believe in fate. Because you can do so much, and if it's not meant to be, and that's what I felt with the boat and the shop, the shop sold like that and we managed to get the boat, and it all worked out fine. It has been really good. I mean we'll overcome this obstacle. We've got to. But it's just a bloody huge inconvenience, it really is.

You want to get one of those politicians out there in a bloody gale force wind! I tell you what, I'm glad we don't have a mortgage on that boat, I'm glad we sold the shop for it, because you would really struggle. At least we haven't got the boat to pay for, 'cause a lot of the big blokes have got mortgages on.

What I miss when I'm out on the boat, is my ladies, if you're busy they'll say "Do you want a cup of coffee, Trace?" And they'll go and make you a cup of coffee, and they'll sweep the floor for you, on the boat I'm the chief coffee maker. In fact I take a flask now, 'cause I'm sick of dropping cups of tea everywhere. You put the kettle on and you fasten it on, and then you get another wave and it's just gone!

We usually go on at about half six, and we get in at about four. It is a long day, and it is bloody tiring. I don't get half as tired hairdressing as I do fishing. It's about an hour steaming out to the Met ground. Most of the fishing happens on that Met ground, I don't know why, I don't understand it at all, but when we go out tomorrow, the soles will be on the Met ground, and then when we go back whelking after Christmas, that's where the whelks are. It's strange.

Yeah, we have had nets caught in the wrecks. I think it might have been the Empress, it has a bit that sticks up, and a big metal thing came up in the nets. That made a huge hole in the nets.

These nets? They come in 300 yards, you join them up so there's 900 yards a go. You usually have about 5,000 yards of net, last year we only did three, and this year, because he's got another chap he's taken on, Tom, he's going to do 5,000 yards, but until we work out whether we can go and fish out of Poole, we'll have to wait and see.

We're not allowed to whistle on the boat, apparently that's really bad luck. They all find it strange because they see me in my oilskins, no makeup, I've usually got a hat on, because I can't be arsed to do me hair, there's no point if I'm out at sea, and then I walk in the pub with a skirt and my hair done and makeup, and they say "Have you really been fishing today?" I'm like 'Yes, I just scrub up well.' They do laugh at me. When I first started they said "You won't stick it, you won't stick that Trace, give you a couple of weeks and that'll be it," and that made me more determined, but I did enjoy it. You've got to try these things, haven't you?

The Ailsa Craig was a defensively-armed British merchantman that was torpedoed on the 15th April 1918, 13 miles from Portland Bill.

The M2 was an enormous submarine that had an aircraft hanger at the stern for a sea plane. On the morning of 26 January 1932 the M2 was taking part in submarine exercises in the eastern region of Lyme Bay, she dived and was never seen again. She was lost with all hands. It is thought that the hanger flooded.

Moidart was a small collier that was torpedoed on 9th June 1918 by UC77. She was on route from Barry to Rouen with coal. Fifteen were lost.

HMS Empress of India was a Royal Sovereign class battleship of 15,500 tons. She was superseded by Dreadnoughts and was used for target practice in November 1913 and sank quickly. In 1896-97 a certain young officer called Robert Falcon Scott served on board her as a Torpedo Lieutenant…so, in a sense, both went down under within a year of each other.

24. Margaret Ralph – Deerstalker & game dealer, Lyon's Gate. Born 1931.

It's very rare that you run into poachers. They operate entirely differently, usually with lights, vehicles at night, dogs at night, we only operate in the daylight. At the moment it's against the law to shoot an hour after sunset and an hour before sunrise.

I was born in Somerset just under the Mendip hills in 1931 in Easton, near Wells. We were only there for about a year before we moved to Crudwell, near Malmesbury in north Wiltshire. Everybody in my family, on my mother's side and my father's side is in farming, beyond that I don't know. They're all farmers. We were tenanted because father didn't buy, he just moved on. Things weren't right in Somerset so we moved to Wiltshire, he was having trouble with the cows, so we moved to Dorset.

I was down into Dorset before I was five. We came to Poxwell. I know a lot of people pronounce it Poxwell, but the old way of saying it was Pokeswell. It's between Osmington and Warmwell Cross. It's an old village, they say the name come from Puckswell. They did an archaeological dig up there a few years ago, up towards the barn on the Osmington side. Manor Farm at Poxwell, there was only one farm at Poxwell village, the other farm was Lower Poxwell, which is only a little village with 14 houses. There was a church in those days but they pulled that down in about the late 1960s, they decided the spire was unsafe. For a little tiny place there's a lot of history.

Somewhere along the line, probably in my teens, my father Arthur Masters decided to go into dairying in a big way and we reared a lot of calves, like 100 a year, and then he selected the best out of those and started a reasonable sized dairy herd. He had pedigree Friesians, and then he put in a milk machine, he was quite cutting edge because when they started testing tubercular cattle, he was right in there at the beginning when it was voluntary, before it became compulsory. I can't understand all this business about the badgers and the TB, and the cattle and the TB, the whole country was eradicated of TB in the cattle, so where did it come from? We didn't have so many badgers then because they weren't protected. It was great fun if you could catch one because the skins were worth a bit of money because the finest shaving brushes was made from badger hair.

Father died in 1956, it was tenanted so we had notice to quit. We had 18 months from when he died to move out, so we moved out of there 1957. Got married in the church there the month before we moved out. We married at the end of August and moved out in September. We were there 21 years.

I went to school at Warmwell, Owermoigne, and then finished up at Weymouth. We had air raid shelters at school, and we used to have to do practice drill into there in case there was an air raid. It was filthy. It had duckboards, muddy water and these dirty smelly tunnels. I can remember all the ships in Weymouth harbour the day before and in the morning they were all gone. I said to my mother, Jane Masters, when I got back from school 'All those ships have gone,' so they knew it was all about to happen.

Americans. Oh yeah, they were about because us kids we always used to go to the road and wave, 'cause they'd throw you out a bar of chocolate or a sweet. Wartime rationing on the farm, we had agricultural workers and doing the manual work, they used to be able to get a little bit extra, so my mother had to apply for this, and it would be like so much cheese a week, she'd have this lump of cheese, and however many men it was, she'd have to

Margaret Ralph with Terry — Robert De Niro watch out

divide this cheese up into these little tiny bits that everyone was allocated, and I can remember helping her pack up the cheese. It would also be sugar, butter, and all stuff like that, so all these little bits would be packed up and George would have one and Ted would have one. She had her scales, she used to weigh it all out carefully, she was a very straight woman. Being on a farm you were better off because you had your milk and pigs and everything, you weren't supposed to but the odd one used to disappear. You don't absorb the anxiety as kids. I didn't used to like the planes going over at night, and you'd hear the sirens go, I didn't like that. I remember one field, we went up there and there were two bomb holes up there, only little ones, and like kids, you're looking around for shrapnel, but there was nothing there, and then there was a big outcry, because these were still unexploded ones. There was about seven bombs on the farm altogether, the closest one was not too far from the manor house and that was an unexploded one. It landed in the spring and tipped upside down in the water, and they had a tremendous job getting it out. They had these pumps going day and night, we were banned from going anywhere near, but as kids you want to see. And then I can remember all along, the posts, they were scaffolding with barbed wire, all along the beaches. Blooming stuff, once they'd cleared it and we could go on the beaches, there was always rusty scaffolding and bits of barbed wire and rusty iron everywhere, you had to be really careful, 'cause we used to go to Osmington Mills, we'd learned to swim in the seaweed and the rocks.

Nowadays a kid's got to be taken somewhere and entertained, we did nothing like that, we spent Saturday and Sunday round the farm, you might go bird nesting, that was a great thing with the kids then, collecting eggs. It was the done thing. Everybody had their collections, and you used to swap to get one you didn't

have, we used to spend the weekend damming up the stream or building a den, you amused yourself, you had your own little three or four of you to do things. We never even listened to the wireless. But I can remember them all gathering round when the end of the war was announced on the wireless, and Gracie Fields singing on there which was always special. We had one of the rooms as a playroom, 'cause it was a very big house and we didn't have it all furnished, so one room was dartboards and I don't know what else, after we'd finished our meal we'd go and have a game of darts, I can throw a good dart.

I was at Weymouth Grammar and I didn't leave till 15. I think the age then you could leave was 14. Just after the war, yeah. I just came back and worked on the farm. Helped milk the cows, we were hand milking then. We didn't have that many cows at that stage, probably about 30 or so. Everyone would knock off for an hour, go and milk the cows and then go back to doing whatever they were doing.

The milk went to Milborne St Andrew. They would come round and pick up the churns. We came out of there in 1957 and it was still churns then. There used to be rows of churns ready to be lifted up, and all of these had to be hoiked up onto the lorry by hand, one person on each side, ten gallons in each churn. Usually the blokes did it, but if something was happening and nobody was there you had to help do it. You always used to check the churns when they come in empty, because if they hadn't been washed properly you had to watch out. They were normally ok.

I stayed on the farm. Then we had to leave and I married Brian, and they were farming at Alton Pancras so I moved up there. We lived there in Keeper's Cottage for seven years, I helped a bit. I used to take the calves to market, then we moved down to Alton Mill, which is the deer farm now, and we moved out of there in '83, something like that.

It was a little farm, Brian came out of partnership with the others and that was about 100 acres we kept on our own. We kept beef and we kept pigs. They were making money then. I remember someone going in saying "I don't like that smell." I said 'That smell is money!' We did have the ups and downs to a degree but you didn't have these sudden changes like they had later. We had Saddleback sows crossed on Landrace for porkers. Mostly we sold weaners, we didn't finish them, just sold the weaners on for somebody else to finish.

When I was quite small Father always had ferrets and he always shot 'cause if he went out Mother would say "I want a rabbit for the weekend." There wasn't hardly any pheasants about then, so we used to go out with a ferret before we could even shoot, so I didn't start shooting until I was in my teens. If you caught a rabbit you had a bit of pocket money which was useful, because there wasn't much money about in those days. We'd sell them. They didn't make very much, there was a firm called Horace Friend in Wisbech, all the things like birds wings, little skins, we used to save it all up and send a parcel up every now and then, get a postal order back which was quite exciting because you didn't get much money in those days. When we started work we had everything found, clothes, food and everything, we had 15 shillings pocket money, then it went up to two pound and you had to buy your own clothes. That was hard, but it makes you learn to economise and look after things. We didn't feel hard done by at all, t'was only a few pence to go on the bus into Weymouth.

Badger skins. Oh yeah, the old boy, Willy Willment, who used to work for Father, he showed us how to skin them properly. You didn't have to dry them or anything, you put them in the post. They'd send it quite quickly. You didn't have to do any salting or anything like that. It was good money in those days.

We used to borrow Father's 12 bore gun, there were so many rabbits. The myxi came before he died, but before that we used to go out with a Landrover after dark, Mondays and Tuesdays. You'd shoot 50, 60 rabbits a night, and we used to take it in turns, me and my youngest brother, John, one drive, one shoot, and then change over. I used to get recoil on my finger 'til it ached, and then we'd go back and paunch all these rabbits and hang them all up, and then on Wednesdays we'd take them to Dorchester market.

They used to sell well at Wimborne because people used to come out of Bournemouth. We took 'em to Dorchester. I suppose they were about two shillings, two and six, something like that. A cartridge only cost three or four pence. We used whatever Jeffrey's in Dorchester decided to stock. There were hundreds of rabbits but they all used to sell. In those days, t'was all cages along, be full of chickens and rabbits and ferrets, all the live stuff, rows of it. Dorchester used to do it till it shut, I can't remember when they shut it but it was a big market. All these little towns used to have markets in those days.

I was a good shot with a 12 bore. I borrowed my brother, Bob's .22, going out shooting rabbits, then he said "It's time you'd better have that rifle, I'm getting another one." So I gave him £5 for it, and I had my own .22. I was in my 20s. You just kept at it. A friend of my father's, Wilf Miles, had a shoot at Bere Regis, they had quite a few deer at the Wareham forest and he had his shoot there, so he used to invite me. At the end of the pheasant shooting, then they used to do the deer drives. Everyone did it in the big woods, half the guns would stand and half the guns would walk through and shoot the deer with the shot guns. That wasn't until the 50s, I had a firearms certificate because I had the .22, but they gave us a Labrador puppy for a wedding present, so I used to go over there with this dog, helping pick up the pheasants. So it wasn't until '57 that I started shooting the deer over there. We only used to shoot seven or eight a day. We'd have two or three days, do all the different patches of the wood, some was roe, some was sika, same as now. They formed the British Deer Society in 1963, and Wilf said "That's it. We're not shooting the deer with shotguns any more." He said "We're going to do it with rifles, we're going to do it properly." So he bought me a rifle, a .243. And that was it, I used to go with him over there, he coached me on, and that's how we started. When I had my rifle, we were living at the mill then and there was nobody in the area who had a deer rifle. I had telescopic sights on there, 'cause you're often shooting at dusk and dawn and if you've got a good quality one it picks up the light. I changed me rifle a couple of times, I did go up to a .303, it was a military calibre in those days, and this copper recognised it and said "You can't have that." The .243 was the low limit on what you can use on the deer, but there's no upper limit. I've got a .243 now, that's all I've ever used. Some people say it's not heavy enough, but where I go to in Scotland, the keeper there always uses a .243 and he finds it quite adequate for the big deer.

I never aim in the head, because you could hit its eye, its jaw, the head moves so quickly. When you're shooting on the farm for people that rear deer, farm deer, when you go and shoot them in the field, then yes you've got to shoot them in the head, and if by some unhappy occasion you don't hit one properly you can go again, but in the wild it's gone, so you've got to make sure you get it. We normally go for a heart shot, because if you're stalking properly the deer won't know you're there, and if you go for a heart shot you can wait till its front feet are forward, both front feet so the bullet goes into the heart, and it won't do any damage to the venison. I've shot deer in the neck, which when they've been very close, anywhere in the vertebrae and they'll drop like a stone, and sometimes you're that confident, that close that you can do it, but normally you'll go for a heart shot. They don't drop instantly always, if you hit it exactly on the top of the heart they'll drop, but if it's anywhere else they might run a little bit before they fall over, it's the adrenalin.

With stalking the wind is the most important thing of all. We take out paying guests, Belgians, French, Danish, different nationalities, and sometimes they say "Haven't you got any high seats?" We do use them more for the sika, because the sika have different habits, and we say 'No, we specialise in the approach.' So it's the wind, make sure they don't see you, and move quietly as well, we usually wear camouflage or modest colours so you blend in, you don't want black because it's a stark colour, it shows.

There's stalking all over the place. You can buy it, lease it, we've never done it much on our own land because it's not big enough. At the mill we had stock everywhere. We still rent Alton Pancras, the whole estate. We've also got the Warmwell Estate, we go up into Somerset on Shapwick Heath where we've just got to control the deer. You're ducking and diving there, to see there's nobody about. It's the people that hang about when it's getting dark that we don't like.

We pay them for the carcases. We gradually went into a game dealing business, because there's always someone wanting venison. Otherwise you cut one up, somebody want a bit, another person want a bit and in the end I said 'I'm not doing this.' We used to have a deep freeze room, and we used to pile them in there till we had about 50, and then we used to ring this firm up and they would come and get them. Then I started a pheasant shoot at Alton Pancras. Some of it's exported, the continentals prefer the roe, so we sell to one of the firms in Hampshire and they export, we sell to another one in Hampshire and a lot of theirs goes to London. Now everything's got to be labelled, so we're starting to do that. It's got to have the location, date, time, sex, weight and damage. Also a declaration that the deer was alright when you saw it still alive and no abnormalities on it when you shot it.

It's very rare that you run into poachers. They operate entirely differently, usually with lights, vehicles at night, dogs at night, we only operate in the daylight. At the moment it's against the law to shoot a hour after sunset and an hour before sunrise.

Dorset is one of the best areas for antler growth because of the chalk hills. Sussex is good, one chap showed me a German book on deer and even there it talked about the fine trophies in Dorset. All the estates let stalking. The estate decides how much people have got to pay, and that's it. They can shoot what they like. I wrote an article for the deer magazine about it. Money rules everything.

There are more and more deer. Years ago we used to think 'We didn't ought to shoot too many,' now it's 'Did we shoot enough?' Nowadays everyone wants to stalk so they're banging on doors asking "Can we have your stalking, and how much are you going to pay me?" You've still got the odd one where they like the deer and they don't want you there. They're definitely on the increase, normally with the roe they'll have a twin, the Deer Society did a count a while ago and they reckoned in a year they could increase as much as 45 per cent on a good year.

The combination of chalk and woodland is very good for deer. In the winter you've got the nice sheltered woodlands, we've got one on the edge of the estate, it belongs to the Woodland Trust, so you've got all the pheasant shooting on one side and all the Blackmore Vale on the other. We shot 16 does around that area last winter, and then we went there the last week before they went into season, and we saw 16 deer!

The shooting seasons are different. All the females are from the first of November to the end of February, but the roe bucks are from the first of April to the end of October, the sika, red and fallow are from the first of August until the end of April, they're only closed for three months, the roe bucks are closed for five. I don't know why. And the muntjac, we haven't got them here yet, but we'll know when we have. Odd ones have been seen and shot, they will come in season within five days of giving birth, and then have another one within seven months. You can't make a closed season for them because they're breeding all the time. Chinese water deer, I'm not sure what their season is.

I've never got involved with hunting with hounds. I can't see that the animal, when they've finished with it, is of any use, because stress causes adrenalin and makes the meat tough. If someone shoots a deer and it's not shot dead and they've got to have another shot and it's left for a little while, that venison will be tough. There's one chef down at Sherborne, and he could look at that and tell you which was stressed meat and what was ok. My partner, Mandy, her knife is very pointed and she gives the meat a prod which tells her 'that's alright and that's tough.' If it's anything that's likely to be tough, we'll put it in for stewing meat. They want the best and you don't put it in if it isn't right.

You can't do anything with the skins except for the Scottish red deer, there's a company up there that deals with them, shoes and handbags and various things I've seen on a stand at game shows. By law, we're not allowed to bury them, they've got to be binned, and there's a firm now that we send them to at Chewton Mendip, it's all got to be incinerated. I don't see the sense of it. It's a natural product so why shouldn't they go in a hole to break them down naturally. The leaves from a tree drop down and rot away.

For the foreign trophy hunters, you test them on a target

before you go to make sure that they can shoot properly, they vary. They usually bring their own rifles. We get visitor's firearm permit forms so they can use their own rifle because they don't feel happy about using ours.

Generally yes, they do have larger rifles because over there if they've only got one rifle they use it for wild boars, so it's got to be heavier. I've been to Belgium shooting wild boar but not here. Individually for deer, it's a one to one, because they might bring a friend which is always a nuisance. Peak weeks are mid-April to the end of May, so you've only got six good weeks when they want to come. A lot of them for roe will come for the week.

I charge them an outing fee 'cause you've got to be out there. But alone you'd probably come home with a deer. With them you end up coming home with nothing. They're usually quite obliging. Sometimes they want to gut it, but I'd rather they didn't, they don't half make a mess. We've got loads of deep freezes and a big chiller up there as well. Sometimes you can drive a vehicle down close to where you shot it. If it's long grass you can drag it along on the grass, but if the gateways are muddy, you've got to carry it.

You're up early so that you can be out there before it gets light, and then you go out in the evening, couple of hours before it gets dark. With the roe if you've got a good wood for shelter and some nice grazing for the deer, you know that sooner or later they're going to come out. They mightn't come out every time, it makes a difference if it's moonlight, they feed more at night, it's all to do with the weather. Sometimes you think it might be perfect, but it isn't, they're not out, 'cause they don't go to water to drink, they like the food to be moist, it's like a rabbit, if you want to go out shooting rabbits at night, you go out when 'tis a bit misty, damp, and they're all out because they love it. The grass is much more succulent when it's wet, and the deer are the same. They don't want it raining, but when the dew comes down they seem to appear quicker. That summer dry wind is a waste of time. I don't know how they manage but I suppose they lie quiet and conserve their energy, and when it's warm you don't need so much to eat anyway, do you?

In Weymouth there was deer in the trading estate down there, and it just got lost, and a couple of years ago there was a sika on Lodmore reserve because it's a herding animal and there were no others it palled up with the cattle. They had a photo of it there, it was licking the neck of this cow. About a month ago there was one knocked down one Sunday afternoon right in the crossroads at Charminster. My brother picked it up, it's amazing where they end up. We've got a scheme going now with the police, Dorset was the first to start, they got in touch with a lot of the stalkers and we went over for a meeting at the police headquarters. They've got a wildlife officer and he set it all up. What they do, if there's a deer knocked down on the road, they ring one of us, because by law they're not allowed to shoot on the road, they have got to be 50 metres from the centre of the highway, so we've got a card authorising us to shoot them on the road. We've got a reflective coat and everything. We have to use our discretion. If you ring the police and say 'There's a deer knocked down, it's a hazard,' they'll ring one of us, if it's still alive, we're deer dispatchers, if it's dead, we've got to move it, and we do what we want with it. It's a good scheme, it's working quite well.

I use binoculars all the time, because a deer lying in the grass, might just have the antlers showing, you wouldn't see it with the naked eye, my eyesight's not as good as it was. There might be just an ear showing by a hedge, so before you rush out into a field you always stand in the gateway so you're a bit obscured and have a really good look round with your binoculars first. One of the chaps said about the Chinese water deer, they'll lie like a hare, he said "You could look out there and you can't see anything, and as it gets to dusk, they'll get up." We don't stalk in the woods very much, but if you look with your binoculars through the trees you might see the outline, but with the naked eye you wouldn't see it, even with the best eyes in the world.

Deer are curious as well, sometimes if you've been walking, the deer will have a sniff, they don't seem perturbed that ten minutes ago you were there, you're not there now. The white fallow down Bridport way, down Powerstock, we used to shoot down there, but it's all changed now. People say "You shot a white deer. Fancy shooting the white deer." I say 'There's dozens of them.' We get the fallow coming right up to Batcombe, but they don't come down this way. They go across that old Sherborne road in the summer. They seem to move about a bit. With the sika, they've put radio collars on, at Arne reserve, and they can look at any time to see where they are, and they don't go very far, they stay on there. It's the stags that go and come in for the rut, because they're a herding animal and they live separately all through the summer, and they'll be rutting in October. And suddenly, there was a sika hind at Alton Common, and you think 'Now where did she come from and where is she going?'

The roe stay in their family groups yes, but not the sika, they're a herding animal. We're not experts by any means because we're learning all the time. You're still seeing things that you've never seen before. You just spend all your time out there looking. The sika deer will go miles for maize. When we kill them, quite often we look in their stomach to see what they've been living off, and sometimes it's acorns, we've shot them at Warmwell and I don't even know where the maize is to, but they've got maize in their stomach. But you don't see that with roe deer. I've seen corn, where they've been on the stubble when the corn's cut, eating that, and they'll eat off the pheasant feeders as well.

Venison? We eat it regularly ourselves. We've also got a lot of private people who come in for it, as well as the deer we shoot, we'll buy in as well, because it's a collecting point here, and then I sell on to some of the big processors, but we cut up quite a lot to sell locally. If you want a whole deer we'll cut it up for you. We also deal in rabbits, pigeons, a few pheasants and hardly any partridges. But it's only local stuff, we don't bring in quail or grouse or nothing like that. Hares are just about holding their own, and that's all. There was a white hare on Alton Pancras estate a few years ago, I don't know what happened to it. I never allowed the hares to be shot when I had the shoot there, none of them do, but the odd one gets shot. If we need hares we get them brought in from Hampshire. Around here we don't get hardly any.

The cross-bred terrier in the photo is Terry. He is the most recent in a succession of second-hand dogs which I have trained to accompany me out shooting. People ask me when I am going to retire, but why should I stop what I enjoy?

25. Dawn Warr – Gamekeeper, taxidermist and artist, Bradford Abbas. Born 1960.

All I ever wanted to be was a gamekeeper. It never crossed my mind that it wasn't a woman's job.

I was born at Ringwood, Somerley. I was 18 months old when we left and went to Pentillie Estate in Cornwall, and I grew up there until I was about 13 and a half. My father was underkeeper at Lord Normanton's estate and then when we moved to Pentillie he took on head keeper's job for Captain Coryton.

My father's father was a groom for the Crutchleys at Eggardon, and I think my other grandfather worked on the farm. They were both dead before I was born unfortunately, but they were both characters. Me mum, before she married, worked at Gundry's, the net making company in Bridport.

Pentillie was lovely. We were about 100 yards up from the banks of the river Tamar and at its widest point there it would be about 250 yards across when the tide was in. We were above Cargreen and below Halton Quay. When we were there first they still had all the market gardens on the big steep banks, and they were all run by old cars with the wheels that worked like winches and they all had short handled hoes because the banks were so steep. I remember strawberry picking, the daffodils and potatoes. It was beautiful. The whole of the banks was market gardens. I remember the spindle-berries, spindle-berries are my favourite. They look lovely.

The estate was about 3,000 acres. That's quite a lot of keepering. Nice when you're growing up. I went with Dad keepering ever since I could walk, and I can remember before primary school, we were at the umpteenth gate, because there was so many gates in those days, and Dad said "Get out and open it, Dawn." And I said 'No, I ain't getting out, I've opened enough.' And he said "No, you get out." And I said 'No.' So we sat there and sat there and eventually I got out and he said "I knew you were going to open it," and I said 'No I'm not, I'm going to walk home,' and I did, and left him there. I'd have been about five I suppose.

Primary school was St Mellion where the golf course is now, and the comprehensive school is at Callington. We used to have to go about a mile to catch the bus, which was all up hill but all down hill on the way back. But my brothers, they brought me up learning how to fish and to shoot, same as Dad, and identifying all the eggs and birds' nests and tracks and things like that. All I ever wanted to be was a gamekeeper. Dad tried to talk me out of it, he said "Trouble with being a keeper, Dawn, you're a woman." He said "You'll build up muscles like a rugby player," which I did but they've all gone a bit south now. Unfortunately.

The estate world is male dominated but I never even actually thought about that to be perfectly honest. It never crossed my mind that it wasn't a woman's job. When I used to go with Dad they were still using broody hens for the pheasants, hatching the eggs. We used to go right out round Gunnislake, and Dad would say "Have you got any broody hens?" "Yeah, yeah," the guy said. "Do you want any more?" he said. "Yeah." "Well hang on, I'll go in the house." Dad said "What do you go in the house for?" "Oh, I've made the spare upstairs bedroom into a chicken house." And they'd bring out broodies that way.

And then we used to use Rupert brooders after a few years. He would raise about 1,200. It's more commercial now. They were all private shoots and all guests, whereas when you're on a commercial shoot now, to make the money, you do need the bigger bags. Your cost is the same whether you shoot 50 or 500.

The pheasants would have been in release pens from say the

Dawn Warr with Rebel, Buster, Squirt and Chum, Bradford Abbas

beginning of July, and release pens are placed in the wood, they're six foot high, netting, no top to them, the birds are about six and a half, seven weeks old when they go in there. Over a period of a couple of weeks they begin to fly out and get used to the terrain. Everything's wandering but they do go back in at night. The instinct is to move on, and with autumn being plentiful with acorns and beech nuts, they don't really need to rely on us for food, so you tend to have to drive them back in. So that's what you'd be doing now.

Softwood is very cold, dark and dismal. You can't beat your oak trees and beech, but of course they take longer to grow. You can shoot pheasants beginning of October, very few people do because there's too much leaf on the trees. Most people would shoot middle to end of October, right the way through. You can last shoot a pheasant on the first of February.

It's quite a military exercise, shoot day. People don't realise quite how coordinated it is, you have to have stops out, which is people who stop off certain hedges to stop the birds from running down there and out of the drive that you're trying to do, you have to have your beaters in a nice line, and you have to have your guns placed in the right place, and obviously pickers up behind the guns to pick up dead and wounded birds that there might be, so it's quite an organised team. I think what a lot of people don't realise, they think it's the guns' day, but it isn't, it's everybody's day, because the beaters get very little money for coming out for the day, but they come out for the enjoyment, same as the pickers up with their dogs, they come out for the enjoyment of the day, so the whole process has got to run smoothly and happily, without too much tension, which is the keeper's job to do.

Most of the time it would be between the owner and the keeper who plan the shoots. On commercial shoots it would be slightly different because the keeper knows exactly where the birds are and roughly how many they're going to kill per drive, so the keeper would be more in charge.

We would shoot fortnightly, where they might shoot a dozen and the bigger days where they might shoot 100. Quite often birds would go across the Tamar! There were three beats at Pentillie, and we used to have one cock pheasant who lived near our house, 'cause we were in the centre, between two beats, and if he thought you were shooting one side, he'd be the other side, and if he thought the opposite, he'd be back the other side, and if he wasn't sure, he'd fly across the river and wait till the end of the day, so there are some quite intelligent ones every now and again.

Game dealers tend to buy most of the pheasants, so you used to hang them in the game larder in braces then the game dealer collected them the following day. The thing about the shoot days, is like an athlete through training, you do all your training and the race is the main thing, and that is what keepering is, your shoot days is what you aim for. After February 1st you'd try and get a holiday in, because it's about the only time you can have a holiday.

You also then need to catch up laying hens, which is your hen birds that's left, and a few cocks to go with them. You have to take out cages to catch them, so that's quite a feat on its own, and once you've caught those, they have to go into a laying pen and be fit and healthy. Once they start laying, which is usually the end of March, you might swap cock birds with a neighbouring shoot or one further away to bring in different stock. So once you started that you had to collect your eggs three times a day, wash the eggs, incubate them, or put them under the broody hens. You could put about a dozen to 15 eggs under a broody, depending on the size, or later on you'd put them in the incubator, then you'd hatch them for the rearing field, and once you'd reared them they were in the release pens and the process went on. You had good years and bad years. The hatchability is fairly level, but of course weather has a big effect.

There were salmon there and we used to have people netting then. Foxes were a problem, but you used to do predator control, tunnel trapping, snaring and shooting foxes. Snaring is quite legal to use, but it's very difficult with the badgers. Now we're overrun with badgers. We used to have vermin drives at the end of the season, once the shooting had finished. You used to have a team of beaters with guns that came out so you'd drive the woods for foxes, with two people stood forward with guns, but also for jays and crows. You used to go round when the crows were nesting and sort the pairs of crows out, and the magpies, and tunnel trapping for the stoat and weasels and mink and squirrels.

There were no red squirrels down in Pentillie, but at Somerley Dad saw red squirrels there but they had quite a hard winter and I think they died out. When the grey squirrel was colonising occasionally you'd get them swimming the Tamar, 250 yards across, they'd only swim it when the tide was in. They did make it over the other side but they were really tired. And we saw a stoat swim across once. Long way to swim when you're a little animal. We had a few otters down there, and the funny thing was when I went down there to visit last week I walked along the shore and there was otter tracks in the mud. They are coming back, very much so. But I think with anything like that, fisherman are more likely to see an otter than anybody because you need to be just sat there quiet, not walking along or anything, just sat there quiet.

We used to have a cormorant roost. Mum thought she saw a Golden Oriole there once, a migratory oriole, but that was years ago. Where we shoot now, we've got egrets there all year round.

They got me a ·410 and they threw a can up in the air for me to shoot things flying. I was about ten or eleven, and I had an airgun before then that we bought in Trago Mills for £8 which I've still got, a .22. I shot all sorts of things with that. I remember once we used to rear duck as well, and we had a breeding pen for ducks, and you clip their wings when you put them in there and when they grow their feathers, they used to fly off and we had this drake turned up, outside in the hatching yard and I said 'Dad, can I shoot him?' and he said "Oh go on then," and I took me air gun out and he said to Mum "That drake's as safe as anything." I come back, and I'd shot it straight through the eye. 'Look Dad! Look what I've got!'

I used to go out with me air gun rabbiting a bit and Dad'd take his rifle. We always had ferrets when I was growing up, Dad'd do a bit of ferreting. You don't want to starve 'em before you go hunting because you don't want 'em to catch a rabbit and stay down the hole. In the early '70s girls shooting were few and far between. But now so many youngsters are anti-shooting and killing anything. Then you could have quite openly talked about what you do over the summer holidays and what you shot and nobody would worry at all, whereas if you said that now there'd be an uproar. So times are different.

Father was at Pentillie around 12 years. I didn't want to go, but of course I had to. Keepering wasn't a very well paid job, you'd have struggled to afford to buy a house, and the new boss took over, the son, and a letter came round to say that anyone who was over 40, which Dad just about was by then, wouldn't get a house on retirement. So he decided that he'd go for a job somewhere else that had a house on retirement. Because keepering, you tend to be a personal servant, so they always used to look after you in retirement, and that was how life was expected. But of course things change and these big estates have got to support themselves, so when that letter come round he thought he'd find a job where there was a house on retirement, so we moved to Dorset.

We moved in February '74, to Melbury Park near Evershot which is a 5,000-acre estate, and Dad took on head keeper's job there, and I went to school at St Aldhelm's, which is now the Griffin here in Sherborne, which I hated. I can remember we had a parent teachers' evening, and I remember the English teacher said to Dad "What can your daughter do?" And Dad said "Well, she can skin a deer." I left in '76 when I was 15, and that was when an under-keeper's job was available at Melbury. I applied and was lucky enough to get it. But I'd have struggled if Dad wasn't working there because women in the keepering line were very few and far between.

Just me and Dad. A real family affair. When we were there it was still very much a private shoot. There was a syndicate but that was the boss's friends and so it was still a very small shoot compared to a lot of places. We used to put down three and a half to four thousand birds, and that didn't alter very much over the years really.

There was a lot more deer because it had its own deer park, and then you had the wild deer outside, roe, sika and fallow, so it was heaven for a youngster who loved wildlife. We had to help out with the deer, but eventually they got a full-time stalker. We had to do a bit of the culling to keep them in sensible numbers.

There was probably more poaching of pheasants in the Pentillie days than there was in the Dorset days because pheasants were worth more in them days. And there wasn't the deer down there to poach, whereas on the game side, now there's more stealing. People will steal poults and you tend to get more deer poaching. It's mostly dogs, but occasionally a bit of shooting. We had a bit of trout poaching as well in the lakes. The dogs are usually cross-breds, lurcher types. We caught one lot from south Wales who went right round the South West. It's very difficult, no matter how well you know your ground, it's at night that the poaching's done on deer, they have a light and a dog, and if you look down the valley, they only flash the light every now and again, so you can be half or three-quarters of a mile away, and you've got to get from here to them, and you've got to know which way they're going, and you can be in a field you know really well and you can get so disorientated, it's unbelievable. But also, all they need to do if they know you're after them is sit down quiet and you can walk right by 'em and not find 'em. It's not easy to catch them. You need a lot of luck on your side.

We've had the Dorset police out with the dog handlers on several occasions, and the trouble is if you catch them on the road without any evidence, it won't go to court, so it's nearly always on their side. But we have caught them. Your worst poacher is a local person, because they can flip off quick and they know your routine, and they can do it 24 hours a day. I always had an Alsatian with me and I think you do need something with you at four o'clock in the morning, especially if you're female. And this particular morning, about four o'clock it was, I was stopped in this lay-by surveying the valley, on the main road and this red Landrover stopped opposite me, and at the time, this red Landrover that had been reported, mainly around Wimborne and all round there, poaching. And I thought 'Oh yeah.' As it stopped the Alsatian got up, they saw the movement and took off. So I chased them and 'course it takes a lot to build up speed in a Landrover, so I caught up and took their number, just to report to the police. The police phoned me the next day and said "Ere, Dawn, what did you do to that

Landrover?" I said 'I didn't do anything, I only chased it to get the number.' And they said "Well after you chased it, it went straight to Yeovil police station and gave itself up, it's actually a stolen fire brigade Landrover from Shaftesbury," they actually gave themselves up.

We had several lakes, and we had a lovely lake that had wild brown trout in, and as I was driving by after doing the birds at about nine thirty on an autumn evening, I just saw movement on the landing stage where the steps go down and I thought there was somebody there, so I walked up. They were hiding in a bramble bush so I pulled them out, really mad, I was, I pulled them out this bramble bush and said 'I'm going to search you,' and they said "No you're not," and they'd hid this fishing equipment, and I couldn't hold them 'cause it was only me and these two men. I pulled them out by the scruff of their necks, and I said I'd meet them by their car, so I met them by their vehicle and they threatened that next time they'd come, they'd kill the dogs. Anyway I took their number and went back down, found all their fishing equipment and the fish, and I told the police and they come and collected it all, took them in for questioning, and they said "God, Dawn, you didn't half frighten them!"

Before mobile phones we had CB radios, I was Calamity Jane. Poor Mum was the home base, so if we were on poacher duty she heard every little crackle, and she never used to get any sleep, poor woman. Dogs. Yes, we had Springer Spaniels, Labradors and Golden Retrievers. Springers are very multi-purpose. They have to be if they're a keeper's dog. They've got to be able to do anything, because when the birds wander in the autumn and you have to drive them back, the dogs have got to be able to chase the birds but not catch them. On a shooting day, they aren't allowed to chase them and they're only allowed to pick up wounded birds, so when they're working through the undergrowth they aren't meant to pick them up at all. They're allowed to flush them. So a keeper's dog has to be dual-purpose.

Modern springers today they tend to go for the field trial type, which is quite a fast dog that will work quite quickly, quite biddable. Now if you're a keeper and you're running a beating line on a shoot day you don't really want too fast a dog because a fast dog will cover quite a big area in quite a small amount of time, and I used to have the big old-fashioned springer, I wanted a slower, ploddier dog, and I used to work three in the line. If you've got a slow ploddy dog and you're talking to the beaters on your left and your right, a slow ploddy dog will only go a few feet, whereas a fast spaniel will whoosh, be gone before you've even realised you can check him back. So my preference was always for the big old fashioned, slow, chunky Springer Spaniel, They had stamina, used to work several days a week and they were good.

Dad retired in '93. I took over then, I was single-handed. I did all the rearing and hatching. The only reason I left, we had change of management and I knew things weren't going to be the same. They couldn't sack me 'cause I did me job, but they made it very difficult. Also if you've built up a good reputation, a good reputation can be lost so easily, and not easily regained. I had a house there, Dad still had a house on retirement, even though we had to move from where we were. But as his health was deteriorating we decided Evershot would be better because Mum wouldn't be isolated there. Though as soon as Dad died she had to pay rent. At least she's got a house and she's happy in the village.

My eldest brother, Harry, he keepers Wrackleford shoot at Grimstone, the Oliver Pope shoot, where our shoot is now at Sydling St Nicholas, his shoot is a field away. And he drives his boundary like hell to keep his birds from coming up to ours, even though I actually supplied them anyway, 'cause they're the ones that I did here. There's nothing like a family feud, is there? No, we get on very well. We have put rings on pheasants up until this year, because all our neighbouring shoots, being friendly like they are, they ring me up and say 'I just shot one of yours, Dawn,' it's lovely, we decided this year we wouldn't bother.

I was at Melbury 18 years full-time, then I left and went self-employed. I took on a part-time keeper's job and I did taxidermy. I had bought a book and taught myself. That was about '82 so for about 12 years I was doing taxidermy on winter weekends or winter evenings as a hobby. So when I did give up keepering I had something I could do, as well as the portrait drawings, 'cause I've drawn all me life, drawn several beaters' dogs. I like photography, so I didn't give up keepering without a bit of thought. I ended at Melbury April '94.

I'd love to get into sculpturing but I haven't had a chance to do it all. But there's lots of work with the portrait drawings and the taxidermy. I use coloured charcoal pastels, so what I do when I go to shows, I do a display of taxidermy, drawings and photographs. I draw while I'm there so people see me doing the work, and then they commission me. Christmas is quite hectic for me, 'cause we do a few geese at Christmas as well,

Keepering can be such a lonely life if you're out there almost 24 hours a day with your dogs, they're your friends at the end of the day, but I love that life. I still rear pheasants and we still run our own shoot. I've got five dogs, an alsatian, a springer and a sprocker, which is a springer-cross-cocker and me other half's got the other two springers. Whatever I'm doing, they're doing, rearing, fieldwork or skinning something. They have a good life really, 'cause if I'm drawing and it's a fine day, I'm out under the plum tree, so they sit by the side of me in the shade, me with a glass of water and me portrait and them just soaking up the rays, so it's quite a good life really.

26. Claire Fowler – Taxidermist and horsewoman, West Bexington. Born 1974.

Taxidermy…I'd always been fascinated by it from when I was a child. I remember dissecting mice and birds that the cat would kill…call me gruesome, but I'm just a bit curious.

I was born in Taunton, most of my childhood was spent in South Chard. My father is a lorry driver for Axminster Carpets has been for at least 25 years and my mother's a part-time carer. My father was born in Chardstock. My mum's mum used to run pubs in Taunton, the one I remember was the Winchester Arms. I went to school in Chard, Holyrood School, I couldn't wait to leave. I had weekend jobs. Dad insisted that my sister and I get out and work so we had weekend jobs collecting eggs at the chicken farm, picking tomatoes and things like that. There was a fruit farm in Chilson Common.

My love was horses, that was it, nothing but horses. My parents would never let me have my own horse, Dad said it was a five-minute wonder and it'd never last, and here I am, years on, still with horses. The first job was down in Devon, near Tiverton, and then I worked in the Lorna Doone Valley, which I really enjoyed. I worked down the trekking centre one summer. I loved it, great people. That was children and adults, take them up on the moors. It was very interesting when the mist come down, 'cause you'd know the route off by heart, but when the mist was down, it was amazing. You'd think you know where you're going but it's surprising how far you can drift out on some rides, and people were thinking "Where are we going?" I didn't want to alert them that their leader was lost!

I was keen on jumping and really enjoyed my hunting with the Cotley hunt, and then I moved on. I was in Andover for a while and I took on a lot of hunting up there. I became whipper-in to a pack of bloodhounds. That was quite exciting and felt quite a privilege. I'd do the kennel work as well with the bloodhounds, they're nothing like foxhounds, they're very stubborn, independent, they don't work too well as a pack, they like to do their own thing. It's quite difficult to keep them up together but it was fun. There's just folds of skin going everywhere, they're baying, making a hell of a racket. Lovely noise really when you hear them crying, totally different to foxhounds. Lovely characters. I'm not keen for getting up close with all the slobber. All the dog shit has to be dealt with. Oh yeah, all the pleasant jobs! They were fed on dry food. At the time there was about 15 couple, so about 30 hounds that they had.

Then exercising the hunt horses. I had my own by then and she was part of the team. I was in Andover for about 12 years, then I came down to Dorset in about 2000. Took up another horsey job in Portesham, I spent six months there, I'm a bit of a nomad I think. Then I became aware of another yard who were looking for someone just to cover weekends with their horses, so I took that on.

I would just come here at weekends, do the horses, and then I moved in here. It was meant to be for eight weeks and this was four years ago. Still doing the weekend work, and I was flying by the seat of my pants financially because I had no other work and I just took the opportunity and got on with doing more taxidermy.

Taxidermy started in 2001. I'd always been fascinated by it from when I was a child. I remember dissecting mice and birds that the cat would kill, or things you'd find dead on the road, and I'd bring them home and dissect them, or try and stuff them with

Claire Fowler with the 'one that didn't get away,' West Bexington

cotton wool in the greenhouse of all places where it was baking hot. I wouldn't treat the skins. I'd just take everything out and stuff it with cotton wool and of course the thing would deteriorate within a few days, it was disgusting. I used to love burying things and digging them up weeks later, just fascinated by the bones and just to see what happens. Call me gruesome, but I'm just a bit curious. I did enjoy biology at school. I used to like to sit at the back of the class next to the fish tanks. I was more amused by the guppies swimming around than anything else.

Taxidermy is a Greek term meaning movement of skin. Well it's not 100 per cent correct, but *taxis* is Greek for movement, and *dermis* is Greek for skin, so you are kind of moving skin. From a taxidermist's point of view you're doing it to make it look alive again, to recreate that animal as if it was living. It's a never-ending strive to get that result, you're always thinking 'The next one I do will be better than that.'

It was just early childhood messing about, and then there was nothing until I put an advert in the local yellow paper asking for anything on taxidermy, items for sale, books, videos, anything to do with it, and I had one phone call. I was still living in Andover at the time and I had a phone call from Devon and he said he had some books, and I said 'I'm interested.' So I made a visit to pick up these books, it turned out he was a taxidermist, semi-retired, and he could see my enthusiasm and desire. He was kind enough to show me the ropes. So I arranged another visit, it was quite a long trek from Andover to Buckfastleigh, but I made a date and I went back down and I sat and watched him as he mounted a squirrel. I just watched and went back home. My first attempt was a stoat. It may not have been the prettiest but it was successful.

Road casualties. Obviously to begin with it was what I could find. Now I'm flooded with dead animals! Once the word gets about that's it. Well I then made another visit a few weeks later and watched him do a kestrel, because they're very different, dealing with fur and feathers. Instead of being sensible and doing a crow or a jackdaw, I thought 'I'm going to do a tawny owl,' and again, it was successful, I did it.

Self-taught. You could say that, I never had anybody looking over my shoulder. He was there on the phone and I said 'I had trouble doing this, why did that happen?' And he would try and explain. You can do a course in taxidermy if you've got £500 to spend. I don't think I was in a position to afford it. So I was doing it in my spare time. Although absolutely skint, I used the time to knuckle down and do as many as I could, because the more I practised the better I got.

People will ring me up and say "I've picked up an owl off the road today, I've put it in the freezer, is that ok?" Or they ask if they should put it in the freezer, and I say 'Wrap it up in an airtight bag, put it in the freezer and then you're safe. Take your time, decide where you want to get it done.' Put it in a plastic bag, squeeze all the air out, smooth the feathers down, keep the animal nice and compact, fold wings and legs in. Don't try to dissect it. So when I am ready I'll take it out of the freezer, thaw it out overnight, then the following day I'll sit down in the workshop, start to skin it, make a breast incision, all the way down, slowly start to skin it, wash the skin, blow dry the feathers, clean the bones and the skull. So I'll wash the skins and then I'll take the carcass to one side, I'll then make my own artificial body up. I'll use the real one to refer to and start working on the head. I'll insert the eyes, they're glass eyes, you can get acrylic but they tend to have a dull look about them. You can get any eye in the world.

Bird skin is like tissue paper, it's so thin, I apply a powder which is borax based. It's a powder. If you can imagine, at one point a bird will have its wings inside out, head and neck inside out, it's legs pulled out so it's completely inverted. Because I apply the powder I then carry on, model and set up the bird. Then you position the bird, get the pose and then you're setting it. And once you've got it set you leave it, you just let the natural drying occur in that position. The powder will just naturally work into the skin, cure the skin and dry it out.

Once I've mounted the bird and I'm happy that the artificial body which is made of fibrewool but it's a traditional method of binding up. I won't use it for large mammals because it's a little bit on the soft side, but it does work for birds, making bird bodies up.

People have brought me a lot of native birds, the most common are the owls, tawnies and barn owls. They're always road casualties. If I've any suspicion of them being illegally acquired I don't want to know. Then there's game birds, a lot of people will bring in the first pheasant they've shot, or the first duck their dog picked up of the season, it means a lot to them. The very rare birds don't seem to come in. I wouldn't look forward to a swan, too big and really greasy if ducks are anything to go by. God I think that would be hard work!

Dust is the worst enemy for feathers, but they don't lose their colour unless they've been subjected to sunlight. Any fleshy parts on animals will lose their colour. On the beak and around the eyes, that'll go grey, and the legs, so that will all be painted up by hand. Until they've dried, which is about another two or three weeks, because when they're setting they're so fragile and wobbly, and then when they set they become stiff and rigid. From the specimen point of view they are best in a glass dome. You have to make up a bit of diorama. I try to use as much natural stuff as possible. I'd say 60 per cent of my work is birds.

Because of their size, people have got room for them.

Deer skins are totally different. I will actually pickle and tan the skins. A massive stag, that takes somebody with a big home to accommodate one of those. I've done a couple of huge red stags. I've not done a whole deer 'cause the workshop, is tiny. I don't have space to do a whole deer. Muntjac or a Chinese water deer maybe, but not a big stag, so they're shoulder mounts. A lot of the time they tend not to bring me the cape, which is the skin, because they're just interested in the trophy which is the antlers on the animal, and then they just get the skull cleaned, and they'll have their trophy.

I know a couple of chaps who do deer management, and I know I can get a small supply of capes. I have to wait for things to come my way, they can't shoot an animal for my purposes. I wait for the season. Usually I will go up to the larder and skin the animals myself. When they're managing park deer there are culls that need to take place, and I'm a bit of a magpie on the side picking up the scraps if you like, meaning the capes.

It's mainly what they've shot within Dorset or the neighbouring counties. The latest thing I've got to do is a Pere David deer, which is an incredibly rare breed. They're a park deer in the UK, but they were hunted to extinction in China, where they originate from. They were brought over here about a century ago. Pere David are as big, if not bigger than red stags. They're bizarre looking animals.

To cure a red deer skin I like to salt them overnight, I will then pare out the flesh, which is when I'm splitting the eyes, the nose, the ears, I'll turn the ears inside out, and any really heavy fleshy parts I'll remove off the skin, and then I'll put in a pickle, it's made up of water, salt and a bit of formic acid. I'll pickle a skin and then tan it. A thick skin will take about a week. After a couple of days I will go in and shave the skin down, because when it's so thick, like on sika deer, the pickle cannot always penetrate that thickness. There's not a huge amount of fat on deer, not compared to on a pet animal, which I have done, it's more like gristle, it's incredibly hard. Their necks can be a good two and a half inches thick, and I've got to get it down to about five millimetres or less! You have to get it so thin, so there's a lot of shaving to do, which I do on a beam with a fleshing knife, that's very old-fashioned. It's got a curve, it's probably about two foot long, blade on both sides, I use the inside curve and I just put the flesh on the beam and just shave it away. Women have probably been doing this for thousands of years.

They must have had to shave the skins down to wear them, even in the ice age. You couldn't do anything with skin that thick because once it goes hard it's absolutely rigid. The thinnest you can go is as soon as you can see the hair follicles through the skin. When it's tanned, it's white, and when you're shaving the skin it'll change colour. The closer you go to the hair follicles, it goes a pale blue, or like a grey colour. If you start cutting the hair follicles from the flesh side you'll lose the hair. They'll start falling out.

With deer, stags and bucks, it's best to get them when they're rutting, the rutting season for roe bucks is in the summer, and unfortunately towards the end of the rut you don't get such nice capes, because where they've been scrapping so much their coats are pretty rough. When sika are in rut, which is October, their necks swell up and they're like bulls. That's the time to get them because again that's when the hunting season is.

I once had a chap who brought a pine marten down from Scotland, it was the smallest pine marten I've ever seen. It must have been a youngster, it was so tiny. I've mounted an albino badger, I had a phone call one morning, running up to Christmas in 2004 and a chap said "I've just come back from Dorchester,"

this was Dorchester to Bridport, the A35, he said "I think it's an albino badger I've just seen on the road." I said 'When was that?' "Just now." I said 'Was it there yesterday?' "No." I said 'right, I'm getting in the Landrover now.' So I jumped in the Landrover and I flew up onto the road where he said it was, and the roads were busy with Christmas shoppers and I thought 'It won't be there,' but I couldn't believe my luck, I saw the badger on the side of the road and the first thing I looked at was its eyes, pink eyes, and it had this creamy biscuit coloured coat and ginger stripes and he had a pink nose, definitely an albino. I was so excited, so I wrapped him up in a blanket, people must have thought "What is she doing on the road?" I tried not to look at the traffic, scooped it up and took it on. She was in perfect condition, she had black tyre rubber marks or soot marks, probably from being under the vehicle, but she was there for everyone to see and I couldn't believe nobody picked her up before me.

Fish and reptiles don't do it for me. I have been brought a leopard to do, which they wanted into a rug, but a rug really isn't my speciality, so I had to turn that away. I've done springbok and gehmsboks and bushbucks, I've done a few African things. I've done a Caracal cat, lovely cat that was. The Beast of Bodmin that would be great!

Otters we can't touch. Even now you, as the finder of a road casualty, if you were to take it home and put it in your freezer you are illegally possessing an otter which is kind of sad because it's a road casualty and it's a shame it can't be preserved. The last otter I mounted which was the one and only otter, I had to prove that it was acquired before 1994 which was very difficult and there were endless letters to and fro from Defra, I deal with the Bristol office. They know I'm a taxidermist, because I have to submit and apply for licences for birds of prey that I want to sell, but the commission side of it is really taking off.

Once you've mounted a variety of birds, you naturally know their poses. How a duck would stand is different to how a partridge would stand. Their anatomy's different. You have to take note of their posture, 'cause I'm naturally artistic, the flair of it all coming together, it just happens. It isn't hard work. There still is a degree of eye and skill and putting the two together. I remember doing a kestrel once, he was just another road casualty, but what I found was that inside he had wing bones that had broken and had healed. They'd crossed over and stitched together again, and a broken leg that had fused itself together, and it's amazing how some survive such injuries. I've never had a Dorset raven come in. I had a Devon one come in. Some friends picked it up, they thought it was dead but it was sort of dying in front of them, it was being mobbed by other birds and because his body was such a mess I only managed to do a head mount of this raven. The beak was a good five inches. They're massive.

I get lots of foxes. They're another favourite along with the owls. If someone just wants a fox I'll make sure I supply them with a lovely fox. Some people are quite happy to accept that their trophy isn't perfect, that's fine because that's the animal they acquired and that's all that matters to them. I've done hares, and I've got slots of deer or boar, sometimes it's just the foot of the animal and I set that up on the shield and I'll apply a little plaque with the date and the place.

I've done one pet, I've done a collie-cross spaniel. I wasn't sure how I was going to feel. I guess I had a bit of a build up to it because the bloke had said a good year before the dog was even dead that he was enquiring, for when the time comes, and 'course it goes quiet and then you get this phone call "We're going to have him put down at the weekend, can we bring him straight to you?" And I'm thinking 'Oh my God, they're going to do it,' and

I'm like 'Ok,' so I made sure I had space in the freezer, 'cause it's quite a big dog, and then 'course the day arrives and I'm thinking 'They won't come here. Soon as he's put down, they won't come here,' and then I couldn't believe it, they were coming down the drive 'Oh my God, they're bringing it here.' They took him straight from the vet's to me, and I was more concerned about how to deal with the people, because I didn't know what state they were going to be in, I weren't worried about the dog so much. He seemed fine and they left the dog here and he was in his cardboard coffin, and I thought 'Poor little thing,' anyway, they'd gone on and the dog was still warm, it was a cool evening and I had to cool him down before he went in the freezer, so I took him out of his box and put him outside on the cold slabs outside my door and every time a car was coming down I was running outside, put the dog back in the cardboard box, 'cause they'd have a fit, anyone who saw a dead dog on my doorstep, so he was in and out of this box until he was cool and then he went in the freezer. But when it came to skinning him I didn't know how I'd feel, but it didn't bother me at all. It was no different to doing a fox. I felt nothing emotional.

Well I have my rule on pets, I will only do them lying down and I'll do them asleep. I don't agree with having them sat up or moving up or eyes open, any silly poses, on their hind legs, anything like that. 'The dog's sleeping in its basket,' and if you walk by and he's looking at you, it's eerie. Its soul's gone, and I think the most pleasant thing is to have it lying down asleep, so they had no choice about that. But they were happy. It was unknown territory for me, how to deal with the people.

Funnily enough I still do the horses. But I'm lucky to be flexible with the hours. It's pretty good, though you get the odd day when it doesn't quite work out, but on the whole it's fine. But because my taxidermy work is increasing, something's going to have to give one day, space is an issue for a start. So for now it's a tad cramped in here.

In the first few years I did the Axminster flower festival, I've stuck with the West Country Game Fair for the past few years, that's in Shepton Mallet, I don't travel further afield, I am in Yellow Pages, and I have the website, but I don't advertise in magazines. I answer sporting questions for Shooting Times magazine, so that's quite nice. I'm finally earning my bread and butter!

27. Jane Carmichael – Horse dentist, Waytown, Bridport. Born 1964.

I do tend to do the practical things…I was on holiday once and got all my messages forwarded through to my mother-in-law and a chap in Axminster with toothache phoned up and said 'I'm in desperate agony, please can you help, I know you're a horse dentist but…!'

I was born in Havant in Hampshire. My father was a pottery teacher at Monkton Wyld. We lived in Wootton Fitzpaine, that's the earliest memory, in a fantastic cottage right in front of the forest on the top of the hill, Charmouth Forest. You had to drive through a farmyard to get to our cottage, it was in the middle of nowhere up a track. It was beautiful. I have fond memories of that place. It was called Spence Cottage.

My two older sisters both went to school in Wootton, I went there for a few months, just before it closed down. My parents split up when I was about five. My father went to London and became a pharmacist. My mother stayed down here and was an art teacher. I went to Chard school. Funny place! Every weekend I escaped to the countryside, I used to get on my bike and cycle to friends who lived in Hawkchurch, and I used to stay there virtually every weekend. That's where the horse connection came in. Westhay House in Dorset. That's where my interest grew. I didn't have a horse of my own until I was 13.

Earliest job, I was in the sixth form at school waitressing in a pub, and I was there on a weekend and we had a very heavy snowfall and I couldn't actually get home so I thought I'd just stay there. I didn't ever leave! That was my first job, so they gave me accommodation at the pub. This was at the Greyhound in

Staple Fitzpaine. I was odd jobbing for many years. I started a stencil business, so I was doing more traditional stencils rather than little flowery things on the walls, I did big ceilings in Victorian houses, got into paint finishes and lime washing, that was the fashionable thing at the time. My husband worked at St Blaise. And then I had my daughter, I was 22 when she was born, and she was born at West Bexington on the organic farm. We were living down there, so that we could have a home birth. We were working on the Pearse's farm, we did a few hours a week in return for a cottage down by the sea. We weren't full time because Angus, my husband, was a carpenter, timber framer, and it was just a fantastic place to live, and great people to live with.

Horses. Well I would always be riding other people's. When we left the Pearses and moved to Netherbury, I brought one of their horses with me, as a loan, and I've always kept up riding, it was a passion of mine so I'd borrow other people's. They were delighted to let me exercise them. Especially when they're youngsters that need bringing on a bit. Then my husband and I decided to get into driving horses. So we bought our first horse together, and I was keen on the riding and he was keen on the driving so finding a horse that fitted both of those interests was quite difficult and he won! He got the heavier cob which wasn't so much fun to ride but you put her behind a cart and she'd trot for miles and miles. We didn't have the money to have two.

We had friends in Symondsbury and we used to go on big pony treks together with them driving their carts, we could just scramble over the fields, usually end up at Shave Cross for a pub lunch, and then drive home again. We had a flat bed cart with artillery wheels, it wasn't a lightweight racing cart. It was good. Our horse wasn't well behaved enough for weddings really. We used to do cart rides for the village fete, you'd strap people on the

Jane Carmichael with Fedora 'Open Wide'

back and keep your fingers crossed that they weren't going to be taken off around the field!

We then lived in a marquee for a year, we wintered in there with a stove and we lined it with rugs. We had a massive plastic sheet on the floor and carpets and a bed that was raised off the floor, our daughter was living there, she was a year and a half, and our friends used to come round and visit us in the evening and think it was freezing, but we had got used to it. We had a wood burning stove in there and it was fantastic, you'd be asleep at night and you could hear everything that was going on outside, the weather and the animals, it was superb. And in the summer it was blissful. You could open out the sides of the marquee and actually be living outside. And then we built a one-room house and stayed there up until my daughter went to school, and then we thought 'Right, we'd better be sensible now,' and we rented a house down at Slape Manor. A little tied cottage, again we were working for the rent.

I did waitressing and my husband did odd jobbing. It was only for very few hours a week, he was working at St Blaise at the time. I was basically a mum, but I did carpentry as well. I made a lot of these chairs, and we made a whole set, all out of green oak, so no glue at all. My stepfather's a basket maker and so he showed me how to do the seats out of willow. We ended up making 150 of them for the National Trust. They went down to the restaurant down in Castle Drogo.

It's a very simple one ladder back for a back rest, and you're following the grain of the wood so they're not totally symmetrical, the legs and the rungs, and there's no glue involved because it's wet wood, so the wood shrinks onto the rungs. You use a draw horse to make the legs, with a draw knife. You're going with the grain all the time, they just stay together. I do tend to do the practical things.

Yes. Netherbury, we've definitely fitted into village life and got to know the locals, it's where we wanted to stay. This cottage, a friend of ours, her grandfather owned it, he moved to Bridport because he was elderly, and it had been empty for maybe ten years. She stayed in it for a while but it was terribly run down, the granddaughter, it didn't have access to it, the farmer and the neighbours made out that there never had been access to the cottage so we managed to buy it relatively cheaply and we had to walk up and down the fields for five years from the pub, so all the shopping and everything came up in a wheelbarrow. We had water, we were lucky and had a council grant to do it up, so we replaced the roof, rewired it, damp proofing. And then we got it to a certain point and it works now, but it's still not completely finished. We disputed the access. The chap who used to live here had a lorry and delivered vegetables around the local area and his van was still in the garden, so we knew there was access, and he had photos of the track as it used to be 20 years ago with his car parked down here. So it was a five-year battle with the chap who used to own the farm, who's now moved, until we won. The chap who used to live here had ducks and chickens and I guess he grew vegetables as well but there was more of an orchard out there originally. His name was John Garrett and he's got a daughter who lives in Bridport and a son who lives in Salwayash, his wife used to be the secretary at the village school.

No land for horses, no. I haven't got horses any more. As soon as the business kicked in I didn't have time. When my son, Oscar went to school, I thought I would be a bit selfish and have some playtime, because I had been a fairly full-time mum, so I went to work for a woman called Jabina Maslin who works on the other side of the Beaminster tunnel. She has a big show jumping yard down there, and I worked for her for about three years, doing a lot of mucking out, exercising all her horses. She's schooling other people's horses and also using her own for show jumping on the weekends. So I worked for her part time for a couple of years and then full-time for a year, it was great fun, we had a fantastic time. I used to cycle up to work because I enjoyed the cycling as well, and then whiz back down the hill, which is the right way round at the end of the day. It was exhausting up there, we did work very hard, but I loved every minute of it, it was great, we got paid peanuts, but it was for the fun of the work rather than the money.

I had my own horse up there and she was a great at jumping but she was always a little bit sharp, especially on one rein. A dentist came to do all the horses at Jabina's, and I'd only thought of dentistry as being for older horses, this was about seven years ago, and I didn't really think of it being necessary for the younger horses. My mare was about six or seven but as all the other horses were being done I thought I'd get mine done as well. I was interested in what he was doing and I wanted to understand it.

From the outside each horse was having exactly the same treatment. I just saw him getting on with the work, very physical, fast work, but I wanted to feel inside my horse's mouth so he put a big speculum on, it's a gag that goes on the mouth, the front incisors rest on these plates, therefore you can open it up with little ratchets at the sides of the mouth so you can get your hands inside the mouth and feel the teeth, and the teeth go right back to the eye of the horse so your arm's in up to your elbow. I had the worry that this contraption wasn't going to hold the mouth open, so I felt inside the horse's mouth, and I ran my fingers too quickly along the edges of the teeth on the outside and came out with my fingers all cut, because they have very sharp little enamel points on the outside of their teeth. So if you do run your hand too quickly along them you cut your fingers.

They get ulcers on their cheeks and she had little ulcers where the points had been digging in.

It's the result of a number of things, through domestication we've changed the type of food they graze on, their chewing patterns, because if we give them different feed it changes their chewing pattern, they don't wear their teeth in the same way, also we're expecting to put a bit in their mouth and a bridle which puts pressure around the mouth, I think these points have become more aggressive through domestication, and we're expecting to add different contraptions onto their heads which naturally wouldn't be there, which complicates things further and causes sores in the mouth.

They chew their hard feed and hay in a different pattern and also the type of grass that they eat here is a lot softer, it doesn't have such high silica content which is sandy particles in the forage, and they chew much more up and down, they don't grind their feed in the same way. They chomp it up and down and that creates ridges on the surface of their teeth, and the points become more exaggerated which leads to ulcers and bruising where the bit goes and little cuts.

They have painful mouths. They can have. It's not in every case. Interbreeding complicates things, so a native Dartmoor pony might have a better mouth than an Arab crossed with a Thoroughbred where you've got a small head and a big head meshed into one. You may have big teeth in a small skull, so therefore the teeth get jiggled into not a very good position. Humans can have the same problem. But with a horse, when they're six, seven years old the roots of the teeth are as long as they're going to be so they come right down into the jaw, maybe 8cms long, then the root is getting shorter, so the tooth is erupting all the time and the surface of the tooth is getting worn down. So if there's any unopposed tooth in a horse's mouth, because the teeth aren't lining up, it'll form into a huge overgrowth because the teeth are erupting at maybe two or three millimetres a year, after six, seven, eight years the tooth is just getting longer and longer and longer because it's not getting worn down.

My horse had something called a wolf tooth, horses used to have an extra tooth. You've got the front teeth, the incisors, the back teeth, the molars, and in front of the first molar in the back of the mouth there used to be another tooth and horses sometimes get what we call a wolf tooth which is a very little tooth which is the remnant of the tooth that used to be there, that's evolved out, and my horse had one of these. She had that removed, and had all her teeth floated, we call it floating, when you file and shape them, and she was like a different horse to ride after that. Much more biddable, she always used to fight the reins a little bit, sometimes she'd be fine, sometimes she really wouldn't be fine, she would be evading the bit, and she really relaxed into it, she became much softer to ride and much more willing. Much happier.

It's incredibly important to have sharp tools, otherwise you will exhaust yourself incredibly quickly, so sharp tools means quicker work, which is more comfortable for the horse not having to stand there for hours on end, and it makes it possible to do more horses in a day. You've got to know where you are in the mouth because if you're hitting soft tissue the horse isn't going to stand there! Imagining where the tool is in the mouth is absolutely vital, you can use head torches, and I do use head torches, but it's all on feel, you can't be constantly looking where you are in the mouth. You can feel the shape of the jaw. The first thing I do is have a look in the mouth or just feel, if it's a horse that's five, six, seven years old, you're almost guaranteed that things are going to be pretty straightforward in the mouth. I will feel the horse's mouth first because a bright torch in the face isn't always a very easy way to start for them.

Half the skill is in calming the horse down. You've got to read the horse right from the beginning, how it's reacting to you, how it's going to be, because it is a dangerous business. The tone of voice is important. I think horse whispering is actually just understanding an animal. The owner you usually get to stand on the other side of the stable door because they can be more complicated than the horses! And if the horse is going to move it's safer just to have me in the stable because I'm at the head end and I can get the horse to move around me but if there's somebody else standing in there they're probably going to get walloped. I have a halter on the horse, which I just tuck the end into my belt in a loop so that if it pulls away I'm not tied to it in any way, it can go, but it's long enough so that if it does start moving I have time to grab it. But I'm not tied to it.

The dentist was Anthony Tory. He was from Blandford, he was an ex-jockey. I was fascinated by it. I started looking up information on the computer, I've been doing this for three years, I found a very good website with information that was thorough, it was a female equine dentist so I felt I could write.

She was in the north of England, and she was fantastic. Basically there's nowhere in this country that does a good training and she said the only place to go was America. She's actually a vet, but she did specialise, she went to America and worked with one of the best horse dentists in America. I asked if I could train with her, and she was actually on maternity leave because she'd just given birth, and said that I possibly could the following year, but by that time I was ready to go and I wanted to train so I booked into one of the schools in America and trained there. It wasn't very cheap but it was something I wanted to do and it suited. It's a three-month course.

I came back fully confident, but it's a different thing putting yourself out there, and people phoning you, wanting your business, I always want to give the best that I can achieve and I'm a bit of a perfectionist on that score. If I do a job I want to do it well. I don't like to do a half-hearted job.

There are different times when you need to sedate a horse. I try to work with a horse as much as I can, I don't try to restrict them in any way, I try to get them to have confidence with me, so I'll be talking to them, trying to get them to calm down, there are different areas in their mouth that are more sensitive than others so I'll start off maybe with the speculum off and just access the outside teeth, so as unobtrusive as possible. You can see it in their eyes and their ears, the way they're standing, the way they're breathing, whether it's a horse that you're needing to calm down, whether it's a horse that's not particularly bothered, they give you an awful lot of signs as to how they're feeling, and you know when you can go onto another step when you can ask a bit more of them because you can read how they're feeling about it.

The speculum's the main thing, which means you can get into the back of the mouth. I've got a range of hand tools which have got very sharp tungsten carbide blades in them and they come in all different shapes and sizes to get to all the teeth, you've got something called a molar roller which rounds off the teeth and accommodates the bit, you've got different grades of blade to take off a greater or lesser amount of tooth, and for finishing the tooth you have to use a finer blade. They have to be sent off to be sharpened and it's bloody expensive. I tend to send them back to America because I can send them in bulk and at the moment the exchange rate's pretty good. That's where I buy my blades.

It can be a dangerous occupation. It's the horses and how they react. About three-quarters of an hour to do each horse, roughly. If you're taking out a tooth it might take an awful lot longer.

Because it's a very physical job I often get comments, "You're not a big hairy milk maid type woman," because I am small, but it's more mind over matter. It is a very physical job and I do get tired and sometimes my arm will get stressed or my shoulder or my back, but I've spoken to men who do the same job and they have the same problems. I have a physio I go and see, I strap my arm up…I would never do more than eight in a day. When they're younger their teeth are softer and you can do a faster job. If it's a horse I've done the previous year then I'm not having to establish a whole new mouth.

Horses' teeth change shape. As the root is erupting from the jaw, it's got different marks within the structure of the tooth, I'm talking about the incisors here. On the surface of the tooth they have different patterns throughout different ages of their life, so you can read the patterns. It's a bit like tree rings. They also get a groove on the corner incisor which appears when they're ten, and as they get older it moves down the tooth until they're in their 20s and it's grown out. The angle of their front teeth changes, it becomes sharper as they get older. The shape of their teeth is much rounder when they're younger, and they become more pointy and they get gaps in their teeth as they get older.

I was on holiday once and got all my messages forwarded through to my mother-in-law and a chap in Axminster with toothache phoned up and said "I'm in desperate agony, please can you help, I know you're a horse dentist but…!"

28. Rosie Young – Biba twin, typographer & second-hand bookseller, Bridport. Born 1946.

We were fairly naughty at art school too, so we didn't stay…Biba was the first boutique…We were at Biba wearing very short skirts, and that's what they wanted. We were known as the Biba Twins. We were in the Bridport News…

I was born in Burnham-on-Sea, my family were living in a little village called Edington Burtle in a farmhouse called Pines. My grandfather had bought it and my parents were living there. He had a tea plantation in India and retired to Somerset. It was the '30s in the crash, he lost a lot of money. He wanted to be a gentleman farmer and then he'd go around poking things, wearing his farming outfit, braces, looking like a farmer. Funnily enough, when I go to the Somerset Levels, it seems like home in a funny way. It is a backwater, it's rural, it's unchanged. Lovely, low land, lots of sky and it's different. It does seem more forgotten. Curiously enough my father's parents were also in India, but at the different end of the social scale, they were missionaries.

My grandfather was in southern India. He was a very handsome man. My mother's family were in Darjeeling and were called Peacock. My father's family were Young. That's my name now, I never married. They were missionaries. When they returned to England they were living in Chilton Polden, quite near to Edington, so that's how my father met my mother.

During the war he was in the Royal Navy and talked about torpedoing the enemy. He taught for a while before going to London to work for De La Rue, also in tea. That's what he'd done in Java before the war. He was in shipping tea and was also a tea blender. During my childhood he was always on the floor with a newspaper with lots of different tea, piles of tea, mixing them together. Great fun. Yes, he was a sweet man my father. So curiously enough both sides of the family were involved in tea. Then we were born, my brother is only 17 months older than us, I'm a twin, so there were three of us quite little. An Irish writer who also lived in Chilton Polden, had a daughter, who then became our nanny, she's still with us and she sits with me in here, in Bridport, Libby.

I remember my grandparents' house, because they moved to Thorncombe, bought a farm there, Herridge Farm and we often stayed there when my parents were busy with the hotel. Mother's brother, took it over and now his son has it. This side of Forde Abbey, past the turning to Holditch, where my Uncle John used to farm, beautiful place, old with that tower.

My grandparents moved to Dorset first and we moved there in 1948. We were in London, my mother was unhappy because being a country girl she didn't like living in Harrow. And my grandfather who was a bit of a mover and shaker rang them one day and said "I've found a little tea room that Philip" my father "could come and run" so they came down to look at it and it was actually a 13-bedroom hotel in Charmouth, seven acres, house, outbuildings, orchard etc…

A man called Squance had turned it into quite a smart hotel. The house had originally been built for Gertrude Evans, quite unusual architecturally, a Danish architect, it was right by the sea, we had a triangular field and a garden with vegetables, it was lovely, tennis courts, big lawns, croquet…and my mother looked out and she thought "This is where I want to bring up the children, better than smoggy old Harrow." My grandfather bought it and so my father spent a long time paying him back. They ran it as a rather Fawlty Towers type family hotel. People

Rosie Young, cover to cover, Bridport Old Bookshop

in those days had family holidays. People would come for two weeks at a time, families, the Rice-Oxleys, Seymours, Bridgers, Bomfords. I know all their names. They would book in for next year when they left. And we'd look forward to the children coming to play.

Libby was the maître d'. She stopped being the nanny and was in charge of the guests, very bossy. They loved her. It was odd, we had no reception area, guests just came in and went up to their room. I remember the Bomfords with Zuky the dalmatian dog. Brigadier Bomford, he snored very loudly. And kept everyone awake. We loved it, loved the guests because we had such fun, and one year I remember my brother said "I'm going to be a ghost." So we told the whole hotel that the house was haunted and the ghost would appear at seven on the lavender lawn, we had all these different lawns, the lavender lawn, I remember all the guests coming out and while they were watching my brother in a sheet, completely see-throughable, my sister Susy and I went up and made all the beds into apple pies! This was a hotel! And when the guests brought their children and they brought toys we used to hide the toys so they'd forget them.

This was the early '50s when people only took holidays in England. They played tennis and they had the sea, it was idyllic. There was Lyme next door, Golden Cap and Portland. We used to go mackerel fishing, and there was Jake the fisherman. Every week we'd have fresh salmon and lobsters brought up to the door by Jake, he fished from the village. Salmon was always on the menu, lovely sea salmon and you know, halibut. We were happy.

We went to a private school in the village run by these three Victorian sisters, it was a real dame's school. My father used to push the three of us and a friend on his bike to the little school up Lower Sea Lane. We went at four, till ten. Six years. It was very

old-fashioned, a wonderful school. We weren't taught to a formal curriculum, we didn't know anything about fractions, decimals, we just did 'sums', English, composition and grammar, French and Latin, and performed plays. So I was very good at writing but we couldn't do arithmetic, so therefore we failed the 11 Plus. So we went to Leweston Manor from ten till sixteen. I wouldn't say we rebelled but we were a bit naughty at school. I always remember my brother's very good friend in Charmouth, the chemist's son, George, a bit of a beatnik and said "The trouble with you twins is you're too disgustingly normal" so I think we were quite average.

We were quite pretty as identical twins, little girls with our fringes and bobs, we were taken notice of at school. We got into trouble. We were popular with older girls which made our peer group jealous of us, so they could sometimes be a bit mean, and I remember coming back from holidays with tales of parties and at one point they went to the headmistress and said "'I think the twins are not behaving themselves" this was our peer group, so we were called to the headmistress's office and asked if we were being a bit naughty at home and going out with boys and smoking. So we were put on a blacklist in a way, but I always got a feeling that the headmistress really quite liked us, they were nuns. It was cosmopolitan, Leweston in those days, there were a lot of foreign students so we mixed with girls of different nationalities.

We weren't very good at qualifications. I wouldn't say I was cleverer than Susy but I was more applied. I got eight O levels, then in the first year of A levels we were asked if we'd leave because of this business of being naughty with boys, so we went to art school.

Just going to parties. It was very stupid really, I think the nuns thought we were a bad influence. I was dying to go to art school anyway. Bournemouth was the nearest. We both went, we were always together. We were asked to leave as a unit. In '63 I went to art school. But we were only there a year, we did a foundation course, so we thought we'd go to art school in London because by then of course it was the Swinging Sixties.

After we'd left art school I was fed up with being in Charmouth, I thought 'I'm going to look in The Lady and I'm going to be an au pair in London.' I looked at all these advertisements, rang them up, borrowed my friend's Chanel suit, put my hair up, went up to London with Susy for support. The final situation was in Prince Arthur Road in Hampstead. I rang the doorbell and it turned out to be Morley Berry who was head of Hornsey College of Art and his wife was at the V and A, the head of silver. They had one precious boy and they wanted somebody to look after him while the very strict Scottish nanny was ill. "Oh we'd better employ you both." So we were there with Chippy, a little boy aged about eight. Really our only job was to walk him to school and pick him up again. We both did it together as they were employing us both. Then Susy got measles, it was around the time of Winston Churchill's death because I remember the fly-past of planes. 1965. We both got measles and they started looking after us. So then we were quietly shoved out and Shaw the Scottish nanny came firmly back into control.

Susy had a boyfriend in London, so we then moved in with him and his friends in Emperor's Gate opposite John Lennon's flat. It was all very exciting, The Beatles were everywhere. John Lennon lived in the same little square as us. You did bump into people all the time in those days. And then, I thought 'I need a job' as we didn't have any money. So I looked in the Evening Standard and I found a job at the 'inexpensive' shoe department at Harvey Nichols, and I remember thinking 'Ooh I've got this job and I don't really want it' but anyway I took it. And Susy was

at home with her boyfriend and I arrived home one evening and she said "Look" she said, "Biba are advertising for girls" and she said "I don't feel very well" so I offered to ring up and pretend to be her. So I rang up, pretended to be Susy and got the job. They asked for her to go along for an interview. Just helping in the shop.

They'd just moved to a bigger premises. First of all they were in Abingdon Road, off Ken High Street, then they moved with pomp and ceremony to Kensington Church Street. And it was all in the Evening Standard, 'Biba moves' and there were pictures of all the girls and Cilla Black, they knew how to get publicity, so then I was very envious, I was in Harvey Nichols and Susy was at Biba. And so she said to them "I've got a twin sister" and so they said "Yes!" I was employed too.

So we went to Biba. We weren't really models, we were just twins. We were photogenic rather than models. We were at Biba wearing very short skirts, and that's what they wanted. The Swinging Sixties, we were photographed all the time, so whenever anyone like Paris Match or Stern from Germany or any of these continental magazines came along…

It lasted two years. But it was a very intensive two years. I remember the excitement of famous people coming in, Brigitte Bardot and royalty and pop stars, film stars. Window shopping? No. They bought things, everything was terribly cheap. I interviewed Anna Wintour, she is now the fashion queen of the world. She's editor of American Vogue, incredibly important. This young girl came into Biba to be interviewed for a job. Susy and I were by that time managing the girls. I had complained because I thought they were being badly treated. At one point Fitz, Barbara's husband said "The girls can have the Bank Holiday day off, but they'll have to work their usual day off on Tuesday." I said 'That's not fair, Fitz, the Bank Holiday should be as well as and they're all getting very upset.' So he put me in charge of the girls' welfare.

Biba was one of the first boutiques. Boutiques were very new things and I remember somebody coming in once and saying "Is this what you call a bouquet?" Anyway, it was a very new word and concept. Before that everybody shopped in the big stores which usually had a small corners for teenagers. In those days you went from your school clothes…almost into your mother's clothes. There was a real gap.

The miniskirt? Well that was Mary Quant, the Ginger Group, Mary Quant, her shop in the King's Road, she started it. We were hot on her heels. In fact Mary Quant was the other boutique. Biba was bigger than Mary Quant. At the beginning only seven or eight girls worked there. The clothes were very cheap, they were seriously cheap. Barbara designed them and somebody called Anne Bear also helped.

Fashion magazines? Yes, definitely. There were teenage magazines, there was one called Petticoat, and Susy and I were on the cover of Petticoat because we were Biba, and then inside "Petticoat suggest what Princess Anne should wear," and on the strength of that Princess Anne came into the shop one Tuesday morning. She caused a frisson, everyone came out of the back "Princess Anne's in." She must have been about 15. She came in with a lady-in-waiting. She and Brigitte Bardot caused the most stir. Brigitte Bardot came in and that was amazing and I remember ringing my friend who was a photographer and saying 'Brigitte Bardot is about to appear out the back of Biba' and he took this amazing picture of her clad all in Biba clothes and sold it to the Daily Mirror or something.

Everything was starting, the music…Yes, the music, I remember the Stones coming in and The Hollies and The Searchers. It was all very dolly bird, and suddenly boutiques sprung up all over London and we weren't on our own for long. People would come in and say "We want to photograph miniskirts" and so they'd take us off, usually Susy and me. We were known as the Biba Twins. And then, if a club was opening they'd want us to dance there in our miniskirts, everything overlapped and then we'd have our hair done by a hairdresser in Kensington and they'd become famous because the Biba girls went there.

No, we never dressed identically actually. Not at all. We did look alike. I've got lots of pictures of us in the Biba days. We were given a dress a week in lieu of wages. We were paid seven quid a week, even in those days that was very little, but then we got a free dress and a free hairdo every fortnight. We had hundreds of dresses but we burnt them when we left. We came home and burnt them. It was like a ritual.

We were there for two years. It seemed like ages. We left just before we were 21 'cause I remember we came home for our 21st and invited lots of the Biba girls to our 21st. Oh no we weren't sacked. Oh no. We'd had enough. Yeah and we'd had enough of it. Then we went to Kensington Market, we wanted to be more hippyish I think, you know, we weren't allowed to smoke dope in Biba, and it was pretty regulated by him. Stephen Fitzsimon. Fitz he was called and he was really just a businessman. Loads of photographers. In fact we did a film for David Bailey. The Life and Times of GG Passion, What happened was that he was making a film, it never did very well. It was not great. It was about a pop singer, Eric Swain. We were his fans, we'd have to go 'eeeeh' we were all on a bed with him, it was ridiculous, but of course Bailey came into Biba and said "I want her, her, her and her," about five of us were in this film.

My parents were sort of innocents "Oh the girls, people are taking lots of pictures of them, you know," sort of proud. We were in the Bridport News. We were famous down here because of being famous in London. And then when it all died down, when I got a bit older I thought 'I don't want to do this, I want to be clever, I want to do something creative.' A friend took me out and said "Why don't you do something sensible with your life?" This was when I was in Kensington Market. "What do you like doing?" I said 'Well I like lettering and I like writing.' He was a designer and said "Come and work for me for a bit." So I went and worked for him in Knightsbridge, and then I found a job with another typographer. I was his assistant, so I never went back to art school. I became a typographer.

We did posters, I did a bit of film work, letter headings. It was more graphic design than typography really, but he was a typographer, Eric, and we did work for the Petersburg Press and Editions Electo. I worked on Hockney's little book of Grimms' Fairy Tales. Doing all the type, this was done in offset litho. All I did really was endless little mock ups of what it would look like to show the Petersburg Press. Editions Electo, which was doing limited editions of screen prints, Joe Tilson and Jim Dine. I actually really enjoyed it but I always had my heart in Dorset, I had fun in London, but my parents still lived here and we'd come down a lot. They still had the hotel. My brother helped them run it then. We'd come down and stay and have blissful times.

I did typography for another two years! Susy was working at the Chelsea Cobbler which was bespoke shoes. Lovely, in Sackville Street. The thing is with the '60s was that to work in a shop was 'trendy'. People were relatively wealthy, we'd never had it so good, had we? People like photographers who were once considered just artisans became very important and famous. So photographers were almost like pop stars. There was a whole world of trendy people…We made our own rules, there were pop stars, fashion designers, hairdressers, all sorts of people who in the '50s wouldn't have been considered anybody. Vidal Sassoon was up there, we all went there to have our hair done. We had our own culture. It was very easy to be famous for five years. If you wanted to make clothes and sell them in a shop in King's Road you could do it. How could you do that now? Things were cheap, rent was cheap, materials were cheap, individual people could do things quite easily in those days.

After working for Eric, I came back to Dorset, '73. We came back to Dorset and lived in Brimley Mill at Stoke Abbott with Peter Glidewell. We used to come down a lot and meet local people, I remember Peter Glidewell sort of homed in on us and said "Oh I can make a film of you two." I thought 'Oh God, I've heard that before.' But because we got quite friendly with him I remember him saying "You could have the Mill House for two pounds a week." And so we thought 'Ooh that's what we want to do, we want to leave London.' We just left London and moved into the mill, and also the '70s were hippie days of self-sufficiency anyway, everyone moving out of London.

We worked at the hotel, we were chambermaids at my parents' hotel. My brother was running it with my cousin. So Susy and I used to zoom over from the mill, past Shave Cross, through the back roads to Charmouth, do the chambermaiding for a bit, do some sunbathing, have a swim and then go back and meet John Symonds in the Gollop. We loved it. That was our move back to Dorset and then we bought the bookshop in Crewkerne. The Little Bookshop.

Yes, I was always interested in books. When we were very little there was a bookshop in Charmouth called Badger's. It wasn't a bookshop it was owned by a dear woman who'd opened her library to children in Charmouth and we could borrow books for a penny to read. I loved it. They were her own books, and she had a room lined with them. Funnily enough she sold it to somebody who opened a bookshop and called it Badger's Bookshop who then moved to Yeovil and became quite big and well known.

On the strength of that we went home to our hotel and opened our own library to the guests. Charging them a penny a book! As a typographer I started collecting books. I'd always liked type to be honest, I mean I'm visual and I can draw, I could have been a painter, I could have been an artist but I didn't continue it because I was side-tracked. I was drawn to illustrated books. Yes, particularly children's books, the type balances the drawing, and I just liked the look of books and children's books are very appealing.

Before I left the hotel I used to write the menu everyday. I loved writing the menu. I loved writing. I liked type and writing, I liked looking at the written word on the page. The shop in Crewkerne was in North Street. It was a sweet little shop and we bought it from Thomas Gray who was from Lincolnshire. I had quite a collection of my own books by the time we moved back to Dorset, then I would visit The Little Bookshop and we got friendly with him. One day he said he wanted to sell it. My father had sold the hotel, it was only £3,000 and so my father bought it for us. We bought his stock as well. And at that time we were very keen on buying antiques. Junk, we used to go junking, so we had antiques as well, and then VAT came in and because books were zero-rated and antiques weren't, so we got more and more into books.

The Crewkerne shop was about four years I suppose. I then sold the bookshop and so I and my partner bought Oslehay Farmhouse in Whitchurch, in the Marshwood Vale and then my children were born, but I always went on selling books. We just did book fairs and market stalls, then I eventually had another shop, in Crewkerne again, in the back of Oscar's which was an antique shop. And then I had a bookshop in Charmouth for a bit, and then I took this shop over with two partners. I had always wanted this. Eight years ago, I came here and I've been here happily ever since. I do two and a half days. But we are in a brilliant position. It is one of the best in Dorset, in England I should think. Middle of a busy market town, we are lucky.

People still value the physicality of old books. We sell real books to real people. That's trying to get people back. I think it'll turn around even more. There have always been collectors of old books, but I've always specialised in children's books and books illustrated by painters I like. Illustrated books I like books with wood engravings. Yes, we have had our moments with rare books. Yes, we have a lot of people bringing in mediocre stuff, occasionally there's one good thing. Books about the land? Yes, they are interesting. I really like country books. I like books on the land. Books about farming are popular.

Food is the thing right now. Books on specific country activities are good, bell ringing, pigeon racing, poaching, those sort of books are popular. They definitely sell, and books about Dorset. Shell guides and Pevsner. Books do have a sort of fashion. People in Dorset are still reading. I think people will always want books, they want to hold them, they want to open them, they like the smell of them. A book is there on the shelf for you to pull out and browse.

Bookselling is quite a social activity. Yes, it's the social side that I'm good at. I've always been sociable, I've enjoyed talking to people. I'm glad I know London, I would not have wanted to be here in Dorset all the time. One had to break away but there is a curious draw, people do want to come back to Dorset. Sadly the hotel in Charmouth has been erased. And now there are lots of little boxes all over our lovely garden.

29. Catherine Streatfeild – Outside Event Manager at River Cottage HQ. Born Denhay 1980

Running around, initially a researcher, that is what it was on the credits...They really needed someone who knew West Dorset. I also helped them come up with some ideas. I never thought I would have a little stint for a film company.

I was born at Denhay on July 22nd 1980. My father has always been a farmer and my mother worked in the BBC for a few years. She worked in Television Centre for the Controller of BBC1 and Director of Programmes, then moved to the Natural History Unit in Bristol, from where she went around the world on a film crew including to Australia tracking camels.

Denhay is our family farm. My grandfather, known as 'The Commander' was invalided out of the Navy in the late 1940s and bought Denhay with Alexander Hood, a merchant banker in 1952. The farm was overrun with bogs, brambles and bunnies. I think the first thing they did was put up a fence to stop all the rabbits; then myxomatosis hit the country and they had to open all the gates to infect their healthy rabbits. They established Streatfeild Hood and Company and in 1958 my grandfather started making West Country Farmhouse Cheddar, a traditional farmhouse Cheddar using the milk from our own and neighbouring farms. We had pigs to complete the traditional West Country cycle with the milk from the cows going to make the cheese, the whey from the cheese making going to feed the pigs and obviously the muck from the pigs going onto the land.

I am really sad that I never met my grandfather because I hear a lot about him. Both he and my grandmother were very much a part of the community: masters of the hounds and very involved with young farmers and parish life. I do not know what made him go into farming originally, but I suppose cheese making is a natural extension, you have to do something with the milk haven't you?

At the end of the '80s, my parents realised they should be adding value to our pigs. They did a trip round France and Italy researching charcuterie products. On their return they decided to try and make an English version of a Parma ham, but not a lookalike. There are still only few people in this country who make an air-dried ham. It was quite adventurous to start a product like that, but once going they got quite involved in pork, and started making bacon, dry cured bacon, which is a very traditional method. It was quality that was always foremost in their minds. Visiting the Langhirano Valley, where Parma ham is produced, was an inspiration. They visited factories where hundreds of thousands of hams were hanging up, but felt there was an opportunity to develop English recipes in a continental style. Their developments of the air-dried ham started in our garage at the bottom of our house. It is really small and not quite as romantic as Italy, but as the business grew they then moved into a larger ham house on the farm,

I think they have always just loved those kinds of products. The uniqueness about the pigs was that they were whey fed; that was what gave them an extra flavour. I used to go and help feed them. My sister Ellen and I were put in our overalls and given our summer job of feeding the weaners every day.

The backbone of the farm has always been cheddar making. We make mainly block Cheddar but also make a few traditional farmhouse cheddars where the curds are put into cylindrical moulds, and pressed over three days. After this, they are put on wooden shelves and turned every day. A natural mould forms on the rind. We also make little cheeses, the Dorset drums, and Ellen

Catherine Streatfeild with air-dried ham, River Cottage HQ

and I spent hours just turning them. All the cheese production is done on the farm and it is now all our own milk. The cheese making process hasn't changed that much in 50 or 60 years. We are such a predominately dairy area and making cheese is a natural process.

Denhay now makes up five different farms, about 1,600 acres. There are dairies at Northfield Farm, Beaminster, Meerhay Farm, Wootton Fitzpaine, Boarsbarrow Farm, Loders, Beerlands Farm, Whitchurch Canonicorum and at Denhay itself. I was brought up on cheese and milk. I did a bit of milking, but we were more involved with the cheese. I remember going out with my father every Sunday morning driving around the farm when he was more of a practical farmer than he is now. We took a lot of interest in the farm and driving around in the back of the Landrover.

I first went to the local village school, Symondsbury, then I went away to Port Regis, near Shaftesbury and then to the Royal School in Bath. After school I took a gap year and spent six months at Denhay packing bacon and earning some money and then went travelling for six months. I went to Australia and signed up to an organisation called GAP to do five months volunteer conservation work in Australia. I started in South Australia, We worked on a number of conservation projects funded by several mining companies. The work involved fencing a conservation reserve to keep out foxes and cats which where very disruptive on the indigenous marsupials. Then we moved to Perth in Western Australia were I did some energy conservation workshops with children which was really interesting. We worked in a few aboriginal schools which was quite an eye-opener really. In the schools we where given some amazing performances from real aboriginals who were keen to show us their culture. They told us stories of their history through

performances, dressing up as native creatures such as the emu and kangaroo. It was really a special experience.

On my return, I started college in Birmingham, studying an HND in Food and Consumer Management for two years. It was really interesting to be living in a city because I had been brought up down here in the country and for us, Bridport was the 'bright lights' so that was one of the reasons that I chose to go to Birmingham, to get a view of the other side of life, and Birmingham is a great city. I chose the HND because I knew that I wanted to go into food but I didn't know where or how. It covered a broad number of subjects from marketing to cookery demonstrations, from packaging design to health and hygiene.

Then I did an internship in America for three months in a supermarket called A&P, I thought it would be interesting to see how an American food company worked. I stayed with my aunt and uncle in New Jersey. It was a great experience, I got to experience how Americans lived and worked, and it was just ten days after September 11th, so that was quite an experience in itself. The internship was to designed to give me an idea of how the whole company worked. They put me through a schedule, which included working on the tills to working in the marketing and sales departments. It was interesting to see a different lifestyle, many people ate out, rather than cooking at home. I didn't really see a huge range of local products, I found food culture was very different from the one I am used to.

Then I came back, I worked a month or so with the West Dorset Food and Land Trust in Bridport before starting work for Taste of the West. It started as a summer job but two years later I was still there. Taste of the West is a group representing food and drink producers from the South West, working with small to medium-sized businesses. We where there to give advice and run various projects.

In my first project I was helping with Objective 5b funding projects. Producers from West and Mid Devon could apply for marketing grants, so I was helping with applications. I then moved on to projects such as organising 'meet the buyer' groups, bringing together smaller producers to meet the supermarkets. That was the good thing about Taste of the West - we were the interface, working on behalf of producers helping them to get to where they wanted to go. If they did not want to go down that aisle, literally, we would also set up similar groups with farm shops such a Darts Farm.

I also worked on the Taste of the West Food and Drink awards. I really enjoyed the judging day, which was really interesting. We would help steward various classes, therefore tasting a wide range of products. I learnt a lot from the judges and tasted a great deal of delicious food. It is just amazing how much wonderful produce we have in the South West. The awards are very high profile now and a great marketing tool for producers.

My last project at Taste of the West was helping to organise the first year of the Exeter Festival of South West Food and Drink. It was a fantastic event, working with over 40 food and drink producers from the South West.

It was great to work at Taste of the West as my parents had set up Dorset Harvest in the middle of the '80s, which then merged with groups such as A Taste of Somerset and Devon Fare to become Taste of the West so they have been heavily involved in these producer groups.

Then I left Taste of the West and found out that River Cottage had moved to my village. I found the number of the programme producer, just gave her a call and said: 'l don't suppose you are looking for anyone?' I was very lucky, that week they were looking for a runner/researcher. I was just in the right place at the right time. I was really just a gopher, initially they needed someone who knew West Dorset and to help come up with ideas and to find characters to film. It is almost what my mother was doing when she was at the BBC.

I never thought I would work for a film company. We were filming the fifth series of River Cottage, set at Lower Atrim Farm in Broadoak. So this is River Cottage HQ, where Beyond River Cottage was filmed. But now it is something more than the television set. We run courses and events, people can learn about the importance of using local and seasonal produce.

The filming was pretty honest, which is why I think so many people enjoy watching it. It was very manic at times, driving round the countryside, but I did get to know the small lanes of West Dorset well. We had one mad morning where we were driving over the hills with the film crew and John Wright our mushroom expert, filming Hugh paragliding with Eddie Colfox. They were trying to find parasol mushrooms. They ended up finding a fieldful in North Chideock.

I also got to meet some wonderful characters, such as bee keepers and local cider makers. One memory in particular I enjoyed, was when we where filming the bees being installed at River Cottage HQ. Hugh wanted to set some hives up at HQ with the help of Ken Bishop, a local beekeeper. That week Ken found a swarm on Hooke school gates and so we collected them up and reintroduced them into the hives at HQ. I was just blown away by them – it is absolutely incredible. Since then I have done a beekeeping course at Kingston Maurward. So hopefully I might keep bees at HQ.

Once we finished the filming for Beyond River Cottage, I became the Outside Events Manager for River Cottage. This means I organise taking River Cottage on the road. We attend agricultural shows, food festivals and markets. River Cottage does the Bridport Farmers' Market every month.

This year we have attended the Exeter Festival of South West Food and Drink, the CLA Game Fair and Bristol Organic Festival next month and we are going to Abergavenny Food Festival which I am really looking forward to. Attending these events involves talking to people who may not know about River Cottage. I have been brought up doing these types of show with my parents, from an early age, I do really enjoy it.

River Cottage HQ is moving to Park Farm, a 65-acre farm near Uplyme. The majority of my time is now based there. It will be the permanent residence for River Cottage HQ. We all move there at the end of the month.

Here currently at River Cottage HQ in Broadoak, we have air dried hams hanging up curing, a vegetable garden, a couple of pigs and goats and a few chickens. These will all move to Park Farm at the end of the month, except the pigs, I want them fed well, because I need them for sausages for an event I have next month.

This farm was a dairy farm, the barn used to be where the cows lived and outside the raised beds were cow sheds. We hope to replicate what we are doing here at Park Farm, but on a bigger scale. We will have Hugh's herd of Ruby Red North Devons plus an increased flock of chickens for eating and laying, and a herd of Saddleback pigs. Malcolm Seal, the River Cottage gardener, has been doing a great deal of research into the farm already, looking into all the families that used to work and live there, and he's already reverted the kitchen garden at Park Farm back to its former glory.

We are not going to have a restaurant. Hugh is very keen that it should remain as this. All our courses have an educational element to them, so it is not just about sitting down and eating and then going away again, it is about learning about what you are eating. For example, we run a 'pig in a day' course, where you start with the whole carcase of the animal. It is for people who want to learn about butchering and processing a pig (sometimes their own) rather than getting it sent off to be butchered by someone else. It also gives the opportunity for people to learn charcuterie skills such as curing bacon and air drying hams.

All sorts of people come on the courses at River Cottage HQ, it is really interesting to meet them. We get people from the city, who aspire to live the River Cottage life and maybe will one day move down or move to the country and we do actually get people attending courses who have done the move and given up the city life. They have the property and want to learn and get ideas for their land. And there are people that watch the programme and are interested to see what it is all about.

We also run evening events, which start with a demonstration by Hugh and the River Cottage team. This is followed by a four-course meal, using the very best local and seasonal produce. Visitors all sit together on long tables. There is always a great buzz at these events, as everyone chats to each other, often sharing ideas and stories.

I have been working here for about two and a half years and really enjoy it. The job is exactly what I want to do. The whole philosophy is really what I believe in. I guess this will have stemmed from my upbringing. Within River Cottage, including waiting staff, kitchen porters, there are about 30 or so of us. Pretty much everyone here is local, it is a great team to work with. The success of the brand is down to Hugh and the team's passion, we completely believe in the whole idea and that is what is making it so successful.

The future? I am enjoying living in West Dorset, there are so many interesting people here, it is such a hub for art and music and food. It is a very special place, very dynamic, and all sorts of new people coming in with new ideas, there are so many different things going on. You don't know what is going to happen in the future. I am certainly enjoying what I am doing at the moment.

30. Anne Beckett – Shepherdess and sheep shearer, Milton Abbas. Born Wimborne 1968.

There's nothing like being with animals in the middle of the night. It's a wonderful time…just sit near them and listen to them cudding, just that noise of everyone cudding.

I feel eternally young. I grew up in Wimborne, later the family moved to Corfe Mullen. Mum kept producing so we had to move to a slightly larger house. Dad had done farm work as a young lad, also showed dairy cows. I grew up seeing pictures of him as a child the idyllic lifestyle, gathering in hay with heavy horses. That made me think when I was a kid 'I want to go into farming.' When he got married to my mum he became a lorry driver for Texaco, drove tankers.

The Brandreth connection is on my father's mother's side. Her maiden name was Mabel Brandreth. I spoke to my dad's sister today. They've been in touch with Gyles Brandreth, he's keen to learn more about the Jeremiah story in the family. Jeremiah Brandreth was the last man in England to be sentenced to be hung, drawn and quartered. In 1817 he led the last English revolt against the Government in Pentrich near Derby and he killed somebody. In the end they let him off the drawing and quartering and only hanged him and then beheaded him half an hour later. My aunt said to me on the phone this morning, "I always said that you had the Brandreth eyebrows." So I can see where my attachment to the land and the fire in my belly comes from!

Dad worked for the National Trust at Badbury Rings just before he died. Later on I kept sheep there. I wish he was around now so I could talk to him about it. When you're in your teens you don't question anything, you're just having a good time. It's not till you get older that you want to start questioning people. My mother's family had pubs in Bournemouth and Birmingham.

My first experience in farming, I was about 15 and you do work experience. I had two options. I was either going to work with a thatcher or work on a dairy farm in Wimborne. I chose the dairy farm, and that was it. I was attracted to both of them, because I knew I was going to be an outdoor girl.

That was milking. I was working with a dairyman and his son, they were both absolutely hilarious. As a female you've got to have a sense of humour. That dairyman chased me round the parlour once, do you remember the Abertay Sacks calendars? There used to be a half-naked woman, he chased me round the dairy once with his Abertay Sack calendar, half of me was quite scared, and half of me was just saying 'Oh humour him,' 'cause you do get a lot of this sort of stick. If you're a young girl going into a man's environment you're going to get a lot of male banter.

Yeah, I was going in at the bottom end with the dairymen, so I was learning to milk cows, I was calf rearing, they were all Friesians, I was really struck by the bull, I know now with AI not many people keep a dairy bull, but I remember being really upset, the whole window had been boarded up and you could just hear a chain moving in there, and he was attached from his nose to a chain that ran the length of the bull pen, and that was all he could do, walk up and down, and they all used to tell me he was really nasty and I can remember thinking 'I can see why.' And he didn't get much use when I was there because they were just starting to introduce AI then.

I signed myself up to agricultural college and did what was then Phase One Agriculture at Kingston Maurward. I had to get myself a placement on a farm. So I got on my push bike and cycled around all these farms. One guy actually said to me "Oh

Anne Beckett with fleece, lorry and Storm, Milton Abbas

come on darling, why don't you consider cheese making?" And I remember cycling up the road and thinking 'This really isn't very fair.'

Eventually I managed to get a place on a sheep farm in Swanage. Paul Loudoun and he had a flock about 400 Dorsets. He's got a National Trust farm, I went and had a look, met the guy and thought 'This is great.' It was a real rufty-tufty farm. Just the place I wanted to go to experience shepherding. Absolutely gorgeous, medieval, the farm itself was in the Domesday Book, and the inside of the house itself looked like it's still in the Domesday Book. It was very rough and ready, all the working dogs pretty much lived indoors.

They had about six or seven hundred cross-breds and a flock of Dorsets. We were January lambing the Dorsets. Purbeck is another world. Believe me. Met some real characters. I started there as I was just coming up 17, and I stayed there a couple of years. Paul taught me to shear. I hadn't been shearing all that long when I went out with a bunch of guys on Purbeck and sheared 100 in my first proper shearing day. They were clean-bellied mules and I didn't have to go in the catching pen, a guy who can pass you a sheep, as soon as that one's run. If I wasn't shearing I was rolling and catching for three or four shearers. By the time I was 18, I mean look at these muscles, that's what you get from working with these beasts!

There were some really interesting characters on Purbeck. Up in Langton Matravers there was a guy, he used to keep turkeys in his house, in the bedrooms, and he used to keep lambs in little tiny water butts. He used to milk the cows at night because he was blind, so he said it didn't matter what time of day it was, but I always remember, as a young girl it really did amaze me. I mean it was a brilliant time.

My working dog at the time was born under the bed, because a lot of the collies used to live in the house. I knew this little bitch which was Paul's best bitch, Floss, she was a little pocket rocket, she was in pup, but I heard all this noise in the night, I had a stack of Farmers Weeklies under the bed, I heard all this manic noise under the bed and she was ripping them all up and she had her babies in the night. It was just a nice little hidey hole. So my boy was born under my bed. We used to do a day's shearing and then all end up at the Square and Compass, drinking cider. It was a community, I remember with Paul, if you sheared someone's sheep they would come and cut your hay, 'cause Paul didn't have a lot of farm machinery. An exchange of skills.

There were two events that I used to think were fun, turkey plucking and shearing, 'cause turkey plucking, everyone had mince pies and whisky, everyone would have a laugh. Shearing was the same, the lady of the house would come out with cider and home-made cakes, that's changed a lot now.

You learn a hell of a lot of veterinary stuff with sheep because they are quite good at suddenly getting ill. Paul taught me how to stop a prolapse by getting a bit of bailer twine, he reckoned if you got it right, up by the back legs you kind of stopped a nerve, that would stop them pushing, and it did seem to work, and then you tied it up on top of the back. I think it's better than a lot of the harnesses.

Lambing was wonderful. With the Dorsets, I remember one small group we were lambing outside, and because it was my first shepherding job I was determined that nothing was going to die. He said "Just go up and check them" but I thought no, so I took an umbrella, it was teeming with rain most nights and I just sat in the hedge with an umbrella all night long, and every five minutes I was going round to see, and with lambing outside, if a ewe is going to lamb she's going to take herself off to the farthest most distant point. Then all the other lot were lambed indoors. I used to sit up in the bales. There's nothing like being with animals in the middle of the night. It's a wonderful time. You often find with lambing that it goes quiet about five o'clock onwards. Just sit near them and listen to them cudding, just that noise of everyone cudding. We used to get a little fox that would nip in and go all around the feed troughs in amongst all the sheep, and the sheep never blinked an eye at the foxes, which I used to think was quite interesting, because if it had been a dog they would have gone absolutely bonkers.

So lambing I absolutely loved. I've got nice long slender hands. Dorsets are terrible sheep. Terrible to shear, terrible to work with, they're exceptionally lazy when it comes to lambing, they'll give one or two pushes and then look at you as if to say 'do you want to help me out here? I really can't be arsed any more!' And then when you shear them they have that particular stomp, don't they? A lot of shepherds call it the Dorset stomp, when the back legs just go dang dang dang, they've got energy then! But I did like the Dorsets. They were Dorset Horns, and of course you've got problems with the lambing with the horn buds. The cross-breds were mostly mule crosses and they were a lot better. Paul, bless his heart, love him to bits, would go and buy broken-mouth mule ewes, 'course, come lambing time when there's not a lot of milk about and you've got these mules producing triplets, you're just doing your nut. He was obviously keeping a lot of young ewe lambs back, but we did have a struggle with the old girls.

Wilton Sheep Fair was wonderful. Every year you go there and you get to know everyone. Two years at Paul's then, I signed up for my NCA course at Kingston Maurward. There was only 22 of us, absolutely loved that, but I got very frustrated at the way they didn't ever seem to teach you anything about the mental side of farm animals, it's always about growth rates,

which is odd really because surely an animal's going to do much better if you're taking care of it mentally. I was renowned as the girl that constantly whinged about animal welfare standards.

In my younger days, I had a boyfriend, he was a poacher, he poached just about everything. We used to have such fun, so while most youngsters were going out having a romance, he bought me a little Baikal, 12 bore shotgun, and we used to go out rabbiting and ferreting, he taught me how to cure skins, how to paunch a rabbit, how to paunch a deer. He did teach me loads. I remember one morning early, a real cold winter's morning, he was shooting rabbits and I was hanging them round my waist, sort of leg 'em, through the hock, and he used to break his gun down and put the barrel down his trousers. It was so exciting because we got chased by a Landrover once, and he broke his gun down so if anyone saw us we could pretend we were just walking down the road doing nothing, and as much as I was scared, it was one of the most exciting things I think I've ever done. We used to ditch the rabbits and come back for those later.

Most landowners would be grateful that you were taking the rabbits. I don't know why it was such a terrible thing. Perhaps this lad just enjoyed getting into trouble, but if he'd just gone and asked they'd have probably said yes. We used to shoot pheasants and deer as well. Then we used to go home, the pair of us and we used to salt all these skins out, we did foxes as well, salted them out. I used to love ferreting. It was really exciting,

As much as I love working with animals, I don't kill anything unless we're going to eat it. I think that animal should have a decent life. The situation that we're at now, where meat has absolutely no value whatsoever, and these animals are living appalling lives, and there is this obesity problem, we shouldn't be doing it. I think it's very wrong. At agricultural college they talked to us about pigs, and I can remember this lecturer showing us a pig, and I said to him 'Look, her back's really dipping' and when she walked she could have almost gone round the corner and left her back end round the other side, and he said "Well that's the drive to breed longer pigs, because if you've got a longer pig it produces more bacon." I remember saying 'But she's really suffering with her back.' These are the sort of things I've always felt really passionate about. For me, I'm convinced I'm a reincarnated cavewoman. I'm heavily into Native American Indians and their whole way of thinking, I just love everything to do with this whole land-based eating your own food, and it's an instinct. It's something that comes up from inside.

I then took a job on the Drax estate, behind the big wall, I was excited to see what behind the big wall was like. That was another experience, I didn't stay there very long. We were running 3,000 sheep and I was the under-shepherd. We were breeding our own Welsh mules from Beulahs and Blue Faced Leicesters. The Drax family were absolutely mad about hunting and shooting. I was basically told by the shepherd "Whatever you do, you do not upset a drive because it is the Drax's most favourite thing and the people that are here are paying an absolute fortune for a gun. You do not ruin a drive." I had a little cottage to live in. A gorgeous place to live. To go off in your tractor and see stags in the mist early in the morning is quite stunning.

I got up really early one morning, went up to the sheep unit, and I looked across the road and there was a red car in the middle of a ploughed field. I immediately thought to myself 'That doesn't look very clever,' so I walked over there and it was a big red Escort. The rear doors were both open and they'd got a stag on the back seat and the horns were tied to the bumper outside, they were obviously driving him at high speed but got stuck so decided to bale out, but they left this stag. You were always

waking up in the morning finding lurchers running around, the guys would bring them down with dogs in the middle of the night and they'd just smash them in with the hammer. They were a pretty nasty bunch, I don't think you'd want to come across them in the night.

After that I went to Melcombe Bingham. Somebody told me that there was a woman was looking for someone to milk her Frieslands, she was selling milk to Mr Michael Murray in Yeovil who makes ice cream and yoghurt, so I went for an interview there. Beautiful farm but it's falling around their ears. So I started there.

I worked there a long time until I got pregnant with my oldest. Doesn't go well when you're right in the middle of lambing, so I had to quickly go. All through this Jack and I were together, he's always been a pig man, so he was doing his pig thing, working near Blandford, and all of a sudden Jack said "I'm going to have to get us a job with a house," because I'd always got a house with my sheep jobs. He managed to get a job in Gloucestershire, near Cirencester. I hated it. It was all polo horses and really, really rich people. I'm just not the sort of person that can sit in the house and say 'Oh I'm delicate and pregnant.' I've got some pictures of me getting the straw in a week before I had Bridie, I was putting the bales on the elevator, so we stayed there until Bridie was probably two or three, and then we went to another pig job in Wimborne.

A Dalgety research unit for testing their feeds. A gorgeous house in Dean's Grove near Colehill. So once again we were on pigs. I got myself a little flock of Jacobs, because with this house came a paddock. I just couldn't believe my luck. When my dad died I had some money so I got myself some Herdwicks and some Jacobs. Sometimes I helped Jack, it was an awful place, they did chickens there intensively, testing out chicken food.

They were putting herbs in feed to see if it would make the meat taste interesting.

One funny thing happened there. We were killing a couple of lambs once, I used to have a big garage with beams in. So Jack shot them and we would quickly string them up and I would just cut their throats over a bucket, anyway my Border Collie who had been born under my bed, was absolutely petrified of guns. Anyway there was a BT man working down the road, and I was just getting to grips with skinning this sheep and I heard this voice say "Hello?" So I came out the garage, and I had a massive knife in my hand, blood all down my front, and I said 'Can I help you?' and he said "Oh my God, are you alright?" I said 'I'm just doing a sheep.' He looked absolutely mortified, he said "I'm just repairing the wires. I've got a dog in my cab and I can't get him out, he's shaking like a leaf." I said 'Oh, that's my collie. He hates guns, and we've just shot a sheep' and this man left shaking! It was so funny!

We were there about five years. Then Jack was called in the office just as I found out I was pregnant with my boy. It was the same day. He'd been made redundant, and I can remember being absolutely mortified. We didn't know where we were going to go or what we were going to do. I sold my sheep and panicked, they went into market. Luckily they all had lambs at foot. So they did get a bit of money. They went into Shaftesbury market.

While Jack was working for Dalgetys he'd taken up hurdle making. He'd been out into the woods and spent a lot of time with Mark Harris and Fred Curley, wonderful characters. He learnt a lot off those old boys. So when he got made redundant, Jack just looked at me and said "I'm not going to go for another pig job I'm going to go into hurdle making." He already had some coppice anyway. The cheapest rent we could find was a house in West Chelborough, beautiful place, exceptionally rural,

we took about ten chickens there, and that was all we had, £200 a month rent. There was no sanitary drinking water because all the water was coming from his own bore hole. I was pregnant with this little lad, and got really ill with a stomach bug and then had a letter came from the water board saying "Please do not drink the water, it's contaminated with faecal coliforms." I was furious about this water.

So anyway I was pregnant, helping Jack in the woods, trimming while he was hurdle making. He was making really good hurdles. We advertised in the Blackmore Vale. We had a bit of copse over at Piddletrenthide on a steep hill. In fact I was carting wood up that hill the day before I had him and I was back in the wood when he was about three days old because we had to pay the rent.

A lot of people would say "Why didn't you get benefits? Why on earth did you go into the woods?" But we didn't know any better. We never even considered benefits, but my God we struggled. We had hardly any food, luckily we were able to shoot things to eat, we were really poor, and had no drinking water in a cottage that was falling round our ears. To say it was depressing is an understatement. I just remember saying to Jack 'I've got to leave this place.'

We ended up over at Winterborne Clenston. I was doing part-time shepherding which was nice because I could take the baby with me. The two girls were going to Winterborne Stickland Village School. I was glad of a bit of work. I loved shearing time there. Simon Conio used to come with his crew. We had such a laugh. He used to call me a woolly hat. Hardcore shearers call girls like me woolly hats. I ended up rolling for him. I always had to disappear to go and do school runs. This is the trouble when you're a woman, isn't it?

So did that but then I started helping the lady who I'd been milking sheep for. Jack was also doing logs for the fuel company that sell in red nets on garage forecourts. I just wish I could explain to people how hard we were working. We were up on top of Turnworth Hill and he got a contract, they used to buy 1,000 at a time. We used to stack them on palettes, so he bought this log splitting machine, so we would stand there all day doing that, and then the next day we'd have a stack of logs the size of a house, and we used to fill the nets.

Also at this time I'd just weaned the baby and he got a cow's milk intolerance, so the doctor said "You ought to put him on goats' milk." Well being me, I thought 'I ain't buying goats' milk, I'll go and get some goats.' So I got a couple of goats, we were milking them for the house and I was also walking them. People think you're a freak, but all the goodness they're eating out of the hedgerows is going into my kids. So we had these two goats and we had the chickens and we were working hard, it was ok, we weren't making very much money, but I think it was a good standard of living.

And the lady I milked sheep for offered us the house again. Now this is really coming up to date. She said "I'll give you a low rent if you do just a bit of sheep work and your horse keep." We were there six years and then we suddenly had to move out and find alternative accommodation. Well I had 20-odd chickens, two horses, two nanny goats, milking both goats that were keeping the whole family going. I was really attached to those goats, they'd been milking for us six years, providing the whole family with milk, really attached to those goats. They all had to go apart from the horses and the dogs.

We now live in the village. A modern house… that isn't falling down around our ears. So we got in here just before Christmas and we had the most wonderful Christmas. The kids said it was like a hotel. When you imagine what those kids have lived in, 'cause they've lived in some serious shit holes, I can tell you, my oldest daughter, she's nearly 16, she's never brought friends home. So I just couldn't believe it, but in the meantime Jack set up a business online selling woodland stuff and survival kits…He's also set up the Dorset Coppice Group…a passion for woodland.

I'm going to be plucking down at the Coleman's, doing the geese, well it's waxing. So hopefully I'll be going down this Christmas. What I really want is some ground of my own. I want some long horned cattle, some Portland sheep, and some outdoor chicken. I'd really like to kill it all myself. I'm really into keeping small numbers of rare breeds, they're such fantastic animals. They're hardy, the meat tastes fantastic, with the Portlands, you see, I wasn't killing those till they were 12 months old. Not like these commercial sheep that are killed when they're babies and taste of nothing. Portland is lovely, really dark, looks like venison. I've got the Portlands' skins upstairs, I immediately cured those three that we did, and they're really nice, 'cause they've got that orange tinge all around the leg area, and around the belly. When the lambs are born, they're bright orange. They look like little foxes in the field, and then the creamy wool comes through. I did a whole lot of goat skins last year and I sold those skins to a man who makes quivers for bows and arrows, 'cause they were beautiful little black, brown and white goats.

This is my first time ever I've been without sheep. I'm going to put an advert in the Blackmore Vale Magazine 'Female shepherd for small flocks.' I've got veterinary skills, I can shear, I can cure skins, I can kill animals and joint them, why the hell not? It sickens me to watch all these TV chefs furthering their careers on this new-found interest in the countryside. This is good for people understanding where their food's coming from, but why can't they use real people to do it? I've thought about running courses teaching people killing. When we kill our own sheep, by law, I have to consume all of it. I've never sold any. I can put my hand up and say I've never killed more than three at a time. And I've often given the skins away, people line their dog beds with them.

All I want to do is teach people where their food is coming from. I really, really want to do that. I think it's vitally important that people stop hiding behind the supermarket shelf to get their meat. I believe if you're eating meat, you're responsible for the deaths of animals. But they've all turned their back on where it comes from. People are horrified by it. I don't know how a course in killing would work, I'd have to get some sort of slaughtering licence.

The other thing I do is ride my horse naturally without saddle…bareback, barefoot and bitless.

31. Cynthia Walcot – Home birth midwife, Beaminster. Born 1946.

By the time I got to her, it was February, it was dark, it was raining, it was cold, and we got into this bender and she was well into labour… as I knelt down on the floor, it was a tarpaulin and you could feel the mud underneath squelching, the light was a candle…

I was born in Templecombe in Somerset. My father was on the railway, so he didn't go to war. He was a wheel tapper and an examiner with carriages and wagons. He started life in Hampshire, went to London and when he got married he decided he wanted to get out of London. So from Clapham Junction he came to little old Templecombe station, it was the Somerset and Dorset line then, Slow and Dirty.

His father, George was in the army, in the Royal Horse Artillery, he was in India but came home with malaria and died soon afterwards. My dad was only about four when he died. I never knew my grandparents. Mother, she was a Londoner, she was a Cockney and so to her, coming out to rural Somerset was wow, a big experience. It was just before the war that they moved.

My mother's father, Thomas Henry Butler was a bus driver and I've got beautiful pictures of him with his bus. He went from horse buses to the motor buses in London. He came from Battersea Bridge garage, where he drove the Number 19. My mother used to tell me wonderful stories about him driving the horses with his leather cape and his leather whip, that he used to come home and carefully hang it over a special frame in the hallway to keep the leather right, you know. I've traced them back to north Hampshire. So they've gone in and come out again, as most families do, with London.

So I grew up in Templecombe. Wonderful, it was very free and easy, we'd go off for the day, me and my friends, and we'd wander through the fields and the lanes, total and utter freedom which is so different from now, helping with the cows being milked and the butter being made. I do remember the ration books though. I remember going shopping with my mother and not being able to have this, that and the other. Because my father was on the railway we got free passes, so I can remember being lifted into the goods van and going either to Yeovil or Sherborne, where the shopping places were. It was still steam. Oh yes! The real thing.

School? I started off in Templecombe, then my father got a better job and we moved to Bagshot in Surrey which I hated. We escaped because my father went to work in Basingstoke. The house went with the job. Mortimer, which is near Reading, and that was much nicer.

When I left school my first idea was to go into the RAF. I wanted to do the travelling bit, so I even got as far as the medical and then you had a sheet of things that you could do in the RAF. I went through the sheet and I ticked three and I went to lunch with my godmother and she said "What did you tick?" And I said 'Oh, I think photography,' thinking of navigation, something else and nursing. She said "Why did you tick nursing?" And I said 'Well I was good at biology and I like people,' so she said "You need to do your general training and then go in as an NCO, you'll get more money that way and a better training." She knew what she was talking about because she was a nurse as well. So I went back and told my headmaster this, Mr Nation who was a wonderful man, the sort that knew every child, and he said "Oh yes, nursing, that's just what you need." So he got me an

Cynthia Walcot with a view to retiring. Beaminster

appointment with the matron at the Royal Berkshire Hospital in Reading.

I dragged my mother along, "You can't do this" she said. As far as she was concerned I was going to work in Woolies. So I went to this interview, and the wonderful old matron sat there with a little white hat on her head with a bow under the chin, "Why would you like to be a nurse, my dear? Would you like to do a pre-nursing course? We've got one going in a place called Blagrave" which is a little convalescence hospital outside Reading. "Give you a taste of what you might like to do." And within weeks there I was in nurse's uniform in this little hospital and that was that.

Looking back, I didn't have this vocation, 'I want to be a nurse.' I'm a great fatalist. I believe things happen as they're meant to happen. Then after a year, when I was 18, I went to the Royal Berkshire Hospital and did my general training. To go from the country to the town was quite a shock to the system. We're into the '60s now. As one of hundreds of nurses, we had a fairly wild time, but not completely wild... More wild than my mother? Well no, she was fairly wild in London, she used to go off dancing and come home at two o'clock in the morning carrying her shoes. It was there in the genes. Oh yes, and my daughter's got it now.

This was state registered nursing, so to complete the training, you do midwifery. It was an extra add on, so I applied for midwifery. And the first one to reply was Bristol, so a few weeks later, I was at the Bristol Maternity Hospital facing the Downs which was wonderful. Beautiful old Victorian place which has now closed down. I was there for a year, tea was served on a silver tray. The only problem was running up and down the stairs because there were three storeys.

After two weeks I knew that this was what I wanted to do for the rest of my life. Midwifery was the thing, being with women and babies. I wanted to be my own boss. Yes. Certainly that was beginning to click in my head. I came back to Reading because of my parents and I was offered a job in the Royal Berkshire Hospital in the new maternity unit. Within six months I was a junior sister. I worked there for two or three years, got myself a flat, learnt to drive. Nurses' pay was reasonable, but I was beginning to feel that the Royal Berkshire was a sausage factory. You never saw a woman twice, she came in, she was induced, she was delivered, I couldn't bear that. I worked on the antenatal ward, on the acute ward, on the delivery suite, on night duty, on day duty, everything, but there was no continuity at all.

Home births? Yes, they were still around. Certainly when I was at Bristol they were still the norm, so there was no problem getting ten home births as part of my hundred that I had to do in my training. Very often grandmother was in the background. There was much more of a family support network.

All over Bristol? Oh yes, on my bicycle. There were steep hills and big roundabouts. When I drive round them now I can't believe I went round on my bike but I did. In fact I'm still in touch with one of the babies I delivered. He's 36 now. But it's wonderful to get Christmas cards from him, he's married, got two kids.

You do get the sad bits but mostly it was very happy. Once I'd learnt to drive I thought 'I need to get out of this, I want to do something in the community' and I was offered a cover job in Tadley which was in north Hampshire. The following day my father died, so I worked in the community as a district nurse midwife. We had to do early morning insulin injections and bed baths and get people out of wheelchairs, and quite nasty things as well as the midwifery.

Yes. I had a Morris Minor. A navy blue one which was my

very first car and I bought it for £99. I loved it. It had the flickers. Better than a bicycle. I wanted a permanent position in the community so I was offered one down in New Milton in Hampshire. I'd go into the New Forest, opening and shutting gates and fending off ponies, and that was really exciting. At all times of day and night

But still there wasn't enough midwifery for me. So I went back up in North Hampshire again, attached to a GP's surgery, with a big area to cover. The decision for a home birth was really the woman's choice, but if I advised her that it wasn't a good idea she would probably go along with it, as long as she could understand why I said 'Not a good idea,' so there was still that respect, I wouldn't say power. The doctors I worked with were lovely. About a 30-mile radius. All the rural bits. And of course all round Aldermaston and the AWRE place. A lot of the men who lived and worked there died of cancer. Although it's never been proved, we know that there was a nuclear link.

After my father died and I got into family history and met my husband. He was changing jobs, we could either go to the Gulf States, or Bootle. He had two interviews and we didn't know which job he was going to get, so we decided that we'd better get on and get married so that we could get the passport. So we went off and found the registrar, she said "Oh yes, I can fit you in on Wednesday how about that?" So I had three weeks to prepare for my wedding, which is ironic because my eldest daughter's planning her wedding and she's had a whole year, and she says "Oh there's no time!" Three weeks. And then he got the job teaching in Bootle, on Merseyside so we moved up there. I was going to be the housewife now, I hate that word. I realised within weeks that I couldn't not work, so I rang up the local maternity hospital and said 'Have you got any part-time jobs?' "Yes, when can you start?" The following week I was working part-time.

We then moved up to Southport. Of course I wanted a baby and a couple of years later Catherine came along in Ormskirk, Lancashire. But we really didn't settle up there and the work that my husband was doing was in a very rough area in Bootle and it wasn't unusual for him to come home with a cut lip and a black eye. He taught English and he was in charge of the library, and he was a six footer, he was a big man with a big voice, but he was working in a Catholic school where the boys could do no wrong. So when he was offered early retirement he took it.

We decided that we were going to run a family history study centre and a guest house. We were just outside Ilminster on the old A303. But we didn't have enough capital to hang on in there and the bank eventually said "I'm sorry, but you've got to go." So I went back to work again. Caroline was a year old when I got my job here in Beaminster. That was 1983 and I've been here ever since.

We got offered a flat in Hogshill Street, we had a winter let in Charmouth up on top of the hill and a farm cottage in Netherbury. Then the farmer decided he wanted his cottage back so it was all a bit hairy. Then my husband's mother died and left us enough to put a deposit down on a new house at Mosterton. We were there for quite a few years.

Based in Bridport I worked a big rural area which took in Lyme Regis, Crewkerne, Maiden Newton, Sydling. We would do what we called domino deliveries, we would take the women into hospital, deliver them in there and then look after them when they came home again. When I first came there were virtually no home births here. Most of the GPs weren't happy at all about home births. It wasn't on their remit. They didn't understand that midwives were actually responsible for the births. So I was here a year before I did a home birth and that was on a Bank Holiday Monday, and that was a panicked GP saying "Can you come, she's delivering and we can't move her." So I rushed down to Bridport, delivered that baby, and said to the GP 'Look, it's not the end of the world. If babies are going to be born normally, they're going to be born normally wherever they are.' I think he saw how straightforward it was and how I sorted everything out and how the mother was happy and the baby was happy and he went off quite calm.

So that was the beginning, and then within a few months we had a couple of bookings for home births. This was '84, '85. And the word spread. Some of the people I worked with were completely anti and said "You can't do that!" 'Well actually I can.' And gradually the trickle became a bit more of a flood.

At the time when we started there were just the two of us, so between us we did all the home births and we were on call for our own women. It started with one or two, and then it became five, then ten. Then we were getting about one a month, so sometimes you had three in one month and then nothing for two months.

Memorable births? Lots! Bungalows in West Bexington with a wood stove that was smoking so much that we couldn't breathe so we had to decamp into the bathroom. Trucks on Cogden beach, it was very windy that night, it was autumn and you were exposed down there. Caravans and trailers with baths in up on the hill between Little Bredy and Hardy's monument. Watching the dawn come up. I remember that vividly. It was in June, it was a lovely morning and she was just about to deliver but we thought we'd give her a bit of space. The GP and I were standing there looking at the sun coming up in this beautiful space thinking 'What are we doing in houses when we could be out here,' but that was one of the GPs that did like home births and came with me to a lot of them. Home births with birthing pools, in the garden. We were convinced it was a bit on the chilly side and we really ought to be indoors.

Underwater births? The first few were a challenge but it was just a case of making sure you bring the baby out of the water in a smooth way, and face first, so as the cold air hit the baby's face and it took a breath so it was breathing air in, not water. It's a much easier transition for them than coming out into the air. It's totally natural.

The one in the bender up on the hill here, I'd seen her a couple of days before and she'd shown me where she wanted to have this baby, and I was thinking 'Oh well, yes, ok, we can do this.' And while I was in the throes of explaining to my colleagues where she lived and what she wanted and they're all taking deep breaths and thinking "What has she done now?" the woman rang me up in labour and she was a month early so I said 'It'd probably be a lot better if you went to hospital 'cause you're baby's going to be on the small side.' She said "No, I'm not going anywhere." And by the time I got to her, it was February, it was dark, it was raining, it was cold, and we got into this bender and she was well into labour, we had a wood stove burning in the corner which bothered me, we were in this tent with one pole in the middle and a mattress on the floor, and as I knelt down on the floor, it was a tarpaulin and you could feel the mud underneath squelching, the light was a candle. I had a tiny torch, but as everything does in those situations, it went very smoothly, easy birth, no problem, but because I was expecting a small baby, and because I was where I was, I called my colleague to come, we always have to call for backup…

Mobile phones? Yes. Luckily the ambulance turned up just after I'd delivered the baby, and he came in with this great big torch, and I said 'Smashing, shine it on the baby because I need to see the baby's colour.' And luckily the baby was crying and it was nice and pink. The ambulance men and women in this area are absolutely brilliant. And they thought it was a huge joke with me squelching around on this mud. But luckily all was well.

Complications? I want a healthy mother and a healthy, live baby, I just want to be where it's safest to be, and if I think that's the hospital, that's the advice that I'm going to give. But occasionally now, they don't want to take it, and that makes life difficult.

Any changes ? The babies are healthier. Women have better lifestyles, most of them have a good diet and that's the key. Breastfeeding? It's a myth to say that people don't breastfeed any more, the majority do. It's the minority who don't and it's usually from childhood, and this is why I think it's so important to get this information through to little children at school to see women breastfeeding, and for that to become the norm to them. The NCT are brilliant, they've taken themselves and their babies into schools and breastfed in front of the class so that the children growing up can see that this is a normal and natural thing to do. It is not normal and natural to put a bottle in a baby's mouth, but you go into a shop and buy a doll, what has it got? It's got a plastic bottle. I'd like to throw them all out. Out of all the home births I've had, which is just over 200, just in the Beaminster area, 99.9 per cent of them breastfed their babies and carried on breastfeeding.

Caesareans? Oh yes. There are increasing number of women who want a date and a time, like footballers' wives. They want to go into hospital on a certain day at a certain time, have their epidural, not feel anything and have a baby at the end of it. If it suits them and it's right for them, who's to argue with it? My feeling is that if women want to choose to have that way of birth they should choose to be in a private hospital so they're not costing the National Health because a home birth is a lot cheaper than a caesarean birth. In every possible way.

All we carry are the basic resuscitation tools to be there in case the baby has a problem. We have oxygen and an Ambu bag, which you see the ambulance men use. Our role is calming the mother…making sure everything's ok, staying out of the way and doing what she wants to do and making sure she's safe. If you're at home amongst your own germs it's a much healthier way to be than in a hospital where there's either total sterility or nasty bugs floating around.

Pain? If women know what painkillers are available and at home it's basically warm water in the pool – wonderful painkiller – entonox, (gas and air to breathe), walking around, having your back rubbed, the T.E.N.S. machine, which is an electrical pulsing thing that you put on the back, they are just in the mindset that they can cope with that. It's not a problem. If they're frightened of the pain they won't be at home. Some of them start off with the idea that they want to stay at home, and a few hours in they say "No, I want my epidural now." 'Ok, fine, let's go to hospital.' It has to be a highly trained anaesthetist who does this sort of thing.

Husbands? You mean the partners? We don't talk about husbands. Funnily enough as I started my training in Bristol, men were starting to come in to the delivery room, and to a lot of the midwives working then, that was a shock. "Men in here?" They had to have gowns, gloves, hats on, they had to be completely covered up. "You stand over there, and you don't do anything and you don't say anything." So completely the opposite now, when you get some partners who want to actually deliver the baby. It's gone full circle. But on the whole now it's the norm for men to be around. When I go to them to talk through the home birth situation I say 'Do you realise how busy you're going to be as the dad? You're going to have an awful lot of jobs to do' and you can see them thinking "Oh, I thought I was just going to have to hold a hand." So it is a partnership.

What happens to the afterbirth? Well there's choices. A lot of home births the mothers want to dig a hole and bury it and plant a tree on it, I've never yet come across couples who want to eat it. That's a complete myth. But on the whole it's "Oh take it away, I don't want it," in which case we deal with it, or it's "Yes, we want to keep it and we want to plant it." And I say 'Well if you do it tomorrow, that's fine, but if not, then in a double bag and in the freezer for when you do want to do it. You can't leave it lying around.'

I believe it's a myth that young women get pregnant in order to get a council flat. They either want to get pregnant, or they're totally ignorant, or they're drunk. If you told me that I'd be handing out methadone in the maternity unit 20 years ago I would not have believed you, but now it's normal. It effects the baby because obviously when the baby is born you've got to wean the baby off the drugs, and they go into withdrawal and they can be very poorly.

Concealed pregnancies? Oh yes. I suppose I've known three main concealed ones where the women were actually in labour and didn't know they were having a baby. They were mentally blocking it out because I don't believe any woman with a baby inside them moving around and kicking could not know they were pregnant, they couldn't bear the thought of being pregnant. So it is a shock when that happens. You think 'How can this woman, in this day and age not accept the fact that she's pregnant and deal with it, and get through to labour and deliver?' And the shock you see on their faces when you say 'Push, because I'm delivering this baby.' You show them the baby and they still are not taking it in.

Delivering a baby for adoption? It's less common, in my career it's not happened very often at all. Even if a girl decides that she wants the baby adopted, she will see the baby and cuddle the baby for as long as she wants to. Occasionally they will breastfeed, but on the whole if the baby's going to be adopted they don't breastfeed. It's rare round here.

It's nice to be in the area and see all the babies I've delivered growing up. It's a great pleasure to bump into them in supermarkets and see them all growing up. They recognise me! Amazingly so. Years and years ago and they still remember things in great detail, things I said which is quite frightening. I think it's a woman to woman thing. We are helping women to deliver their babies, we're not doing it for them.

Years ago midwives had to be licensed by the bishops, we're talking 17th, 18th century. I've seen bishops' licences for midwives which are very interesting. It was a character reference. Royalty and the well-to-do would have trained midwives. When Charles I's wife was having her babies, she brought her mother's midwife over from France, who was very well paid, and was always invited to the christenings of these babies.

Invited to the christenings? Yes ! And occasionally weddings now. I've delivered all three babies of one family. That was my hat trick, and very memorable. Many years ago when I was in Southport I delivered the son of the goalkeeper of Liverpool Football Club, that was remarkable.

Music is vital. I couldn't live without it. It is Radio 3 occasionally, Classic FM. I have music in all the rooms in the house. When I retired they gave me a new digital radio from all the midwives in West Dorset. They knew how important it was for me.

My retirement? I only got the travel bug fairly recently, but now I want to go everywhere. I've been to Canada, I've been to Portugal on holiday, been to Madrid, going to Australia probably next year and all places in between. I desperately want to get to St Petersburg to see the Winter Palace and the Hermitage and

I'm writing a book. It's family history. A favourite ancestor of mine is Beatrix Walcot. She was born in Shropshire in 1575, she had two good marriages and her second husband was John Digby who was ambassador to Spain. He was made the Earl of Bristol and he tried to organise the marriage between Prince Henry, James I's son to the Infanta of Spain, and then when Prince Henry died it became Prince Charles, later Charles I. So I now know everything about Beatrix, and I want to write her story.

32. Ruth Thompson – Midwife & barn dance caller, Maiden Newton. Born 1954.

I have a bit of a Jekyll and Hyde existence. It did leak out at work a few years ago, somebody knew, and then I started being booked for people at work

I was born in Dorchester. My parents originally came from Sussex. My father was a chartered accountant and Mum did audit work. My grandparents were all in Sussex. My mother's father worked for the Post Office and my father's father was a carpenter in Portslade. We lived in Dorchester until I was about 18, then I went to Brighton to do nursing training, and then Tunbridge Wells to do midwifery. I stayed in the South East for about 11 years, and then came back.

At the time I trained we had all done nursing training, so we did an 18-month course to be midwives, that course does still exist but most people coming in to midwifery do a three-year course. They're not already nurses. They come straight in to midwifery. I think we were sceptical about that to begin with but no, we've got some very good midwives who haven't got the nursing background. I think it's very hard for them because a lot of them are mature people, a lot of them have got their own families, and how they managed to do that training with young children I don't know. We all lived in. It's now university-based. Not necessarily for a degree course, a lot of people do diplomas but I wouldn't mind betting that in the next few years that'll be phased out.

I started work in Yeovil, and I've been there ever since. I've been working in Yeovil for 24 years. I enjoy it. Yes I do. I was full-time until my oldest son, Roland was about 18 months old, and then I managed to do a job share and I've been job sharing ever

since, picking up extra shifts. It does work quite well. I could be there any time, nights, days, weekends, but not as much as full time.

I thoroughly enjoyed being pregnant. I loved it. I loved every moment of it, come the second one I was a bit creaky and stiff, I was 38 when I had my first one and 41 for the second, but I felt well, I thrived, loved being pregnant, loved having babies, I was very lucky, I had very positive experiences. Women are supposed to have a choice, and if it's their choice to stay at home then they have to be supported by their community midwife. If things go awry then they end up being transferred in, but there are many women who have straightforward, satisfactory home deliveries who could have been advised to go into hospital, and there is still an opinion that everyone should have their babies in hospital, even though there are statistics saying that the success rate of home deliveries is every bit as good, if not better than hospital deliveries because you don't get the intervention, and it's more positive at home, the woman's in her own environment, but having said that I've worked purely in the hospital.

The catchment area for Yeovil hospital is quite large. Westwards we go up to Chard, north up to Glastonbury, Street, and Dorset as well, over to Shaftesbury. A lot of things are much the same. Epidural rate is higher, caesarian rate has soared, very few women choose to have a caesarian, but we don't deliver many breech babies any more, they mostly all have caesarians. Women are given choice, and someone who's had a caesarian before will be given a choice about whether they want to have one with the second baby. I had a caesarian for my first, and it wasn't that many years ago, my son's only 14, but attitudes have changed in recent years. Nobody asked me if I wanted a caesarian for the second, and it's likely that if they had done I would have said 'Yes, please,' because the experience of the first

Ruth Thompson with fiddle, Maiden Newton

one was fine, I didn't have a problem with it, but I'm glad I wasn't given the choice because as it turned out I had a very normal, straightforward delivery, and I'm very glad that I did.

We're involved as midwives up to 28 days maximum, but that tends to stop at about ten days. If all is well we transfer care over to the health visitor. Women go home within 48 hours normally, and in fact women having caeserians usually go home on the third day, I stayed in for eight days and thoroughly enjoyed it.

Husbands and partners have been welcome in the labour ward for many years. I do take issue with one or two aspects of it, men are encouraged to be supportive and understanding of their wife's moods during pregnancy, they're more or less expected to be there at delivery, which I don't necessarily think is the right thing. I think their role should be support, if providing support means being with the other children at home, that's every bit as supportive. Most men will be present at delivery, but as soon as the baby's born they're rather chucked out, and I think that's rather sad. I do like the idea of the labour wards where both partners can stay and go home together.

Attitudes to breastfeeding haven't changed enough. I was horrified to hear a survey on the radio within the last year about breastfeeding, attitudes against, and I was horrified to hear that a lot of people don't like seeing breastfeeding in restaurants. I thought 'Where else are you supposed to feed your baby?' The baby's having its dinner as well so where else can you go? If you're in a restaurant where are you expected to go to feed your baby? That survey really did take me aback.

I think the media has a lot to answer for, how often do you see a woman breastfeeding on Eastenders or any of the other soaps? They just don't. You never see anyone on television breastfeeding. If I had a young baby now, I would be feeding it and you would be interviewing me and I wouldn't have a

problem with that. I first fed my oldest son in public when he was two weeks old at church and the vicar came down and said "You shouldn't be sitting here on your own, come and join the rest of us, would you like a glass of water, can I get you anything?" And I felt totally welcomed by someone, quite an elderly man, actually, but he'd spent quite a lot of his life in Africa, and to him it was a natural thing to do, to get on and feed your baby. I think perhaps as midwives we don't give the downside of bottle feeding enough, the allergy problems, obesity, raised blood pressure, lower IQ, the list goes on and on..

I'm sure there's a link between that and the obesity problem. But of course you always get women who say they bottle fed their babies and they were fit and healthy and slim and had good IQs, but if we're talking about the health of the nation as a whole, I firmly believe that if we had better breastfeeding figures a lot of the problems we have would go.

I don't know what the figures actually are for teenage pregnancies rising. I certainly don't think free family planning has made any difference. I would think that adoption figures are going down, but that's maybe because there isn't the same pressure for a young girl to part with her baby. She's perfectly at liberty to keep her baby, but you can't be judgemental or self-righteous about people who have extremely difficult decisions to make in their lives.

How did music come into my life? It's mainly traditional music. My father played piano and I had piano lessons as a child so I had a fairly classical upbringing with piano. I didn't start playing the fiddle until I was in my 20s, and this sounds a bit scatty but I used to go to a folk club in Tunbridge Wells, and for the first time I met the music session ethic, where people would just bring instruments along, sit around a table and play tunes and I'd never seen this before and I was completely fazed by it.

And I just wanted to do that, I admired these people so much who just wanted to play tune after tune with no notes in front of them and I thought 'I really want to do that.' I'd tried various instruments I suppose in my youth, whistle and recorder and guitar a bit, and then I borrowed a fiddle, thought I'd have a go, and after six weeks, the person I'd borrowed it from wanted it back, but by then I was hooked. I've never achieved a particularly high standard, but I love it, I love playing, I love the people we've met over the years and the whole scene of traditional music, and I found that I could play in sessions, that was my sole ambition, to play in sessions, it was all I ever wanted to do, and having found that I could do that, then other things led from it like being in a band.

I started many, many years ago in a band in Dorchester called The Butter Street Buskers, I don't think they're going any longer, then I joined a Yeovil-based band, and then we formed a band down here called The Raunchers, which I loved, that was really great music, then English Mustard, who were going for many years with different line ups, but they don't exist any longer.

Playing village halls, weddings, marquees, PTAs, cricket clubs, anyone who wants a barn dance. And then we formed a band here called The Casterbridge Band, that's in relatively recent years. I don't actually play with that band, I do the calling, and I started calling when I was pregnant, in fact soon after I'd had my first child, I'd done a few gigs calling, really when bands were desperate and I stepped in.

I really enjoy calling. It is hard work, there's no let-up at all whereas the band can sit and relax for five minutes. The first one I ever did actually was for the organic farm at Godmanstone, many years ago. I was meant to be playing in the band but our caller let us down at very short notice and we had to find another caller. I phoned people I knew everywhere, following up leads, in the whole of the south west of England really, from Winchester to Gloucester, to Exeter and Plymouth, couldn't find a caller, this was at 24 hours notice, then in the end I thought it would probably be easier to find someone to dep for me in the band and I'll do the calling. So that's what happened. So I did that night and I thought it went quite well, and took on a few gigs calling after that, but it didn't really take off until I'd had my first child. I'd been playing in English Mustard with a two fiddle line up, then when I had a bit of a gap the band carried on with the one fiddle and functioned perfectly well and I wasn't needed, so I started doing more calling.

We do I suppose mostly English dances, I'm not one for making up dances, lots of callers make up their own dances. I love Strip the Willow dances. There are lots of modern dances that I use because they flow, they're fun to do, they embody all the good figures in a good sequence, but there are lots of traditional dances as well that are great fun to do. I'd love to do more of the triple minors which are the dances which used to be done one hundred, two hundred years ago, and I think that the reason they went out of fashion was that they were a three couple sequence. You have a long line of couples, one, two, three, and then it starts again, one, two, three, and it rotates so the couples move into different positions, but couple number three, they don't have very much to do. They tend to do a lot of hanging around until their turn comes to the top and then they become couple number one, but there are some really nice dances, but they are a little bit tricky to do. One hundred, two hundred years ago, people would have known the dances. In any village there would have been a repertoire of maybe up to ten dances, but now we know hundreds of dances because we pick them up from other people, we go to dances and we hear a caller doing a good dance and we jot it down and it gets trotted out and joins the repertoire.

Caller and midwife is an unusual combination. I must admit that a lot of my colleagues are not very music orientated, certainly not traditional music, so there's no one I can really talk to about it. I have a bit of a Jekyll and Hyde existence.

I'm not very purist about the dances, and I don't think people used to be either. Was it in Under the Greenwood Tree when Fancy Day was dancing with Dick Dewey, and it came time for casting off, well he didn't want to cast off, because he didn't want to let go of Fancy Day, and he had a little preach from someone who said "If a dance writer had meant you to cast off, that's what you've got to do." I do adapt dances sometimes, if I'm with people who I think perhaps aren't going to be able to do a lady's chain then I'll stick in a right hand star and a left hand star, and if people don't like it, I'm sorry. My job is to keep everybody entertained.

You do get a lot of purists who will object if you don't do it the way they think it should be, but I'm the caller and if that's how I want to do it that's how I'll do it. I use a radio mike. I wouldn't be without it. I'll often do the walk through without a mike. It depends on the ambient noise. I'm often teaching people how to do the dance before it starts. Once the music starts I couldn't possibly…and dances are so much bigger. A hundred years ago a barn dance was a barn dance, and barns really, as barns go they're quite small, or you might have a dance in someone's living room, but now we're talking about cramming 100 people into a village hall. Not everyone's dancing, a lot of

people will be talking so you can't possibly compete with it. I can't anyway. So I'm fairly free and easy.

Colin my husband will very often be playing, but I'll work with other bands as well, and in many ways that's easier with children if you're out at different times. I like working with other bands, I like seeing who's around and what bands there are and what tunes they play. I had seen Colin in music sessions in a wonderful pub in Sussex but we didn't really meet until we played together at a seedy but much loved pub in Sidmouth called The Mason's Arms. We've shared and loved English music ever since. We'll play a good tune wherever it comes from but we feel that most of the good tunes are English.

Occasionally I see people from barn dances at Yeovil hospital. It can be a bit embarrassing because they recognise me and I don't always recognise them, which makes me feel a little bit guilty, but yes, that does happen. And likewise someone will come up to me at a dance and say "You delivered my baby five years ago," and I have to say 'I'm awfully sorry, I can't remember your name.' It's impossible.

But it's great, we've made so many friends up and down the country, people will just turn up on the doorstep and say "Can we stay the night?" Or phone up and say "We're en route to Cornwall, can we stop?" And the same for us, it's great. It did leak out at work a few years ago, somebody knew, and then I started being booked for people at work who wanted their birthday parties, wedding parties, but I did keep it quiet for a long time. I always get nervous when I'm working for people I know well. It's sometimes easier being anonymous.

33. Rev Canon Nerissa Jones MBE — Parish Priest, United Benefice of Askerswell, Loders and Powerstock. Born 1941.

I adore it here. In spite of having done so much in towns, I am absolutely a country person at heart… Outstandingly beautiful, without question, and some of the nicest people that you could possibly ever hope to be amongst.

I was actually born at a place called Walton on the Hill, but I was brought up at Leigh Gate in West Milton. It's very unusual that anyone comes back as a minister to the place where they were born or grew up. My parents first came there in the 1930s. My first memories were of carthorses. I remember so vividly coming up about as far as this black carthorse's knee. The war was in full flow. My father was a fireman, he'd been a fireman in London during the serious times there, and when he came down he used to bicycle over to Weymouth. You went on duty for three or four days at a time. I knew nothing apart from the sound of aeroplanes going back and forth over the top which I didn't like. A child picks up other people's feeling. I remember my father, across one of the large fields, you could see him just nip past a gateway as he bicycled off. It's quite a bike ride to Weymouth. You just take things for granted when you're a child.

The farm was small, but my father owned more land at Kings at the top of Eggardon. Nick Poole's father farmed there later on. Yes. My father was his father's landlord, and my earliest memory in King's farmhouse was living there for a while. Then later on six German prisoners of war lived in it, who worked on the farm. The prisoners of war were very nice to us. I suppose they missed their families. Hundreds of thousands of prisoners never went

back. I remember how very nice they were. They would carve us little whistles and that sort of thing. There were five of us, a sister and a brother older than me with a space in between, and then me and then a brother and sister below.

My father, before he came to Dorset, was a solicitor in London. The grandparents were very medical. His father was an eye surgeon at London in Moorfields, and his father was too. Their family name was Lister, which is a good medical name, and his great uncle was the Lister who was so instrumental in introducing antiseptics into this country. That's where the Lister comes from and my parents adopted Tyndall later on. Further back on that side they were Quakers and therefore unable to go to university. In the early 1800s, they were wine merchants in Norwich. They didn't drink, but they sold to people who did. On my mother's side her father was a soldier in the Coldstream Guards in the Boer War. My parents were quite dedicated atheists. My mother's immediate family was intensely Anglo-Catholic, and the others in the 1880s, largely changed over to the Church of England, although some ancient great aunts were still Quakers.

I was educated at home and in Bridport, at the Grove School. I know quite a number of people still to this day, they said "I know you," when I came back to work here. Growing up here I know where all the houses are and what bridlepaths there are because we always rode when I was little. I know the geography and the contours, I think it's absolutely part of me. I hadn't been back here long when a farmer asked me to sign his gun certificate, which I did, it's part of what you do, there's a little section where you put how long you've known the applicant, and I put 'fifty years' in there, which I thought was quite funny. I really enjoyed putting that.

So there are people who knew me when I was a Brownie.

Rev Canon Nerissa Jones with North Poorton Church

When I was 11, I went to the grammar school in Bridport for three years, and then I went to London, because from a very early age I had wanted to become a ballet dancer.

There was a dancing school here, it was run by a Miss Fairbairn who was originally South African, she must have been born in about 1890 or earlier, she'd been associated with quite a lot of dancers during the whole development of British ballet, during the first half of the 20th century. I started with her and then, of course she also taught in London so that's how it all developed. I was staying with relations mainly. You do two ballet classes a day and an afternoon and evening of lessons, so it's a good mix, but I didn't dance for very long or professionally. I met David when I was 16, he was a contemporary of my brother's at Sandhurst, and my brother was cadet huntsman of the Sandhurst beagles, and in the summer holidays if you had a suitable place you could bring them home, together with the kennel huntsman. He brought them home with this really nice person, David. I was only 16 and then by the time I was 17 we liked each other tremendously, and when I was 19 we got married.

My dancing career stopped. The production I really enjoyed was a musical which was a revival of an Ivor Novello musical called The Dancing Years. This particular period which was '57-'58, was a very peculiar one in the English theatre. All the huge theatres in every town were still going. Two or three years later they'd all turned into bingo halls. It was the last gasp of travelling companies and repertory and large shows that were going round. We used to move on Sundays every other week usually you did a fortnight somewhere. There's no large theatre in England that I haven't danced in. None. This show went on for 10 or 11 months and it was a tremendous experience. I was 17.

There'd been a lot of poverty in Dorset in my day, but what one saw in Liverpool for instance, this was 12 years after the war,

it was quite shocking. It was just the sheer, utter poverty of living in a room which you stepped in off the street with huge lorries going past, belching their beastliness straight through the front doors. I think it's probably hard to remember for anyone now quite how filthy the Midlands were and the Black Country as it was called. We went to Edinburgh and Glasgow. Our chorus was about 50, and of course all the props and everything went on by pantechnicon, but we travelled by train. It was just how theatre was, and we played to full houses. It was extraordinary, and after that, television and bingo and a different way of life, but it was a fascinating era to be involved in.

An army wife? I suppose you have to call it that and I began to have my children. We moved first to Shipton Bellinger. David was in the Duke of Edinburgh's Royal Regiment, he had been a Royal Berkshire man. We went all over the place. I had one child while I was still there, Anna, my oldest daughter, then we went to Malta which was lovely and I had my son Thomas, then when we were back in Aldershot, I had my third daughter Harriet.

We had something like 30 moves in 28 years. Well then we ended up in the army in Ghana, but I had a long gap at home because our youngest daughter is grievously handicapped and I refuse to use any word like 'learning disability' because it insults her. It really insults her. It's not that she can't learn, it's that she's brain damaged, she can't see, she's living in Bridport. So that's another reason why I'm really glad to be here. She was born in '67, she's going to be 40 next year. She loves movement and speed and things and she's going to go to Disneyland in America for her birthday. But looking after her, which I did with help until she was 14, was absolutely full-time.

David having been teaching at Camberley Staff College, was seconded to the Ghana Armed Forces to be the deputy commandant of the staff college there. And that was when

Harriet was offered a place in a home for people with grievous disabilities in Dorchester. It was new and small and really delightful in every way. We took her to see the paediatrician who very sweetly played with her for a little while and then said "Mrs Jones, this is exactly the kind of person we're looking for," and that was so lovely. No one had ever said anything like that about her before, but it was very hard to leave her. She was fourteen and a half. I suppose her mental age is about one in some ways, and luckily, although she recognises us every time and did after the first six months I don't think she pines for us. She's beautifully looked after.

So anyway, we went to Ghana, and that was an extraordinarily exciting time. We were there for two and three-quarter years, it was a time of famine and turmoil, this was in the early 80s, and revolution, it was a very amazing time. Independence? That was '56, it started with Nkruma being head of government at independence and eventually people took over from him because they didn't like the way he was.

Ghana is a very sophisticated country, but matters there were deeply compromised by the famine in West Africa. There were two revolutions to do with Jerry Rawlins, the first one he took over in '79 before we arrived. During that time a new constitution was forged and then he stood down and there were elections. He went back to being in the air force. When we came in February '80, it was clear to us that the governing party were taking all, they were saying "Winner takes all," in spite of the constitution. Things were sliding and sliding. On 31st December 1981, it all came to a head and JJ Rawlins came back. People have to choose very quickly when there's something like that, "Which side am I on?" It was a very interesting period in which David was able to do a great deal of good. One of the main problems was getting the army back under control. A lot of the soldiers who hadn't been paid, hadn't been clothed, hadn't been fed thought "Our time now."

Dreadful, dreadful things were already raging round, you could sit on top of your house and hear arms going off. David was asked to try and help with that, which he did terribly effectively. It really was remarkable, they got almost all the arms in and they got the soldiers out growing their own food and doing army exercises, which actually was what they wanted. They didn't want to go around pillaging and raping much, but if you've got nothing else to do and also no food and no pay and a gun… It was very dangerous too.

It so happened that I became aware that the psychiatric hospital which was right in the middle of the city had very little food indeed. I mean no food, people were starving. Not just starving but they were dying. There was a little bit brought in every day but a lot of them weren't getting it at all. It was a most dreadful situation.

I went there to ask what I could do and they showed me the children's ward, which was a sort of yard around which were rooms with no beds or anything like that, and there was no water. One of the rooms was literally piled high with frightful dirty clothes that they had just stuffed in there, covered in shit. There just wasn't water, so I took them away and washed them bit by bit and told people who had food what I was finding. So I managed to get enough for them to get one meal of rice and protein a day, but they were just dying like flies. It was more to give them the feeling that someone cared. It's very interesting psychologically, I think, that if someone ceases to look recognisably human, people give up on them. So that was the staff too, they would just let people stagger away, what was the point? It was just like a concentration camp. That was exactly what it was like, especially in some of the men's wards and wards for the people they called criminally insane. It was just like that. Lots of people naked, other people with just some dirty shirt on, it was terrible.

Gradually more people got to know that they could help, by giving me something, I would cook it and take it, but that was hopeless. It was hugely overstaffed and so what food did come in by official channels was being used for the staff, and they had their own families. There were 60 cooks for what was meant to be about 2,000 patients. But I think there was about double that at the beginning.

In the end I did get the government interested because they sent for me one morning and I took Jerry Rawlins round on a Sunday and he saw the full horror of it for himself. The full, complete horror and he was tremendously moved and he put in train a team of doctors and army personnel who moved in. He had the kitchen guarded, and you cook a lot better if someone's standing over you with a rifle. And also the churches all helped. All of them. And they decided that each day of the week a whole denomination would come and do what it could. So every Anglican church, with everybody providing half a cup of rice, it mounts up a lot. They did it and the Methodists and the Presbyterians and the Baptists and the Roman Catholics, there were seven days in the week when at least one meal's worth of food was going in.

When we came back David was at the Ministry of Defence in London, and I went to London University to read German. I went to Queen Mary College and did a degree. It was just fun and then I went to the theological college in Oxford.

A conscious decision? I'd known for years before but it wasn't possible to do anything about that sort of thing. It might never have been if Harriet hadn't found the right place to live.

Women could work as deaconesses, which meant you did exactly the same training, and exactly the same selection process, but they wouldn't ordain you on account of your foul gender. I was ordained in 1988 as a deacon, but then there was another five years before the church decided that gender is not an insuperable barrier to godliness and use, and I was ordained priest.

David by this time had seen the job of associate director of Oxfam in the Times one morning and said he thought he'd go for that, "I'll never get it" he said, "but I would like it very much." So he sent off and never heard anything for ages, and then they got hold of him and he had a long series of interviews and competitive entry and got it. So that's in Oxford. I was doing what I really wanted to do and then when I came back to London, I went to St Botolph's at Aldgate. It's the church by the tube station. Being a city church it didn't have an enormous congregation but it had a series of cares and services for people living on the streets which included setting up a doctor's surgery at St Botolph's. The other very important thing that St Botolph's did was being open to Christian people who were gay and lesbian, because the church is usually so particularly foul towards them.

There was a particularly good parish priest called Malcolm Johnson there then, I was very glad to work with him for five years. And then we both left and I went to become the incumbent of St Chad's, Wood End, which was in Coventry. It's an outer city post-war development, which had been good in its time but everything had gone very much pear-shaped, what with the car industry moving out and the unemployment…

Some people moved but a lot of people couldn't and it was very difficult for them. Anything you've ever read about the difficulties of living and bringing up your family in such conditions were more than true there. So I worked there for eight years and did a lot of exciting things. I loved Wood End. Afterwards the city of Coventry gave me their gold medal which is like the Freedom of the City and the people of Wood End put me forward for an MBE.

Coming home to Dorset? Well I was asked to come. I had a letter from all the church wardens asking me to come if I was thinking of changing my job, and there were several reasons why I thought very seriously about it. One is that Anna, one of my daughters lives here and her husband and three children, in West Milton, and Harriet lives in Bridport. So that was very, very high on my thoughts, the other was that I had to decide whether I wanted to stay in Wood End until I retired, which would be another five years if I retired at 65. Nobody would want you for two years or whatever. So it was just the right moment. I left Coventry in July 2001. I've been here five years. This is my sixth year. It is fantastic. I adore it here. In spite of having done so much in towns, I am absolutely a country person at heart.

The parish? It's Askerswell, Loders, Dottery, Powerstock and North Poorton. It takes in the villages of West Milton, Nettlecombe, Loscombe and Wytherston, you waggle about a bit on the roads to get from place to place. In February they're making a new united benefice which will include the parish of Symondsbury with Broadoak and Eype. I'm a priest-in-charge. That's quite important, because vicars have got freehold. I haven't got freehold. The countryside? Beautiful. Outstandingly beautiful, without question, and some of the nicest people that you could possibly ever hope to be amongst.

There are four really important times in the country, they are Christmas, Easter, Remembrance and Harvest, at which time you get extraordinarily packed churches. So much so that you have to have a service in each church. Other times less so but the actual attendance is a great deal higher than the three and a half

per cent which is the normal church attendance throughout the land.

God fearing in these parts? You actually know a great many more people who don't go to church than people who do, but there are times when you become faintly useful, I think. When people die of course, christenings and weddings, but I was thinking in particular funerals. Also, which I think is enormously important, I do get the chance to pass on what I've learnt, both by experience and also theological training. And one of the things that I am deeply interested in is that for hundreds of years parish clergy have not, on the whole passed on what they actually know. I try to pass on what I was lucky enough to learn at theological college, combined with my experience and theirs. I like engaging in conversation. Things are not the same as they were in our grandparents day. We don't think the same and we shouldn't be thinking religiously the same either. Things have changed so much. From education, different ideas coming in, a different make-up in society. Fortunately deference went out, it only began to go out after the Second World War but you know, some people cling to it and long for deference, but they always want to be the person that's deferred to. Is Dorset still feudal? Sometimes it is but it's a bit of a joke when it is, and it's very sad. I would try to undo deference at every turn.

Parish cider? When we married, my father gave us a cottage, at West Milton. I've met older people who lived there or were brought up there, in the cottage. So that's given it a lovely new dimension. It was a sheet anchor and the children attended primary school here for a bit, so it's always been home, and so when we came I think Nick had started cidering. I'd known him all his life, and so I was only too glad to be involved, it's a lovely thing. On the first Sunday in the month, after church, I always look forward to going to the cider shed. I help making and collecting of apples, that has to be part of it. About two thirds of the people in West Milton are involved. An alternative communion? I love it, it is in a way. You see such goodness going on there. And then there's the Powerstock Cider Festival. Oh that's fantastic, yes. It won a prize at the Bath & West this year for innovation.

Preaching? It's a nerve-wracking affair because you want it to be right for the people that are there, you want it to tell them something, you want it to relate to their lives and not just be something that happened in the olden days. I begin preparing my sermons on Monday and think of things during the week that join it all up together.

The working week? Well on Sunday I have two, three or sometimes four services because there's rather a mad pattern which means I have to be able to cover everything, although I've got wonderful Elaine Marsh who farms at West Milton and has trained to be a reader since I came. She can take services which are not Holy Communion, and I have lots of other help in that way but I still need to be able to cover them all in case other voluntary people can't. She can take funerals and is a marvellous pastoral help. And that's really very important, especially as the benefice gets bigger. You can't do it all on your own. So I have a lot of services on a Sunday, and although it's tiring, it's the easiest day of the week because you know what you're doing. During the week there are two schools here which I may be going to for assembly, Powerstock and Loders. I will have Symondsbury.

Clergy are supposed to say their prayers every day, so I quite often go into church here in the morning, and people come to see me, either by appointment or not. I have to work out who I ought to be seeing, people who I perhaps haven't met, people who've moved in, people who are in grief or very ill. Really your

timescale for visiting people is very short. You can't really visit anyone before ten, or at lunchtime, or before two, or much after five, so you've got two hours in the morning and perhaps three hours in the afternoon. And the school is not just a service, there are governors' meetings and parochial church councils.

Blessing of animals? I never have before but we're going to have a blessing of pets service at Powerstock during half-term, so I hope lots of people will bring their animals, just for fun. It could be really good. I blessed the Park Beagles at a meet last year. It was actually a moment of seriousness, because as the Hunting Bill was coming up people were wondering to what extent they were going to lose their jobs. The reality of what it's like for people is forgotten in Westminster. We have country services with rogation, with processions and things like that. And those four festivals really punctuate the year. But the main work is being attentive to people, listening and caring. It's being around, I expect a lot of people will say "Well she hasn't ever visited me," Or "I haven't seen her." I often feel there's so much more that I could do, but there isn't really.

God? I think God is consulted in times of need, or blamed, or asked "Why me?" At other times people don't feel the slightest bit concerned that they don't have anything to do with God. I think less belief probably goes with losing deference, in a way. There have been many generations now of people who find the Church irrelevant beyond words, and haven't been to it and see no reason why they should. But then you find that an awful lot of people have visited the church and left some kind of message in the Visitors' Book that they've felt more than just "it was a nice arch." So we have made a special effort to make our churches visitable and to have them open at all times. It's really important to have it open, and if you've got anything in it that's too valuable to have it open, why? Take it out.

I suppose what led me into the church, to become an ordained person, is a feeling that the group of people who come to it and read the radical teaching of Jesus must themselves be open to a kind of reform, and to being of use in society. So you're starting with people who are a bit converted, including myself! You ought to be able to be a bit encouraging.

An internal conversion? That's what I was looking for in myself, a kind of re-ordering of ourselves within, that would have a good effect for other people whether they think in your way or not.

And the future? I've passed my retirement year, and the diocese did ask me to stay on for a while, and then this came up, the new united benefice. So just at the moment it's impossible to say, except that I don't envisage full-time work until I'm 70 because (a) one must never think that one's the only person that can do anything, and (b) there's tremendous fun to have with David before we both get too old.

What would I like to do? I'd like to ride more, I share a horse with my family in West Milton but I don't have enough time to do it. Nobody minds me being able to ride on my day off. Riding on Eggardon as a child was fun, because the north side belonged to my father and belongs to my sister Sarah now. It was all open, there were no fences. There were more skylarks there then, but there are lots now. You often hear them, it's the one place you can really hear them, and up the valleys in West Milton too.

34. Jane Cotton – Undertaker, Weymouth. Born 1954.

Laugh about it? You have to. If you don't, it can be a very distressing job… Last week, for example, I conducted the funeral of a two-week-old baby and you never ever get used to those…

I'm Jane Cotton. I was born in Burton on Trent, Staffordshire. We're all from the Midlands, my mum was from Ashby-de-La Zouch, my father was from Leicester. My mum was a telephonist. She was also a pianist and Father was a telephone engineer. Later he was a warehouse manager for a tobacconist/confectioners.

I can only remember my grandfather on my mum's side, coincidentally he died the same year as my dad. He worked with tools, a real old village chap, agricultural farming machinery as well, I never knew my mum's mum, and my father's parents, we seemed to lose contact when he died. I was 12, so I never really knew them very well.

Schools, a Catholic primary and then the girls' grammar school in Burton. I moved down here in '82. I taught at the convent here in Weymouth, primary children, supply work and then Weymouth College. When Peter got too busy in the business I joined him full-time.

I met Peter at the Pavilion Theatre where he was stage manager, which he did at the same time as working in the family business. Our school used to take our Christmas productions there, so that's how I met him, I used to see him once or twice a year and the rest is history. He was very hard working. He loved theatre.

Cotton and Son was started by my husband's grandfather in 1912. It was a sideline for painters, decorators and chippies. They made the coffins and boiled up the pitch that they used to use to seal them. They used to call it the coffin shop, it was on Trinity Street here in Weymouth. Peter took over officially from his father in 1990. We've not quite reached our centenary yet, but we're only six years away.

The premises in Trinity Street is now a little holiday cottage, so tiny that you wouldn't believe you could run a business from it. We ran our office from home but downstairs we built a separate little viewing chapel, and behind that was all the working area. Upstairs was the storage and workshop. We had to take all our coffins upstairs and then down again to use them.

I guess really I did it in dribs and drabs. I wasn't terribly brave to begin with and I think it's the thought of it that's more worrying than actually doing it. When we were first together I used to sit on the stairs round the corner so that I couldn't actually see what he was doing and chat to him, and gradually I used to take a little bit of an interest and he'd say "Can you hold this?" And "Can you help me with that?" The first removal I did was by chance really, we happened to be in Dorchester and we had a call for a removal in Dorchester, so it was either Peter driving back all the way into Weymouth to get his chap and go back again, or as we happened to be just close by and he said "Do you want to have a go?" It was just a little old chap that had collapsed and I said 'Yes, I can do that.' And that was the beginning of it really.

There are some times when it's very unpleasant, but most of the time it's just a person. I say to a lot of families, when they're fearful of going into the chapel 'Did he or she hurt you when they were alive?' "No, no, no." 'Well he's not going to hurt you now.' I remember Peter telling me that, and it's actually quite right. Yes, if it's very unpleasant, then obviously it's not very

Jane Cotton with hearse, Weymouth

nice, but most are normal, straightforward.

In the early days, when I was doing quite a lot of removals, and especially for the coroner, there may have been a few raised eyebrows, as if to say "Oh, a lady, I don't see many ladies doing this," but I've never had any adverse comments, it's been fine.

Recently we did a little baby's funeral, I think they came here because it was a lady, they then asked for a lady vicar as well. Only the other day, I went to see a gentleman, and he said "I'm so glad it was a lady who came."

The Coroner? At the moment all of the funeral directors in this area do Coroner's removals on a rota basis. We do two months on call and six months off. And what that means is that we attend sudden deaths, unexpected deaths, suicides, murders, not that we get many, thankfully, road traffic accidents, things like that, where a doctor wouldn't normally be able to issue a death certificate. So we would take that person to Dorset County Hospital where a post-mortem would take place. We are working purely on behalf of the coroner in those circumstances. Sometimes we don't even meet the family.

It's mixed emotions, really. We're all on call 24/7 – you can't go anywhere without the mobile, so it can be a bit of a tie, especially if it's a busy day and you've got a couple of funerals and then the coroner's call comes in, because they don't like to wait too long. You can see some quite nasty sights.

Having said that, it can be quite interesting. Three years ago, we were called out to Portland Harbour and when we got there it was all sealed in a body bag, the police had already done that, so the chap and I picked up the stretcher and thought 'This is very light', trundling off up the beach and back to Dorset County, and when we got there, the mortuary technician opened it up and he looked at it and said "That looks a bit strange," Dave's an ex-farmer and he said "That's a cow's innards!" And what we think

had happened is that somebody had been illegally butchering on Portland and throwing whatever was left over the cliff. It had been washed into the harbour.

We call bodies the 'deceased'. We can keep ten in our premises. It's like you would see in a mortuary in a hospital. When I first entered this profession, the jokes, you can imagine, from friends, even now - but you get used to it. Laugh about it? You have to. If you don't it can be a very distressing job. It's a very rewarding job, but it can be quite emotional. Last week, for example, I conducted the funeral of a two-week-old baby and you never ever get used to those. I think it's the grief of the parents. This tiny little thing in your hands that you're dressing, you didn't know them and you think 'How very, very sad.' But what is really the lump in the throat time is the parents, their grief… it's just, you don't bury your children, do you? So that can be quite distressing.

People without relatives can be so sad because they've had a life of 80, 90 years. It doesn't happen that often but there are occasions when there might be two people sitting in the crematorium and nobody there to see them off.

We don't make coffins in-house, we get ours from a Dorset company, although they have just moved over the Somerset border. Occasionally we need a willow coffin. Occasionally cardboard coffins. I use them so rarely. There are various kinds, there are some which are coffin-shaped, and some which are tapered, but they're a cardboard box, and there's no disguising it really, although there is a company now, where they will decorate them with anything from football clubs to tartan.

A funeral from start to finish. If the person has died at home, the first contact is the removal. They're brought back here, and then it's time to go and see the family. I usually go to them, I think they're more comfortable and relaxed in their own home. So when I visit the family, a few minutes are spent talking about what happened, history and a bit of small talk, to relax them a little. We'll fill in the forms, and then we can talk about the kind of service they want. It gives them a bit of time to think about things. Most people have thought about bits and pieces to be honest. I will then ask them whether it's burial or cremation, and once I've got all the details I need I then start asking them for their preferences. 'Have you got a day or time in mind?' I'll always try and get as close to their choice as I can. It's not always possible but we'll get as close as we can. Do they want a minister? Church of England? Methodist? Roman Catholic? Humanist, which is non-religious, and then do you want to go to church? Or is it straight to the crematorium or burial or whatever. And then there's usually family discussions about that. And then, how do you think you want to get to the crematorium? Do you want to go in your own car? Do you want a limousine? Do you want the hearse to come to your house? Do you want to meet it at the crematorium or church or cemetery?

I would say probably 75 per cent want to see their loved ones. It tends to be family but occasionally a close friend will come. We did the funeral of a young girl, a 16, 17-year-old, and her family said her friends could come, so we had a lot of visitors. I tend to show them into the little chapel and then I'll wait outside unless they want me to stay in. Generally people want some time on their own because they want to talk to them and put things in the coffin.

They lie in a traditional coffin that's completely open. Generally it's the coffin-shaped traditional English type. Yes. I will ask them what they want their loved ones to be dressed in. Sometimes they will say to me "Oh, I've got it all ready. Got a suit for you." Or "Got the dress she was married in." Or "Came to my wedding in." Or they'll say "No, nothing would fit him, he always looked scruffy, put him in one of your gowns." We have what we would call a traditional funeral gown.

If you're dressing someone in their own clothes we would put them on as normal. I know a lot of funeral directors cut them up the back, but we never do unless we have to. They never fit as well, you can never tuck them in as well. The only time we would cut them is when "He got married in this" and that was about 40 years ago and he's now twice the size. But to be honest, if it's badly sized it tends to be the other way. Far too big because they've lost weight. That's easy to deal with, you can tuck it in.

It's quite common to put things in the coffin. Photographs, letters, birthday cards, but quite often we'll have a packet of cigarettes or a drink, although if it's a cremation we can't put glass in. Football memorabilia, teddy bears, toys, those tend to be the most common things. We did one where he was a very keen gardener and they put lots and lots and LOTS of seeds in with him, they thought they would grow. And another one, it was a burial - our poor bearers - it was a solid oak coffin and they put horse brasses in, it weighed a ton. If it's a burial, almost anything can go in if it'll fit. For a cremation nothing with a battery, occasionally somebody will give a toy or a teddy bear that speaks. You just take the battery out.

A lot of funeral directors embalm as a matter of course. We don't. There's not the need to because of refrigeration. But we will embalm sometimes, and those times are if we've got to keep somebody for a long time, it preserves them better. Some funeral directors will do it because they haven't got refrigeration. It's not particularly expensive. I've got what's called a trade embalmer, she's not employed by me full-time, but she's a qualified embalmer. Embalming fluid? It's dangerous if you drink it! But there's new stuff, it always used to be formaldehyde, all sorts of fancy names.

Embalming has to wait until registration is done because if all of a sudden the coroner decides that he wants to have a post-mortem it's a bit late if they've been embalmed. If it's cremation, we don't do anything until two doctors have examined them, and one would be the GP if they died at home, and another doctor would be a doctor completely uninvolved, not known to the deceased. So once that's done we could embalm if necessary. The deceased would be washed and teeth put in if necessary and eyes closed. And then they would be dressed and put in the coffin.

We don't use make up as a matter of course. For men, if the colour is really bad we might use a little bit of powder just to tone down a little bit, to stop a shine. When my father died I was 12, I can remember my mum, when she went to see him she said he looked like a painted doll. We would only use just the slightest hint, just to stop that really very white look, and on ladies only again, the tiniest touch, unless the family ask us. "She would never be seen without her makeup, here it is!"

Sometimes they give us a photograph. A photograph is more for hair, I think. And sometimes again, people will give a photograph. On the day of the funeral the coffin will be sealed with screws and flowers will be put on top of the coffin, then into the hearse and either straight to the crematorium or the church for the service. For a funeral I wear a striped skirt, called a funeral stripe. I wear a white shirt, a cravat, a black waistcoat and a black frock coat. Some ladies do wear top hats, but I don't. I look a bit like Jiminy Cricket!

Well, I've got my bearers. Mark is one, he drives the hearse, Dave works on a casual basis, and then I've got three other bearers, so there's five. Sometimes I need six if someone is particularly heavy. Members of the family do occasionally carry the coffin. The smallest will be at the foot end. Always feet first. Tradition. If it's a vicar they're carried in the same way but they are turned round, so they're facing their congregation. We always carry a body out of a house feet first. Always. We turn round in awkward positions if we have to.

My office manager, right-hand man, woman I should say, and very good friend, is Margaret Sherratt, she's been with me almost two years now, runs the office, runs me, she's been instrumental in bringing the office into the 21st century and she's starting to conduct some funerals. I took on a young man in March this year as a funeral assistant. He's 24, married with twin baby girls, so there's just the three of us full-time, then there's another chap who's been with us five or six years, his name's Dave, and then the other chaps that I have are all casual bearers, drivers and removers.

Well from a physical point of view, the hardest part of my job is doing removals of nasties. Road traffic accidents, someone who's been there two, three, five days, three months, been in the sea for a month, so from a physical point of view, it can be very tough. But we wear masks and they're very effective. Dave's got the stomach of an ox and he never wears a mask. The sight can be very unpleasant, but you harden yourself to it. You have to. You have to think 'This is the job I'm doing, I have to do it.'

From an emotional side, if someone is grieving for their spouse or for their parents you let them get on with it, you're not embarrassed by their tears and you encourage it. They say "I'm sorry" and you say 'You don't need to be sorry. This is what it's all about.' But I think it's a parent's grief that's difficult. And if we do babies' funerals, small children, I always dress them. I do it. I feel that I have to do it somehow. I think that probably stems from the first one that Peter and I did, he just didn't know what to do. He couldn't do it. And so I did it and I was cool as a cucumber until I'd finished, and it just broke my heart then. If they see a tear in your eye, that's fine.

When Peter died I found it very hard in fact. I went back to work very quickly, I came into the office the week after the funeral, just to get my head round the paperwork, and then the next week I started back. It was far too soon but I really had no option. People had to know I was carrying on if I wanted my business to survive..

I think some people, because they knew that Peter had died, found it was easier for them. "You know what I'm talking about, don't you?" And I'd say 'Well yes I do. And you know, it will get better. You'll have good days, you'll have bad days.'

I think people want to talk. I'm a perfect stranger to a lot of them. I'm the Funeral Director. They must feel utterly safe in my hands. You must instil confidence in people. Sometimes you think 'Have I done this right, have I done that right?' And you're panicking like hell underneath, but on the top like the proverbial swan, you're serene on the surface. Inside you're panicking, 'Have the flowers arrived?' or 'Did I tell the vicar to turn up at 11 o'clock?'

It's a bit like a wedding except that for a wedding you sometimes have 12 months to plan it. I have maybe five or six days. People often ask my opinion about children "Do you think we should take so and so to the funeral?" I would ask an age, and I think unless they're very tiny, my feeling is that you should ask the child. It's like anything that's unusual with a child, if you tell them the truth - you don't need to go into all the details, but as much as they need to know, and let them decide. I think if you ban them from going they'll always think it's taboo. Some don't want to go and that's fine. I was 12 when my father died and I chose not to go. I actually regret that now. Subconsciously, I think it was probably my mother's grief. I was all right as long as she was all right.

Increasingly we do more humanist funerals. Of course, there are no prayers, there are no hymns, so we'll have readings, poetry, tributes, CDs, we'll listen to all sorts of things. The range of music is phenomenal really. I've had everything from The Birdie Song, seriously, to high classics, military music, jazz, rock music, Queen - Another One Bites the Dust - a huge, huge range. There is a top ten if you like, Candle in the Wind, The Wind Beneath My Wings, I Did It My Way, all those, but quite a range.

Portlanders often want as much of Portland involved as possible. We did one a couple of months ago where the sons wanted to carry the coffin from the house to the church, which was probably 100 yards up the road, and we had to drive around a little part of Portland because that was where he was brought up. There was a big community and everybody followed because Portland is still a very strong community. I think the same thing happens in some of the villages around, even Upwey and Chickerell. There's a very strong village community and if it's a burial in Chickerell, quite often you'd get a lot of locals there. The church will be bursting at the seams.

In Weymouth we tend to have a high percentage of cremations, 80 plus per cent. There are still four cemeteries in Weymouth and Portland, there's one right beside the crematorium, one in Melcombe Regis, one in Wyke Regis, and one on Portland. Some of the churchyards have already run out of space and closed to new graves unless they've been reserved in the past, and then only for parishioners.

The cost of a funeral. Some people will say "They didn't want any fuss, they told us to put them in a bin bag on the compost heap!" They'd rather the children or the grandchildren have it and so they'll go as basic as they can. Others will say "I want the best, I've got to have the best this, best that, doesn't matter what it costs, we'll pay it." But the majority tends to be "I want it to be decent, I want to do what I think he would have wanted but I don't want to be silly about it." So it's a happy medium.

We have a pre-paid funeral plan, we've got more than 60 of those. I say to people if you want to do it, do it when you're well, not when you've been given three months or two weeks or whatever.

Yes, funerals have changed even in the short time that I've been involved. I think less people die at home and more in hospital. The majority of families don't stay close knit, so the son might come from London or Glasgow or New York or Barbados, they're flying in from all over the world just for the funeral. A lot of people still want a Church of England minister. I think there are probably fewer church services, it tends to be more at the crematorium. A lot of people are moving away from traditional black, they'll even say in newspaper announcements "No mourning clothes please." "Bright colours please." And I think a lot of families try to treat a funeral as a celebration of life rather than mourning a death.

It's never a happy occasion because you're saying goodbye to someone you love, but you try and remember the nice things that happen.

35. Angela Hughes OBE — Otters, conservation and green burials, Hammoon and Shillingstone. Born 1922.

It was kept secret, we didn't tell anybody outside the local landowners…I used to go down every night with the frozen fish.

I was born in London and my maiden name was Angela Pritchard. My father produced all kinds of sports equipment and he had a factory in London, so I got to know quite a few of the well known personalities like Wally Hammond the cricketer and Victor Barna who was the table tennis champion. My father's parents were from Canada, he came over in the Great War, got the MC and bar and never returned. He married my mother who was a Brine, who was from Dorset, funnily enough, near Wimborne, so that's one of the reasons why I came back because all of my ancestors had been farmers or in the Navy. I grew up in London.

During the war I joined the WRNS in the summer of 1942 and entered in the category of 'signals.' I was drafted to Greenock in Scotland. From there I applied to be a coder. I was duly sent on a course and qualified. I was then sent to Great Yarmouth where we operated solely with little ships. MTBs, MGBs, MLs, ASRs (motor torpedo boats, motor gun boats, motor launches and air sea rescue) and mine sweepers. All working in the Channel, I was subsequently commissioned as third officer cypher and drafted to Liverpool. Eventually I was sent to India where I worked in Cochin until returning home for demobilisation at Christmas 1945.

I met my husband in Gloucestershire. He was farming at Lydney in the Forest of Dean. Lovely views over the hills. I always had an interest in natural history. I was also a political agent for a long time. We wanted to expand and we were on the railway line, so all we had to do was hire a train and load everything onto the train and unload here in Dorset. Everything came by train even the cows. We milked in the morning in Lydney and milked in the afternoon in Dorset. The station was still working at Shillingstone, so we unloaded there.

We had looked at 100 farms and eventually we decided on Hammoon. That was in 1955, when there was still very good money to be made in farming. It was East Farm, Hammoon. We had 320 acres, all river frontage of the Stour, which was lovely. We built up to about 180, 200. Pedigree Friesians. It had been a church farm, they hadn't had a dairy or anything, and they sold it to raise money to finance one of their operations. We brought with us a whole flock of Dorset Horn, and a lot of pedigree cows, and a few pigs I think. The sheep got too fat, that was the problem and we had to change the flock in the end because they lambed twice a year.

We enlarged the herd to about 220 I think, and then we built a very modern dairy and silage effluent container, we were very progressive. It was a lovely farm because we had 20 acres of woodland and all this river frontage, and then eventually the disused railway line when that was closed.

Quite a lot of lower fields flooded, and once we had it just lapping into the dairy, and the village was cut off repeatedly. A lot of the houses were flooded. In those days half the village was owned by us and half by the other farmer. There were very few private houses. At our peak I suppose we had about eight farm workers because we bought another farm up at Woolland, on the hill. We owned the property that Dame Elisabeth Frink the sculptor later lived in. We had that farm for four or five years, then I had to sell most of it when my husband died, for death

Angela Hughes with the River Stour, Haywards Bridge, Shillingstone

duties. He died in '68 so I carried on farming for many years, until about 12 years ago, so that was about 40 years. Then my son and my son-in-law gradually took over. My daughter, Fiona lives at Bere Marsh Farm. I bought that actually in the '70s. I also bought a small flock of Jacob sheep because it had a lot of little orchards and small areas which I wanted to graze, and that was very suitable, and I bred them and sold the surplus for meat. They were very good to eat.

There was a cider press at Okeford Fitzpaine, I used to let them have all our apples. A penny a pound I think I got. It was at the top end of the village, near where the garage used to be.

I was always very keen on wildlife, and when we moved down to Hammoon I asked my husband not to cultivate all along the hedgerows, to leave areas, and I took over the woodlands and put up a lot of nest boxes. I was then a member of the Otter Trust in East Anglia and they were asking for farmers who would introduce otters, and so I had my first pair from them. We had two in '89 and three in '91. The Otter Trust built a sort of container by a pond and they gave me a supply of frozen fish. Daily I'd give them about six herrings. I had to unfreeze them, they gave me a really good supply. It was an enclosure dug very deeply into the ground and then we had small boxes for them to hide in. I used to go down every night with the frozen fish, but the exciting thing was that the second night we saw another adult otter outside their pen. He must have heard them calling, so there was an otter in the vicinity, but the dog otters travel about ten miles. I invited all the other landowners nearby, to come and look at them. This was long before there were any known otters in the vicinity, so it was quite a thing. It was kept secret, we didn't tell anybody outside the local landowners.

I was in the forefront of conservation. We kept feeding the otters frozen fish for six weeks. It was a long time. And then we opened the gate and they went down into this little pond and we saw them for a day or two, and then they traipsed from the pond to the river which wasn't very far away, and subsequently you didn't see them very often, but it was very exciting. Now they're very prolific in this area, it's one of the best areas for otters in this part of the Stour, and the Piddle. And I've had various reports and it's monitored regularly, they find spraints and footmarks. I saw them occasionally after we released them. Some of my friends and fisherman have spotted them. The fishermen didn't mind. They were rather thrilled actually. It didn't get to the extent of all the fish being eaten. The Stour is rich in fish. We used to have a lot of crayfish here but then the wretched American crayfish got into the Stour and the last English crayfish seen was ten, fifteen years ago. The Blandford Fly. Oh terrible. We had them at Bere Marsh, we got bitten. It's a horrible little fly.

Otters, they breed at odd times, they've been recorded as breeding in most months. They usually have a pair of young. Young cubs have been seen, and the latest reports have been on Fontmell Parva brook. They like the Piddle, all the little side streams. They migrate from one river system to another because they have been killed on roads, haven't they? And they have been as far as Christchurch. They go up the small tributaries quite a lot, and up to the lakes. They've been up to the lakes at Okeford Fitzpaine. Because they stock it with carp I think. The mink at Childe Okeford. Yes, we used to see them quite a lot. They'd got all my hens once but they used to get into the river but I don't think they did any harm to the otters. An otter's very big compared to a mink.

Otter hunting went on into the '80s I think. What I wanted to do was to get the otters tagged. They wouldn't agree to it but I said 'I wish you'd tag them.' They never agreed so we never knew if they were our local ones or not. The local otter hunt operated from Wimborne, but they were never allowed on our stretch of the river, but I couldn't stop them on the other side, it was only this side. Mr Tucker was the master of the otter hounds, I warned him to keep off. They were still going in '90. They met at Pegg's Mill. He called himself the mink hunt so they must have finished otter hunting. My husband was a keen hunting man but not otters. We had the Portman hunt that hunted round here.

There were other schemes that I ran. I did the nest record scheme for the BTO (British Trust for Ornithology), and I have a large heronry in my wood, and egrets are breeding now. I think I've got the largest heronry in the county, I think it's beaten Brownsea Island now. There have been about 48 nests, they're down to about 37 this year I think. We don't know quite how many egrets, maybe three or four pairs. They nest in the same trees, but it's a slightly more fragile nest, not quite so bulky, and I would say they nest a little bit later.

Curlews. I did originally have a pair that reared its young, but that was soon after we bought the farm and we had a lot of rough ground in those days. We have sparrow hawks and buzzards and kestrels and so on, I think I've seen 142 species of birds on the farm. We've had some pretty rare ones, like black terns, red-footed falcons, curlews, some quite interesting species like quail.

The vineyard. My son-in-law who was Italian put it in and it needed an awful lot of attention. We got quite a lot of nice wine, but it wasn't really big enough to do on our own. We had to mix the wine with someone else's and take it down, I think it was fairly near Corfe Castle where we got it processed. Then eventually we gave it up, but it had this wire enclosure all around it, two acres. It was in a lovely position and I read about somebody having a burial ground on a farm and I thought that it

would be ideal to have one up there, so I got planning permission and we put that in, that was opened in 2000. We rooted out all the vines.

We advertised the burial ground, we have a brochure and then my daughter Fiona developed it still further and I had to visit all the undertakers. They come from all over the country, usually because they've been born here, or they lived here and were very happy here, it's such a lovely position.

We've had an awful lot of problems this year with the drought, some of the trees have been dying and it's very difficult to take water up there because you can't have running water nearby, it's illegal you see, so we're on a high hill without any water.

Woodland burials. I went to see a few. I went to see this one locally, near the coast. I also went to see one in Somerset, near Street, and then there's one that started at Holt near Wimborne, and I think the Prince of Wales is trying to start one at Poundbury. The ground here is clay. There is a small plantation so if they want to scatter ashes they can. The burials extend from there. We've had about 100 burials to date. We have room for about two or three thousand. We've extended the length between the graves a bit because you want the trees to last a long time. We give people a choice of about six trees which are suitable for that area. Oak, not ash because they grow so fast, whitebeam, silver birch, not cherry, hornbeam, that's a nice one, most of them go for oak, it grows very well there and it'll take longer to grow.

People can't choose their site. They have to have the site we give them, because if we're going to make a plantation, they have the choice usually of one or two rows, but we have to crop it, you see, we can't have it scattered everywhere. They're allowed to put wild flowers and plant flowers on the grave. No plastic or artificial flowers and we plant the trees of their choice, stake them and look after them. If they die we replace them. At first we got them from our forester but now we buy container trees, and they're better. But we don't do any tree planting in the summer, we wait until the autumn when there's plenty of rain.

I go down to Fiona's most days, we walk along the railway line, I go to the river, we have barn owls nesting there, we have a farm walk every year, a walk that takes people round, it's a dawn chorus walk. It's a yearly feature. We go round the wood, down the railway line, down to the river, back to Bere Marsh Farm and they see a lot of birds. It's a very sluggish river, we don't have any water voles in the river, but we have quite a lot of nesting duck and moorhen and so on, and every year we get a couple of sandpipers moving through.

As soon as my husband died I realised I was in a wonderful position to illustrate how farming and conservation could work together, so I ran two major conferences based on the farm, have you ever heard of the Silsoe conference? It was to illustrate the effects of farming on conservation. That was in about '69, so the first conference I held based on the farm was 1970, and then I had a repeat conference in 1980, and we brought together farmers and conservationists and illustrated how certain types of farming could affect the wildlife, and which were least damaging. Even the hunts contributed and we had a very good attendance, and Sir Derek Barber who was a well-known organiser of the Silsoe conference, he took the chair and all the local farming community took part and it was based at Weymouth College, they came to the farm first and then we had the conference at Weymouth College.

I remember meeting an old farmer, he said "I don't understand what you're doing but I admire you for doing it." We did very little in the way of fertilising, and I reckon we had

several miles of hedgerows, we never took any out. We used to have a lot of snipe about the farm, and the winters were much wetter and longer. We couldn't really harvest anything after September, and now you're right into October. We used to grow maize and you couldn't harvest it after a certain date because it was too wet. Now they go on and on and it's not much good for birds or anything. We used to grow narrow stem kale, but when it had been grazed off and the field was full of little wet holes, I remember seeing 100 snipe diving in, getting worms, but they have different types now. We used to strip graze the kale. I had three pairs of lapwing nesting when we came. We had an old carter who was a real countryman, and he used to avoid the nests. He used to pick them up, even when he was driving a tractor, and put them back, but they got isolated and the crows got them. We tried our best but they stopped nesting and went up on the hills.

Along the Stour there was limited weed cutting, but we negotiated with the river authority not to dig, not to cut at the wrong time. They used to do a lot of river clearance, and after the conference they made quite a lot of deep pools for us, and inlets, but we wouldn't let them use a drag line in some areas because it used to ruin the banks for any breeding kingfishers, so we negotiated with them not to interfere with some areas, because their responsibility in the old days was to make sure as much water got off as quickly as possible. It was land drainage.

The railway was useful to send your milk off, but it closed in 1966. The drivers used to ring up and say "There's a sheep on her back" or something. It was sad that it went, but on the other hand it was nice for us because we bought our section and then we turned it into a nature reserve and it's been a wonderful area, and we've kept our section. I planted a lot of buddleia all along the side and we conserved areas which had cowslips so we cut them regularly so they're not smothered, and we have glow worms.

We had freshwater mussels in a certain section of a river and the otters certainly took mussels because we used to find the remains, but crows go for them as well. We had the Kimmeridge shale, when the water's low you can see all the shale and that's where the mussels would be. We had two different types of mussels here.

The OBE was for farming and conservation.

POSTSCRIPT

For anyone who has read these stories it is obvious that all these women have great determination and have consciously followed very different paths of their own. Not for them the comfortable office. What is fascinating is that many of them have ended up in Dorset by one means or another. Many came when they were very young and were brought up here. The diversity of their occupations is also remarkable, and very often they have succeeded in a man's world, pushing the boundaries without realising it.

Much of the work that they do is hard manual work or involves being outside in all weathers. Many have an instinctive feel for the land whether they be gamekeepers, poachers, deer stalkers, shepherdesses, ferret handlers, orchard owners, pig farmers, fisherwomen, taxidermists, midwives, priests, undertakers, cidermakers, letter cutters, market gardeners, there is a real hands on approach that I admire.

Apart from making a record of what is happening in Dorset today, I hope that some of these stories may act as an example to the next generation contemplating a career in the rural landscape. Yes, it is hard work, but the rewards in other ways are enormous.

Some people ask me how I choose people for interview. It is a subjective process, but in the first instance I contacted people I have worked with. Ann Hodgson I first met in Fontmell Magna in 1980 on Springhead farm when she was working for Lawrence Woodward and Alice Astor. I heard this voice bellowing out across the downs calling in one of her dogs as she was driving sheep in to vaccinate the flock against enzootic abortion. Her first words to me were "Damn it man, don't just stand there, get hold of that gate…" Within a few months she had persuaded me to buy my first sheep, 24 Lleyns, from the Grants at Alvediston in the Chalk valley. We shared the grazing on Fontmell Down for a number of years and the orchids were marvellous. She also introduced me to many of the men who later appeared in Dorset Man, David Winskill, Walt Pitman, Mark Harris, and of course the hurdlemaker Cecil Coombs, as well as Ruby James. When Ann heard that I could shear sheep she gave my phone number to a number of people who had small flocks in north Dorset and very soon with an advert in the Marshwood Vale Magazine meant that I had a shearing round. The first sheep to be shorn were of course her own…Elsie and Eddy Martin were also on the shearing list and we always had a very warm welcome at Drone's Farm. Lunch was more of a banquet with sloe gin and plum wine. Those were the days of sheep shearing.

Other Dorset Women were friends like Caroline Fowler who helps me with my computers, or Ruth Thompson who appeared at certain wild barn dances at farms above Portesham, Tracey Copp has cut my hair over the years, Catherine Streatfeild worked for Taste of the West, cheese and cider were also natural choices, Peggy Darvill's pork has to be tasted, Tamarisk Farm was another shearing station for many years. The music events put on by Val were legendary. Farriers, falcons, ferrets and horse dentists came out of the wood work as did taxidermy and undertaking. Phyllis Tuxhill I met at a poetry course at Dillington a few years ago, the otters on the Stour I had heard about for years, but never knew quite who was behind it all. Nerissa Jones I had seen at the Powerstock Cider Festival, and Anne Beckett the other shepherdess was recommended to me by

Julie who used to work in the knicker shop in Blandford, but now works in the Dorset bookshop. Often it was word of mouth, and I followed my instinct for a good story. Interestingly many of these women rebelled at school and carved out their own paths from an early age.

Life has changed so much in the last hundred years that any attempt to record it and disseminate those changes can only scratch the surface. Photography is a vital way in which to record the portraits of working people. With the words and the voices you get a real sense of the person behind the image and what makes them tick, what it is that is giving them the inner energy to go in the directions that they have chosen.

As a county Dorset has a great ability to absorb outsiders and in many ways the dynamism of those outsiders coupled with the native knowledge can often make all the difference between a culture surviving and a culture flourishing. Dorset, and West Dorset in particular, is at the cutting edge of a new food culture. Often it is the women making the running. I hope you enjoy reading these stories as much as I have in recording them.

James Crowden *November 2006*
www.james-crowden.co.uk

Photo by Tessa Gilks

JAMES CROWDEN was born in Plymouth in 1954 and grew up on the western edge of Dartmoor. He joined the Army, read civil engineering at Bristol University, then travelled widely in the Middle East, Eastern Turkey, Iran and Afghanistan. In 1976 he spent a year in Ladakh on the northern side of the Himalaya and lived in a high altitude Tibetan Buddhist valley called Zangskar. After studying anthropology at Oxford he worked in the Outer Hebrides, Bristol Docks and North Dorset. It was around Shaftesbury that he kept sheep and worked as a woodman, shepherd and sheep shearer. His first book, *Blood Earth & Medicine* charts the annual cycle of farm work as seen through the eyes of a casual agricultural labourer. He then moved to Somerset and took up cider making in the autumn. Other books followed, *In Time of Flood* and *The Wheal of Hope - South Crofty and Cornish Tin Mining* with George Wright, *Bridgwater - the Parrett's Mouth*, *Working Women of Somerset*, with Pauline Rook, as well as *Cider the Forgotten Miracle*. More recent books include *Waterways* for the National Trust and *Silence at Ramscliffe - Foot and Mouth in North Devon* with Chris Chapman, *Dorset Man* and a new anthology of food poetry called *Open-Mouthed*. James now writes full time.

Photo by Edmund Wright

GEORGE WRIGHT was born in London in 1950. From 1970-1973 he studied graphic design at Wimbledon School of Art and in 1975 he became a freelance photographer. He has worked internationally for many newspapers, magazines and book publishers. His pictures have appeared in *The Independent Magazine, The Observer, The Independent on Sunday Review, Departures* (USA) and *Instituto Geografico De Agostini* (Milan). He has also worked as a stills photographer for Channel 4. His work has been exhibited at the Metropolitan Museum in New York and the Chicago Botanic Gardens. He also has a number of photographs in the National Portrait Gallery collection. His books include *English Topiary Gardens* (1988), *Ceramic Style* (1994,) *Print Style* (1995), *In Time of Flood* (1996), a collection of photographs of the Somerset Levels and *The Wheal of Hope* (2000) about the demise of South Crofty and Cornish Tin Mining. He has lived in Dorset since 1983 and has undertaken many local commissions and arts projects. A large collection of his work is on the permanent display at the Dorset County Hospital. George Wright has also just completed a major series of portraits of council employees – *Council Works* for Dorset County Council.